# In the House of My Bibi:

## GROWING UP IN REVOLUTIONARY IRAN

Nastaran Kherad

Academy Chicago Publishers

Published in 2008 by
Academy Chicago Publishers
363 West Erie Street
Chicago, Illinois 60610

© 2008 Nastaran Kherad

Printed and bound in the U.S.A.

Library of Congress Cataloging-in-Publication Data on file with the publisher

*In memory of my grandmother, Fatemeh Moradi,*
*who taught me to see the world with an intelligent eye,*
*and for her gift of storytelling,*

*In memory of my beloved brother, Mohammad,*
*who is always alive in my heart,*
*and from whom I borrow my voice,*

*And to my mother,*
*for all her undeserved suffering and pain.*

# CHAPTER 1

Dawn creeps in through the iron shutters, but inside it is like night, dark and quiet as death itself. It has been twenty-eight days since I last saw a ray of sun, the moonlight, stars, the sky, gray or blue, crimson or pregnant with lamb-like fleecy clouds.

My eyes are fixed on the wet mop prints I leave behind, tracing the corridor's cold, cement floor. I mop swiftly to fight the growing urge to look up. I do not want to sleep at night, when the nightmares attack, when the urge becomes overpowering, as in this moment. The urge to feel, to smell, to breathe the crisp outdoor air, to reach up high and peer through the stubborn shutters that mock and claim supremacy over me and the others who are locked behind them. *Look at me! The sky is mine with all its stars, not yours*, they whisper. I wonder what color the sky may be. I imagine it a deep indigo, the glistening color of the fishpond in my grandmother's garden under the moonlight. A chill slithers through my entire body. I hesitate for a moment. The mop's wooden handle clutched in my fist, I look over my shoulder. I hold my breath. It is so quiet I can hear the breeze caressing the branches of a tree outside, and I can hear the brisk *thump-thump* of my heartbeat. Two of my cellmates are busy sanitizing the showers, and another is sorting a pile of fruit in the front corridor. The *Sisters* are not here, but their *Eyes* are, the penitents who report to them; they watch every move we make and hear every whisper.

Careful not to make a sound, I put the mop on the floor, tap my sandals off, and tiptoe like the breeze outside toward the iron eyelids of a pair of condemned windows. It is too early for the birds to sing.

1

If only I could see the sky, the fading moon, a gleaming star. I kneel over the accordion edging of the attached wall heater. With my left palm pressed to the wall, I push myself up straight, reach with my right hand and grasp tightly onto the shallow windowsill. My eyes barely meet the shutters' panel. My knees begin to quiver as they sink deeper into the heater's jagged surface. Ignoring the pain, I peer between the hair-thin cracks; only a thread of gray leaks through. I lose my balance as my fingers grow too weak to hold my weight against a cruel gravity. I am grateful that no one seems to notice the tumbling sound.

I walk to the restrooms.

It is my turn to clean, along with three other inmates. The list is pinned to the wall. The names are carefully chosen by the *Sisters* to avoid any suspicious contact between the detainees and to elimi-nate any gossip or plans to escape in the quiet dark. The cleaning schedule begins at predawn, at three sharp. We sanitize the entire windowless restroom, all its coarse cement walls and its three door-less showers, scour the toilets, mop and disinfect the floors in the corridors, and distribute the fruit and occasional medicine that our families bring us on Monday afternoon, the Visit Day. Sharing is forbidden unless it is done under the watchful eyes of the *Sisters*, who sometimes allow us to distribute our fruit when it is about to rot. In the stagnant heat even the best fruit shrivels quickly into a moldy lump. Since the guards search through the medicine and fruit, by the time we receive them the next day, they are already on the verge of going bad. I beg my mother not to bring any, telling her that we have so much to eat that we don't know what do with it. We know that our mothers go out of their way to buy expensive, hand-picked fruit for us. These are not easy times and rationing is strictly enforced. The last thing I want my mother to do is to squander her hard-earned money on kilos of fruit that will rot before I can taste them.

There is not a single piece of furniture in either of the two rooms or in the narrow, L-shaped hallway. The only luxury in this place is a worn-out, brown carpet stained with perhaps old, spilled chicken stew and vomit. Each room is designed to hold ten to fifteen seated people. Tonight, lying cramped next to one another, 128 young women sleep, covering every centimeter of the entire floor. Since there are not enough army blankets for everyone, we fold them into thin mattresses and wrap ourselves in our black *chadors*. The day I was led to this cell block, located in God-only-knows what part of the Sepah Detention Center, the morning list by the door indicated seventy-six women, most under the age of twenty-five. Not a week later, the number of detainees had doubled. The numbers change daily, even hourly.

Here everything happens in the heart of the night. They are owls, vampires, the *pasdar* guards—they come alive after dark. Every hour or so, especially after midnight, the iron double-door opens its black maw and swallows another unfortunate soul. Some are here only briefly, then gone—transferred? Disappeared in a matter of hours. Those condemned to stay remain faithful to any ray of hope, awaiting an unknown destiny.

I am bent over the toilet, scrubbing, when I hear the sound of the iron double-door creaking open. I freeze at once, holding the toilet brush in midair. My two cellmates, too, holding their scrub brushes against the shower wall, exchange quick glances and then resume without a word. Everyone's heart sinks each time the door opens. Anything dreadful is possible: the guard must be shoving in another captive; somebody is going to be called for interrogation or to be lashed; someone has been marked for solitary confinement or to identify another unlucky soul who has just fallen into yet another of the *Sepah's* traps. To save myself from stray thoughts, I continue scouring the toilet. But then there comes a voice.

"It's for you." The *Eye* points to me.

I feel beads of sweat spring on the back of my neck. Without looking up, I surrender to the *Eye*'s tall, black shadow, hovering over me at first, then enlarged and stretched on the facing wall.

"Quick! Get ready!" she hisses. "Your interrogator is awaiting you at the gate." She hurries back to the corridor.

My backbone stiffens. I feel the chill run through me again. I know this chill; I first felt it when I was a little girl. The first two weeks of my arrest, I was interrogated every midnight. What could it be this time? *Adelabad Prison? I thought they were done with me*, I murmur, unsure if I had just thought those words or spoken them aloud. I hope for the sake of this night that the *Eye* did not hear me.

It won't take me long to get ready. We try to stay ready for these moments. Like the rest of the girls, at all times I wear a thick, loose navy-blue *mantaue* that comes to my knees; my feet are covered in knee-length socks under a pair of thick pants, and my hair is gathered in a braided ponytail under a black scarf.

Careful not to stomp on the motionless arms and legs of drained bodies, exhausted from heat, insomnia, and constant interrogations, I hurry to the far corner of the first room. Firmly, I double-knot the scarf under my chin and stretch to reach for my chador, folded and kept in my prayer bundle. Unfolding it, I throw the black *crepe-de-chine* over my head, adjust its elastic band behind my ears, and make sure that not a strand of hair is exposed. I pause: breathe in, breathe out, close my eyes, say a prayer. To stop the trembling of my fingers, I clutch the chador tightly and dart out to the narrow hallway. A black strap in her hand, the *Eye* awaits me impatiently in front of the double-door. I turn my back so she can blindfold me and send me into complete darkness. In her secret code, she knocks softly: two consecutive knocks, one solo, two more consecutive. The door screeches open. I step out. The door screeches shut behind me.

"Follow me!" a male voice orders.

It is not the voice of *my* interrogator. The Voice hands me a short rope, careful not to touch my fingers in the exchange, for he is *na-mahram*; it is *haram* for him to touch the skin of an unlawful, non-related woman. Not only that, I am a soiled dog, so he fears if his fingers were to touch me, he'd burn in the fires of hell. To save him from this sin, to preserve his claim to a cozy precinct in heaven, I hold the rope tightly in my grip. It guides me; it is my eyes. From here, I rely on my other senses, especially my sense of hearing. We walk through the winding, narrow, cold corridors. No matter how the interrogators muffle their talk, their voices echo sharply off what sound like very high walls all around me. The spongy softness beneath my feet no longer feels like concrete or tile. There is a softness that suggests linoleum flooring, the better to suffocate telltale footsteps. Once, one of the cellmates had whispered to me that the corridors are not as long and winding as they seem. She said that the interrogators just walk you for a long time round and round to create that illusion, to prevent you from mapping the interior of the building, in case you get released and want to share this precious information with the outside world.

A minute later, the rope with the stranger at the other end loses its stiffness. The Voice cautions me to stand still. Someone else is approaching. The dragging of sandals is not familiar.

"Good evening," the new Voice greets him in a dry tone. This one is not my interrogator either. The rope is being exchanged. I feel the air become heavier, then emptier. I imagine this guard to be bigger and taller than the last one. He walks faster too. Faster than my steps. Blindfolded, I fall in behind him and try to match his pace. After rounds of walking, winding, and twisting, he, too, stops somewhere, which seems to be the open threshold of a room. Another girl is placed behind me. She reaches for my back, clutching the slippery chador. Now, I am her eyes, the blind a cane to the blind. Along the way, we gather in tow three more girls from different doorways. *Where are they taking us? What is expected of me this dawn? How dark is this place? How deep down under the ground are these corridors, these passages that smell like mildew and suffering?*

Like a mouse in a maze, I spin and spin some more through the everlasting corridors. Suddenly, the Voice ahead of me stops with no warning. I halt abruptly, my head sinking into his back. He dodges quickly; I feel my shoulder hit against a hard surface. The wall. The girl from behind bumps into me, making me lose my balance and fall. She topples over me, dragging others, each crushing into a pile of tangled legs and arms. "Upcoming traffic!" says the Voice, chuckling, followed by quiet laughter from the opposite side. Another guard must be ushering a string of women as well.

"What's happened to your horn, brother?" says the Voice from the opposite direction. "My fault. I should've honked," answers the Voice at the head of my line, amused .

I rise to my feet, and I guess the others do too, because someone's pulling at my chador again. I pull it closer to my face and adjust the elastic band. Once again, I reach for the rope, which the Voice hands me. The roving caravan continues.

If this weren't a pitiless dawn, if this were a game during a happy time or a scene from a comedy, I might have laughed too. The guards play this game often.

"Wait here!" the Voice orders. I hear steps coming from all directions. Someone is definitely in his summer sandals. The other four girls are released from me. I am left alone in the middle of the corridor; the rope is still in my sweaty fist, and I don't know why I cling to it as if it is the umbilical cord of my own life.

How much time has passed since I have been left standing here? Twenty minutes? Half an hour? My eyes are burning and my body feels as if it is weighed down with heavy stones. Quickly, I shift from foot to foot, hoping no eyes are watching. I know this is not allowed and I could be doomed to stand on my feet for hours, stiff as a stick.

After a time which seems like an eternity, the Voice is back again. He takes the rope from the other end and asks me to step forward. He leads me into a room, which seems very bright in comparison to the corridors.

"Face the wall!" a voice commands. It is *he*, my interrogator. A late-twenties voice, deep, and surprisingly kind. The interrogators must have been well-trained and chosen with care, because they all sound alike, talk alike, and act alike, so the detainees won't be able to distinguish between them. I know the procedures. I have done this many times during the last twenty-eight dawns. I turn around and let the wall's angles envelope my body, getting as close as possible to the wall as if it's my protection.

In the triangle corner it is harder to breathe. My heart beats even more unevenly now, my knees weaken as minutes drag on, and my tongue is already a useless piece of leather in my mouth. I am cold and I am hot. My hands are freezing, but my backbone is hot-wet. A line of sweat fades over the arch of my back and rolls down freely. From here, everything is a mystery. How long will the interrogations last this time, what sort of questions are they going to ask me this time over and over, how long before I will be sent back to the cell block or perhaps to solitary, or Adelabad Prison? Am I going to be lashed? Are they going to leave me standing here for hours as they did last time? They offer you a chair to sit on only when they order you to write. A chair with an attached desk, like the one I used not too long ago in high school last year at this time. I will be eighteen in forty-six days. When spring comes. When my grandmother's garden will be in full bloom and the entire courtyard intoxicated with the fragrance of night jasmine and orange blossoms. *Will I ever see another spring?*

"You lied." The interrogator's voice shatters the silence. "Bunch of lies you told me. Did you think I was a fool to believe you? Pretending it all. Playing innocent? You know what we do with liars? No? You will see *tonight*. We send them *to hell*. That's right. Express and one way. You forgot that the liars go to hell? I am here to remind you."

Lie? What did I lie about? He has never used this tone with me before. What happened to his pretend kindness? His trained gentleness? His diplomatic way of mining information out of you? What kind of trick does he have in his bag this time? Someone must've gotten arrested and said whatever to fill in the interrogation papers. To save her back from a lashing, she must have gone along with the lies they ordered her to write, admitted that she is a member of this or that counter-revolutionary party; that she had contact with this person and that person, had gone to secret anti-government meetings that may or may not have actually taken place. I know what people will do under pressure and torture. What would I do if they lashed me? What would I do if they tortured me? I wonder. Would I lie too and write down names that have no faces? Or would I tell them the truth?—Yes, yes, I have met them all in an open meeting, right in the middle of Zand Square. Thousands of them, no, no, the entire city. Didn't you hear us shout: NO to theocracy, NO to hypocrisy. Leave this nation alone! *I pray that the interrogation will end*.

"What is it? You know well when to turn mute, don't you?" He paces behind me.

Boom!

My entire body jolts. Something crashes onto the floor, a notebook maybe, a stack of files. I hear the rustle of papers. I hold still. He picks them up, leafs through them, and hits them at something hard, the edge of a table, perhaps.

"I didn't lie," I murmur. "I don't know anything to lie about. I swear."

"My bowl of patience is filled. I've put up enough with you playing dumb for me. From this hour, you're out of my hands. Someone else is going to teach you how not to lie."

This time, a *Sister* navigates me from one corridor to the next, surprisingly shorter and less winding. She's a fast walker. Her hand is covered in a smooth glove. "Watch the steps," she hisses. Holding to the wall on my left, I walk down the steps. She pushes me inside a room. "Sit down on the floor and remove your shoes!" Without waiting for me, she starts yanking the sandals and socks off my feet. Another female helper joins in. They're very quick. A pair of hands reaches under my chador and gathers the fabric around me; I am told to remain motionless. One of the *Sisters* pushes me down. "Lie here with your chest down on the bed!"

It's a hard wooden board. My feet are bare. My instincts tell me to hold on tight to the board's sides. So, this is it, the lashing that everyone talks about. My skin already quivers. I clench my teeth. More footfalls are filling the room, more pacing and whispering.

"Wait!" yells one of the *Sisters*. "The lights are not dimmed yet, brother."

There must be more than six people walking in the room, mostly men; male lashers who must not see the woman's curves in the bright light.

"*Allah-o-Akbar*," someone shouts.

*Shtttt* . . . Something jerks, pulling at the skin of my bare feet as the first lash licks fire into my skin.

"*Allah-o-Akbar*," voices rejoin in unison as another lash comes down. I hear screams. Is this my voice deafening my ears? How did I learn to scream like that? I bite harder into the fabric of my chador. "Who was your contact? What were their names?" The voices are louder, the beats are faster. My back is burning. I feel the flames rise beneath my skin, thousands of scorpions sting, jerk, and pull at the arch of my feet. Vibrating shocks rush to my legs, spread over my back, burst in my head, and burn the roots of my hair. Irrepressibly, a million bees sting my back. An army of ants crawls under my skin. Tears bubble in my eyes and fall down from the tip of my nose. I press my fingers to the board's edges.

"*Allah-o-Akbar* . . . *Allah-o-Akbar*."

My ears deafen with a whizzing sound. My head is filled with a humming thud coming from a distance, voices stretch and distend . . . *Allllahhh-o-aakkkkbbbarrr*. I spin and spin. Light, then lighter.

A ball of weight leaves my body. My body small, then smaller. My eyelashes have never felt this heavy.

*A soft dew caresses my face. The courtyard is covered in a misty twilight. I do not want to leave my bedroll. My eyes are still full of a sweet sleep.*

*Bibi is at the fishpond. She's folding up her sleeves, getting ready for the ablution ritual for the dawn prayers.*

"Allah-o-Akbar . . . Allah-o-Akbar," *the* muezzin's *enchanting voice coming from the alley mosque's minaret greets the courtyard.*

"Allah-o-Akbar," *Bibi answers the inviting* muezzin's *call in her warm voice. "God is the greatest," she recites. "Come! My child's child." She reaches for me. "Give me your little hand. Hurry to the House of God. It is time to worship the only merciful, compassionate creator."*

*My ears are filled with Bibi's prayers.*

*I stand next to her as she begins her prayers. She prays for a long time and does many rounds of prayer beads. She extends her arms high into a gray-blue sky and prays for seven neighbors to the right and seven neighbors to the left. For all the close and distant relatives. For friends and a list of other people who stop and ask her in the alleys to pray for their afflicted family members. They say Bibi's prayers would be answered for she has a soul as clean as the water of the Well of Zam- Zam and she is a* moshgelgosha, *the resolver of difficulties.*

*Bibi kneels down under the fading stars and prays for all the poor, the sick and the needy. She hymns, "Allah, Allah, Allah, the cure of the ill, the hope of the hopeless, the exigency of the destitute, the only capable creator who can grant everyone's wish."*

*She asks God to keep me under His wings and not to withhold His kindness and compassion from me, a fatherless child with a gypsy mother. At the end, she asks Him to look down on her, just another black-face dog in His immense empire.*

*Her face is as round and silvery as the moon above. I find it hard to imagine her as a black-face dog. But Bibi says a good slave of God is the one who's modest and asks Him for forgiveness of his sins. She asks Him to lead all the other slaves of God to salvation and emancipation as well.*

*Bibi cries hard while asking for forgiveness, and I find myself wondering what kind of sins she could possibly have committed when everyone admires her and prays that she will go to heaven.*

# CHAPTER 2

Humming voices. Noises and whispers. Footfalls. Someone is calling my surname. The rain pours on my face. Water trickles down my nose, droplets fall from my chin. My body is hot-wet. Flames lick the skin of my back. My feet are ablaze. I blink. Blackness everywhere. My eyes are filled with weariness under the blindfold. My head bears the entire weight of the universe.

"You were just supposed to scare her," someone is saying in a frenzy.

I recognize his voice. It is *he*. My memory will trace his voice for the rest of my life.

"I just wanted to make sure that she didn't leave anything out. You know we didn't even get the permission from the *Hakem-e Sharae*."

"*Hadji Agha* would have given you the release, brother," another man says under his breath.

"Her case is different," *he* replies. "You forgot that she's come with her own feet?"

He paces around me, his dragging sandals in my ear. "She's a stew of minced-flesh. I said only the back," he raises his voice a bit. "Why did you lash her feet? She'll be limping tomorrow. Now, I have to cancel her visit till she recovers. I can't send her back to the cell block like that. I need to find her another hole. Just an hour ago I crammed six of them in one solitary cell."

"They're like cockroaches, these fatherless pests," the other man says disgustedly, "reproduce like rats, these infidels."

"Nothing of what's happened tonight should be included in her file," *he* murmurs. "Send her to a solitary! Let's hope that she'll mend fast."

Someone's shaking me. "Get up! You wimp," a male's voice scolds.

"For the sake of Imam, look who we're dealing with," another man says. "Bunch of scarecrow-fearing, scarf-headed crows. Is this how you wanted to topple our Islamic government? Go on and wash your dishes! You traitors. Hypocrites."

Someone titters.

"Hey, you there. Do you hear me?" the same voice asks. He holds my arm and jiggles it harder. I'm surprised that none of the *Sisters* are here and that a male is touching my arm. "You hear me?"

"Yes," I hear myself gasp, my voice muffled.

"Come with me, then!"

"She shouldn't walk like that up the stairs. Let her butt-crawl. What the hell. Damn her. Damn all of you, you rotten-seed bastards."

There are four girls in the cell, all wounded and lashed. The room is two meters wide, three meters long. The cold cement walls and floor smell earthy, creating an unsettling sensation of burial inside a grave. There's hardly enough space to lie down. Arms folded on their chests, the girls squat and doze so that one at a time they can lie down and sleep. There's no casement or venue to allow the light to filter in. The only light in this room is a low-watt light bulb hanging from the ceiling. My cellmates' faces are shadowed, ghostly, yet somehow angelic at the same time.

"Don't lean against the wall," one of the girls says tenderly, reaching for my shoulder. "You need to take off your tops. Nothing should be touching your flesh right now."

Everyone gathers around me, even the one who's lying down.

"How . . . how did you know I was lashed?" I ask.

"You're naive. They bring here only the ones who are minced," says the one to my right, her voice barely above a whisper.

"Your feet too? Back and feet together? What did you do? Blow up the *Sepah's* bus or something? Ah! Those heartless criminals. And they call this Islamic justice?" She shakes her head as she tends to my wounds. "It could've been worse. You must've fainted and that made them stop the lashing. What are you? *Mojahedeen? Fadaee?* Anything at all?"

No response. I look down instead.

"Join the crowd, *comrade*," says the one who was lying down moments ago.

I see. They must be Lefties, most likely the Fadaee guerrillas' sympathizers.

Mohammad's been kept at the Sepah Detention Center for several months now, perhaps in a cell just like this one. I wonder if I tap on the wall, would he be on the other side? Would he hear me? What a childish notion. These walls seem so solid that I doubt even the loudest screams could be heard by God, let alone by humans. I push myself to sit up and try to stretch a bit, but my breath stops short, knotted against my chest. The army of ants and the whizzing bees sting and pull at my skin again. Carefully, the girls gather my clothes over my head. We don't ask each other's names because we don't want to know. Here in detention the first lesson I learned was not to trust anyone. You never know who could be the next *Eye*. I try not to look up or stare, so I won't remember their faces later. They do the same with me. In here we become nameless, blank faces. The one in the good mood gets up, dips a towel in a bowl of water and begins to mend my feet. The bees sting like tiny flames, but two girls have a firm hold on my shoulders.

"You have to tolerate the pain. Trust me, you'll be thanking me tomorrow," says the same girl.

"Right now, cool water is the best remedy," another one says.

With the back of my hand, I wipe the ooze from the corner of my eyes. I have never been good at tolerating physical pain.

"Hear it from me, the experienced one!" the good-natured girl says as she dabs my back. "I had at least three hundred of them, back, feet, arms, you name it." She pauses. "Why are you here in this cell, somebody please tell me!"

"It's obvious they made a mistake," answers one of the girls holding my shoulders.

"They must be desperate for an empty cell to shove whoever in here. If you don't know," she moves her mouth closer to my ear, "they call this the Cell of the Ghosts. You'll see, they'll come and get you as soon as they find another empty hole."

The room's stagnant, sunless confines reek of blood, disease, and infection like a piece of decomposing meat.

Then the door swings ajar and a female's covered arm reaches in with a black blindfold. "Put this on and come outside!"

"It's for you; just butt-crawl." The girl stops nursing my back and pulls down my clothes carefully. "Good luck!" she exhales bitterly as she fixes my chador.

*"If you ever leave alive from this despicable desert,"* the one lying on the floor recites the famous poem, *"to the blossoms, to the rain, send a greeting from us."*

Though a black cloth blinds my eyes, I can see now. My mind's eyes wander to another day, a beautiful day of liberty amidst the splendor of Dena Mountain, when Mohammad recited this poem to me. The knot in my throat grows tighter. In the silence of this dark cell, I feel myself shatter into pieces, remembering Mohammad and his high hopes for his beloved revolution. Blindfolded, I butt-crawl to the corridor.

# CHAPTER 3

"All right then. This is the last time," the interrogator says, standing behind me. Facing the wall, he asks me to remove the blindfold without looking back or to the sides. "Last chance to write whatever you think you might've forgotten. I'll give you enough time to go over anything you want to add. Start with the personal questionnaire and finish up with your relationship with the anti-revolutionaries. Anything you might even think is trite or not worth mentioning."

He pulls a chair with an attached desk toward the wall and hands me a stack of white paper, pencils, and two blue Bics. This is the time they become saints. They offer you *everything* you need: an extra eraser, another pencil sharpener, different pens in case one runs out of ink. Their technique switches 180 degrees. "Ah, your pencil got too dull? Here, take a few more." They even offer you water, which you have to sip and give the cup back to the Hand behind you. It is only at these times that your eyes are open, but you're not allowed to turn around to peek. You never see a glimpse of the interrogators or anyone, or the place they take you. The only time the blindfold was ever removed from my eyes was the first day that they took me to the *Hakem-e Sharae*, accompanied by two armed *pasdars*. The bright light overhead is blinding. It is the writing time. Spit-out-whatever-you-know time. And if you don't know, they make you know. They have you sit in the corner of the room, pen in hand.

I stare for the hundredth time at the questions and the blank papers. I sharpen the pencil a few times, put it down, take a black Bic instead, then a blue one, but I know I can't write down the lies they want me to write with contacts as they say—counter-revolutionaries, their names and places of hiding—the same questions they kept asking me in the cellar.

I read the first question: Place of birth? Even a simple fact such as this seems beyond me. My mind seems to drift, as if in a waking dream. In the solitary there is so much time I don't know what to do with it. So, I summon my inner self to float in an unknown horizon and dream in a different dimension. A rainbow butterfly breaks out of its fragile cocoon and flies and flies. I dream of a place where there's no lashing, footfalls, darkness, and silence, torture and executions. Where there is sky and sky and sky. Think. Think. Think. In my cell, my chest to the cold floor, I lie down for hours, trying to find an answer to the questions ringing in my ear. How did it all start? Why am I here? Why is it that thousands of us are jailed, executed, falling down to the ground like autumn leaves? The lives of the young people of this country have become cheaper than dirt these days. I glance at the question: Place of birth?

The blue Bic is frozen between my fingers. The invisible words chain and join lines:

I was born in a garden . . .

*A lady barges in through the narrow doorway of the house. She shouts at my Bibi. She is that fruit-lady again, bringing her basket of peaches, apples, and pears in exchange for the golden-green and ruby black grapes that droop under a canopy of vines over the vegetable garden. On the path to the garden, she reaches out her hand, picks some ruby black grapes from beneath the arbor, crunches a few, spits them out under the trees and says, "They're too sour."*

*The fruit-lady doesn't look like the others who bring things to the house, calling out when they come. There is the toothless salt-man who comes on his donkey, shouting in the alleys for dried bread in exchange for salt and onions. He never enters the house, but whenever Bibi comes out and offers him an ice-cold drink of lemonade, he prays that she may drink the eternity-water in heaven. And when he picks the grapes from the creeping branches over the doorway, he says, "Bah, bah! They taste like honey."*

*There is the ice-man who brings clumps of ice on Saturday afternoons, and the shopkeeper's boy, who brings yogurt and butter and collects the empty tin bins, and the women with scarves on their heads who tie their babies on their hunched backs and sell syrup, honey, and dates. They, too, pray that Bibi may be a pilgrim to the House of God as she offers them more grapes.*

*This fruit-lady wears white shoes with shiny heels and a knee-length, pleated, poppy-flower skirt with a matching long-sleeved top. A wide pearly belt hugs her waist, which is as thin as my storybook. Her belly isn't like Bibi's belly, rising like bread dough under her cotton dress.*

*Unlike any of the neighbor women with their long, uncombed hair, her short brown hair is curled up around her neck. When she looks at me, she fingers strands and pulls them back behind her ear.*

*Bibi calls her Golrokh, the Flower-face. And I find myself wondering how someone as angry as the fruit-lady could have such a pretty name. Her large eyes look like the eyes of the deer standing next to the man with a ring of light around his head in the painting in Bibi's prayer-room. And when she blinks, her long black lashes move like the lashes of my doll, except that her eyes aren't blue, but a glowing honey brown. Suddenly she walks toward me. She lifts up my hands, yelling at Bibi for letting me dig in the dirt and vegetables. I think she doesn't like my garden of tomatoes, eggplants, and cucumbers, either. She says I look like a village-girl. She wants Bibi to rub more Vaseline on my hands. She wants to know why my cheeks aren't pink and pinches them with her long fingers. "There," she says, "they'll be pink now." When she sees me staring at her, she almost hugs me but gives me a quick kiss on the forehead instead. I become so hot, I know my cheeks are pink.*

*She turns and yells at Bibi again. Bibi cries and tells her if she's worried about my clothes and my hands, she should take me with her. I clutch my bunny to my chest. I can't understand why Bibi wants to give me away to the fruit-lady, even though she smells like Cameo soap. She looks at me again. Then she goes inside the garden, picks the pomegranates— some still in red bloom—the tiny green baby persimmons, and the sweet lemons, packs them all in her basket, covers them with mint and basil from the garden, drinks some lemonade, whispers something to Bibi, and leaves with her fruit basket.*

*I go and hide under the arbor for I don't want to talk to Bibi. But when she comes and hugs me and my lips touch the salty streaks on her cheeks, I'm no longer angry with her.*

*"It is still a beautiful afternoon," sighs Bibi.*

*I go to the alley, looking for Marmar, the next-door neighbor girl, who has hands as white as cotton candy. She tells me that the fruit-lady is my mother. I push her and she falls to the concrete sidewalk, sprawling across a hopscotch square. I yell that I will never play with a liar again, and run to my Bibi crying.*

# CHAPTER 4

This Monday I did not have a visit. It is the third day since the lashing and the wounds on the bottom of my feet have begun to heal, but I still have to push my weight to my heels, so I limp. I know it is forbidden to talk to my mother, my only visitor, about the lashing. Nor am I allowed to talk about it to any of the inmates; it is one of those taboo details we simply don't share. Here, in the corner of solitary, I wonder if I have screwed up my life by coming in voluntarily. I wonder if I will ever again set foot in the outside world. What did the future hold for me? In the past three days, more than anything and anyone, I think about Mohammad and his decision for me to turn myself in. I think about my own decision. What have I gotten myself into? Will it help Mohammad's situation after all? The bonding and the love for him had taken hold of my heart since early childhood, that cold autumn morning when I opened my eyes to see a boy sleeping on Bibi's bedroll.

The first blow of Shiraz wind had just arrived; with it came Mohammad.

Like any other morning, I woke up to the sound of sparrows squawking on the front porch. My eyes were still full of sleep as I sat up on my bedroll, staring at a boy. I did not know what sky he fell from. His arms and one foot stuck out of the blanket, his toes wrapped in a white rag stained with red spots; his mouth, half-open, shaped like an oval hole. I gawked at Bibi as she entered the room, a tray of food in her hands. "Who's this boy, Bibi?"

"Shhh!" Bibi gestured softly with her index finger to her lips.

"Don't wake up your brother, my flower! Poor thing. He walked the entire way to get here. May I die for his bravery."

*My brother? Dear God, not another one*, I thought, and began to examine him more closely to see if I could find any likeness that he might have with Ali, my older brother who came now and then, tormenting me. His machine-trimmed hair was a lighter shade of brown. Only his cheekbones and arched black eyebrows hinted at similarities to Ali. Finally, when I could not find any sign of meanness in his pale-skin face, I let out a sigh of relief and gave up scrutinizing him. After all, with him sleeping in his striped gray-and-white pajamas, and a bandaged foot, it wasn't all that easy to feel any spite.

"What's happened to his foot, Bibi?" I whispered. "When did he get here?"

"Ah! It's a long story, *babam*," Bibi whispered back as she carefully spread the morning *sofreh* on the floor. "He ran away from *that* boarding school," she said. "Poor child. It was not even dawn when I heard him knock on the door. You should've seen him. He fainted in my arms from exhaustion. I'm still amazed how he found this house on such a dark night; him being here only a couple of times. Only God knows if there were any stray dogs on his way. He had only one of his rubber sandals left on one foot." Bibi sighed and shook her head. "Well, as I always said, this boy is sure something else."

Bibi scrambled eggs in a pan over the Aladdin oil-heater, placed a bowl of cream-milk, a bowl of homemade quince marmalade, fresh-baked *Sangak* bread and a jug of milk, and poured herself a cup of hot tea from the china pot over the boiling samovar.

I ate my breakfast without making much sound. Finished, I went to the garden to play and waited for the boy to wake up.

He slept and slept as if he hadn't slept in days. He slept into the afternoon. Now and then, I would poke my head inside the room or tiptoe around him.

Finally, he shook off his winter-long bear-sleep. He jumped to his feet once he noticed me. "*Salam!*" He limped toward me, hugging me joyfully. "Look at you! How you've grown!"

I stared at him. He seemed cheerful despite his limp and bandaged foot, and talked nonstop. My fears left me. He wasn't mean like Ali.

"You know me?" I asked shyly.

"You silly girl," he said, pulling my braid lightly. "Don't you know me?"

I tried hard to remember. Maybe I've seen him before. But I couldn't remember.

"I'm Mohammad," he said, patting his chest with the palm of his hand. "Don't you remember? I always played with you when we lived in Abadan."

My head must be stuffed with hay as Ali says. There must really be something wrong with me, because I still can't remember a thing. This was exactly what Ali said when I saw him for the first time. I wondered why all the boys coming to my house knew my name and who I was, yet I didn't know them.

"Well, dear," Bibi said to Mohammad. "She was a little too young when you all used to live in Abadan. Barely three years old then. You're older than she, of course you'd remember."

Mohammad ate the entire tray of food Bibi had put aside for him and had no problem drinking a second glass of milk. I sat watching him gulp that stinky goat cheese. I looked at his agate-green eyes; his black eyelashes were even longer than mine. I watched his hands, so white, I could see the tiny blue veins. His fingers . . . they were long, like Ali's.

"Thank you God for this blessed food," he said as he finished off his meal. He thanked Bibi too, "*Merci, merci, Bibi,*" as she offered him more food.

Bibi brought pots of hot and cold water, pouring them in a large basin to give Mohammad a loofa-bath in one of the empty rooms. I was not allowed to go inside that room, because she said he was almost a grown-up and naked. She put an old big shirt on him and wrapped him in a thick blanket, washed his pajamas by the fishpond and hung them on the laundry line in the courtyard.

Mohammad treasured the garden, even though it was winter and there were hardly any leaves left on the trees. The garden looked empty. It made me sad; I wished that he had run away in the summertime when the trees were heavy with their fruit and the garden was overflowing with vegetables, colorful flowers, and rainbow butterflies. The good thing, there were still tons of persimmons left on the high branches. He ate so many of them I feared he might get a stomachache. Unlike Ali, who hated Bibi's animals, he didn't even mind the rooster and the bunny hopping around. We kept chasing the bunny, playing the entire afternoon until nightfall when Bibi told us we had to go inside her room.

After we finished off the last bit of Bibi's roasted eggplant dish, cross-legged, we listened to Bibi's stories. Mohammad tickled my feet, making me giggle. I brought my storybook and asked him to read me from the pages with the pretty pictures.

"*Waay!* This is great," he said. "You know how to read. Amazing!"

I was mesmerized by the way he spoke, and by his accent. All afternoon I heard him saying big words: great, amazing, fascinating, magnificent.

He was ten years old then and in fifth grade. I was five and hadn't started school yet, and I could read only the beginning pages of my Farsi book. He said he could read the entire book in less than an hour, so he chose a story from the end of the book. On some of the pages, he held my finger and pointed at each word. When I pulled my hand away, he said that the words wouldn't *electrocute* me. And I knew that I didn't have to be afraid, because he called me *kucho-oloo*, the little one. I repeated the words after him. Bibi watched us, obviously amused. "*Afarin! Afarin!*" she praised. By the look of her frownless forehead I knew that she did not mind losing her place to Mohammad as the night's storyteller.

The next day, the sun never came up. It was too cold, so Bibi forbade us to play in the alley. It was around noon when we went to the garden. When we were tired from running, we lay on our backs, looking at the patches of lamb-lamb clouds. The Old Lady who lived at the end corner of the sky was sour again, sweeping the clouds away from her roof and sprinkling them all over ours until a hideous gray hung over the bare wooden arbors.

"Blue is a great color," Mohammad said. "The sky is blue. The sea is blue. The water is blue. Well . . . not literally . . . water is colorless."

Is that magic in his words? I closed my eyes and listened to his voice, trying to mimic his singsong accent in my head. I sat up as I saw a brown baby worm crawling toward me. I picked it up off the ground and let it glide on the back of my hand. It was the coldest and

slimiest little thing ever. I thought it was lost, so I got up and let it
slither under the pomegranate tree. Bibi always warned me not to
stomp on them when each time after a heavy rain they crawled out
from the soaked soil in search of dry spots. "There's a lot of benefits
to those worms," she would tell me. "They are good for the garden;
they dig in the dirt and the trees' roots get air and nutrition."

"It's good to live in a house," Mohammad said, pulling on a dry,
leafless branch. Leaning on both elbows, he looked around. "I wish
I could live here, with all these trees and animals . . ."

"Don't you like it where you live?" I asked.

"It's not all that bad, I guess," he said, cushioning his arms under
his head and staring into the ashen sky. "We have to share everything, though. We sleep in a big room; each of us has a bed. And
there's school, of course. Lectures. Music. Crafts. Penmanship. Did
I tell you I play chess? Yes. No one beats me. I could teach you, you
know." He faced me. "Ping-pong, too. But, mostly, I read."

"I like to read too. I even spell out the words."

"That's good, *kuchooloo*," he said, pinching my nose. "When you
read, you can go places you've never been, you know?" he mimicked
my talking. "You can fly on the wings of imagination."

*My! How did he learn to talk like that?*

We talked and talked. He told me about the time when the *Shah*
and his queen, *Shahbanoo*, had come from the Capitol to visit Shiraz. He said he was in fourth grade then and that he played trumpet
in his school band and marched on the streets among thousands of
other schoolchildren waving flags for the King of Kings. I remember
whenever Bibi talked about *that* boarding school either she sighed
or cried. But from what Mohammad was telling me, it seemed like a
nice place to live.

"I wish I could live with you at your school," I told him.

"*Naa*, you don't." He shook his head. "It's good to live in a home.
Where I live, they punish you if you don't do things right. Hossein
gets punished a lot. Once, they made him scour the toilets in the hall.
They say he's stubborn."

I didn't know Hossein yet. But Mohammad told me that he's our
brother too, only a couple of years younger than himself and older
than I.

"Do they punish you too?"

"Naa. Well, sometimes." Suddenly, he became agitated. "They *discipline* us. They don't hit me that often, unless I run away." He stared into the sky again. I was glad Bibi was not around, for she would say, "You sure ask lots of questions, girl." But I couldn't help wondering about the place where he lived. "Are there any girls where you live?"

"*Areh*, yes," he said. I used to say *areh* too, but Marmar kept calling me *Abadani* girl, *Abadani* girl, so I started saying *ha* like the rest of the people in our neighborhood.

"But the girls live in the next building," Mohammad said. "I see them on Fridays when Mother comes to visit us."

He called her *Mother*. I wanted to tell him that I never called her *Mother* or *Momon*, or anything at all. I didn't. Instead, I heard myself asking, "Does she hug you?"

For a moment, he looked perplexed. He gazed at me with his huge eyes. "*Areh!* She brings us fruit and Zoo cookies when she visits us."

"Sometimes she comes here and brings me fruit too. She thinks I'm ugly."

"No, no." He sat up. "Don't think nonsense!" he said, pulling my braids.

"Maybe you can come and live with us, with Bibi and me."

"That would be something, huh? I'll be out of there as soon as I finish sixth grade, then I start high school. When I grow up, I want to be like Bruce Lee."

I didn't know who Bruce Lee was. Mohammed stood up and performed some odd movements, chopping the air with his arms, kicking and attacking an imaginary enemy, making even more bizarre noises:

"Chuh, chuh, tehhh, tehhh, haa, hee."

*Tagh, tagh, tagh.* . . . It was the iron knocker.

I opened the door. Two women dressed in dark blue suits entered the walkway. One of them was tall and skinny, the other one was chubbier than Bibi. Looking at them standing next to each other made me chortle.

"What is it, girl? Have you seen a clown in the circus?" the skinny one scolded.

Bibi was behind me in no time. "Ah, forgive her, sister," she apologized. "She's just a bubbly child, laughs even at the cracks between the bricks in the wall."

The moment Mohammad saw the women, he ran to the storage room, hiding. "Don't let them take me, Bibi! For the love of God, Bibi, let me stay here!"

The women told Bibi that it was not his first time running away. When they were searching for him, his mother suggested this house.

I begged Bibi too. "Bibi! Don't let them take him. They'll hit him again."

The chubby woman gave me a stern look. "What prattle is this girl speaking?" she shook her head. "No one is getting punished at our *prominent institute*." Then she looked at Bibi and told her that even though she was the grandmother, officially, she did not have guardianship of Mohammad or me. "With that long tongue of hers," she pointed at me, "we might have to take her away one of these days, as well."

Bibi became furious. "Leave my house this instant!" she shouted. "Don't get too fancy with me, ladies. Don't try to fool me with these phony, colorful names. Boarding school my eye! That's a horrible orphanage you established there. And no girl of mine will go to no orphanage. I may not wear bronze-buttoned suits, but I'm not senseless like my daughter. Hurry up! Leave! And don't wag your tail in my face."

I pushed to close the door, but the chubby one held it with the palm of her hand and flung it open. I hid behind Bibi's legs.

Suddenly, the women became soft with Bibi, telling her that they would not return without taking Mohammad along. "This is a matter of duty for us," said the tall one.

Bibi looked at Mohammad, who was peeking from behind the storage door. She told the women that she'd take him back tomorrow. "I don't have the heart to do it now. Let me convince him tonight, reason with him with a sweet tongue," she argued.

The next day, Bibi's daughter, Golrokh the Flower-face, came and took Mohammad back to his boarding school. We all cried, even the Flower-face.

Mohammad kept running away, coming home in the middle of the night, with lost sandals and torn pajamas, his feet bloody, his body shivering from the cold and from the stray dogs. Bibi continued besieging her daughter to bring her grandson now and then on Fridays. "It's a long commute," Golrokh would sigh, "and the taxi-fare. Besides, what about the other two boys, Rahim and Hossein? It wouldn't be fair."

Eventually, Mohammad came home periodically on Friday mornings with the taxi fare Mother had given him.

# CHAPTER 5

The wounds on my back begin to itch and fresh pink skin gradually surfaces beneath the dead peel on the bottom of my feet. It's been ten days since I have been thrown in the solitary cell. I have seen at least a hundred lashed, kicked, stomped, and tortured young women come and go. Our captor's strategy is to keep the detainees together no more than two or three days. To cause more tension and distress, they keep moving us around from this cell to the next, usually one detainee from each political party, so no one would dare to trust another or think of collaborating. The *Sepah* guard labels the *Fadaee* guerrillas and the *Tudeh* Communist Party *Lefties*; the *Bahai* believers, *kafers*, infidels, and they call the *Mojahedeen-e Khalgh* sympathizers, *monafegheen*, hypocrites. One of the guards is always kicking at the door to remind us of their presence and that they are watching. At odd hours, past midnight, a black-gloved arm reaches in proffering a blindfold for one of us, and the walking through the dark and winding corridors begins. Not that the darkness really matters in a dungeon where days and nights are the same. I have not breathed fresh air and the only brightness I have seen these past days is the overhead dim light. The murky air in this cell is even heavier and reeks more pungently of dried blood, vomit, urine, and mildew.

Yesterday, for the first time, one of the *Sisters* led me to a doorless shower. She sat there in the front area the entire time as I hurriedly shampooed my hair and clumsily soaped myself. Her entire plump, short body was covered in her black chador and for a second, I got a glance of her black, piercing eyes through the vertical opening of her masked face. The water was barely lukewarm and the air was cold, but I was thankful as the water gushed over me and washed off the filth and foul smell of the past days. My hair fell down in a clump and clogged the drainage, making the soapsuds whirlpool in circles. I was thankful that the *Sister* ordered me to have my back to her. I let my tears fall freely, swallowed my sobs, and shivered quietly.

Another knock again.

The blindfold handed in is for me. A male *pasdar* leads me through the familiar winding corridors. Once again, they interrogate me, asking if I have anything else to add. With the shake of my head "No," someone pushes a stack of papers before me on the attached desk.

"Swear and sign here," orders a hoarse voice. My personal interrogator is nowhere in sight, and this one does not give a damn about pretending to be kind.

I have no doubt; I am going to be hanged.

Someone leads me to a car, a Land Rover patrol perhaps. They have been spreading all over the streets of my beautiful Shiraz. The rage and vengeance of centuries in their eyes, the *Basij* armed guard are determined to wipe sinners off the face of the planet. As the eyes and ears of the *Imam*, they drive the newly purchased Land Rovers all over the town. Accompanied by the *Zaynab Sisters*, the Committee of Monitoring Public Behaviors, whose only mission is to enforce the recently mandated policy of the national *hijab* for women, and to arrest sinners, young teenagers, who engage in sinful acts of laughing and joking in public, and God forbid, holding hands.

It must be raining; right before they shove me into the car, I feel a soft drizzle on my shoulders. I hear the soft panting of a spring shower against the window, and the swishing sound of the wipers. What a beautiful scent. The spring of Shiraz seems to have arrived early this year. There must be blooms and plants around here, because the air smells damp and fragrant. With my sight taken away from me, I concentrate on sounds: the opening and closing of doors, the vroom-vroom of a running engine, the whispers, the rustle of the black chador. Two *Sisters* sit one at each side of me. This is definitely not the prison's bus the cellmates talked about.

I am drenched with sweat under the layers of clothes and the black chador. It must be midday. Now I am certain of one thing, I am not going to be hanged. At least not yet. The hangings take place after midnight, when the owls fill the sky over the dark woods of this country called Iran. A solitary cell is not an option either; I have been in one the past ten days.

The thirty-something-minute drive on a straight stretch of asphalt sets off my instincts that this is the way to Adelabad Prison. This is not freedom, yet somehow I am relieved. The interrogations must be over. At least for now.

# CHAPTER 6

The blindfold disappears.

In the cubical security room right before a massive entry gate, a female guard commands me to shed my clothes. I undress completely in front of a *Sister* looking on like a menacing black crow. She examines me from head to toe, behind and front, the roots of my hair, my open palms, the arch of my feet, looking to find any birthmarks, scars, tattoos, anything of the sort. She orders me to bend over with my legs spread wide. I squeeze my fists and break into a frenzy of sweat, feeling the moistness in my palms. On her command, I dress myself again and stand in the corner of the room, waiting.

A few minutes later, she reappears, followed by a middle-aged man in a long white overcoat. *Doctor* is embroidered on his left chest, *Adelabad Prison* under it. The man aims a small flashlight in my eyes, my ears, and my throat. He listens to the sound of my heartbeat and checks my pulse, careful that the tip of his fingers would not touch any part of my body. I glance at him and I see two horrified eyes and a wide forehead under his receding hairline. An overworked, underpaid, miserable doctor, perhaps an opium addict, who at least has found work in this hovel.

Talking to a male voice over his walkie-talkie, a *pasdar* in a brand new green, heavy army overcoat leads me through a wide corridor. The fabric has not yet lost its new oily smell. The walls are a clean cream color, but the air is filled with a pungent sanitizing smell like the one in hospitals. At the threshold of the *siasi* Cell Block 4, the women political prisoners' section, a buzzing sound opens the massive iron door enough for only one person to pass through. The *pas-dar* orders me to enter.

At first glance, the entrance seems nothing but an ordinary office with blank walls. To the left, there is a closed door and an iron staircase which loops up like a slithering snake. A common gray metal office desk is positioned at the base of the wall with a few open folding chairs around it; behind it sits a sturdy *pasdar*, his face dotted with chicken-pox scars. Tapping his fingers to his temple, he converses on the phone in an extreme Shirazi accent, the lower south-of-town people's drawl. He stutters over every few words. A pack of crow-like *Sisters* paces around his desk, chattering. One of them opens a crack between the drawn green tarpaulin curtains. She peeks through the slit for a moment, then turns and walks up to me. Her eyes are oddly small for such a fleshy, round face. For an instant, I see the eyes of a chicken flickering under her thick, un-threaded eyebrows. "Another one?" she says to a woman standing at the desk without removing her gaze from me. "Do you need to talk to her, brother?" she asks the man behind the desk.

He fondles the stack of papers in front of him. "*She is Mohammad's sister*," says the man in a low voice. With his eyes fixed on his huge black army boots, this newly *Hezbollah*-invented sign of modesty, he stands up and motions me to approach his desk. His swollen belly bulges out in his army shirt, stretching buttons to the brink of bursting. He looks at me; gazing longer than should be appropriate for a *na-mahram*, then he looks awkwardly down at the papers on his desk. I can see the glint of surprise and humiliation in his eyes. Perhaps my small body frame disappointed him. Seeing me alive before him, perhaps now it turns his stomach, thinking how four patrols filled with twenty male *pasdars* had miserably failed to catch a small creature like me on that horrible night ten months ago. My escape stirred such turbulence that an army of *Basiji* was called for backup, searching the entire neighborhood house-to-house all night long. The news, it was said, had shaken the prison like an exploding grenade. Apparently, the entire city heard about it. The first day that I turned myself in at the Sepah Detention Center, almost every one of the girls came quietly to see with their own eyes who this escaped panther was. No one said a word. Just a faint smile. I was ashamed; I had failed them.

"I am pleased you were wise enough to make the decision to repent," he tells me in his trained, sympathetic voice. "And not to fall for the deceitful words of those anti-revolutionary traitors. In case you don't know me, my name is Majid Torabpoor. Feel free to come see me any time you need to talk to me." Then he faces the *Sister* standing at his desk and whispers something to her. The *Sister* pushes one of the heavy curtains to the side and asks me to follow her.

So, this is it. Suddenly, the reality that I am in prison seeps through me. The infamous Adelabad Prison. It is said that with the help of Americans the Shah built it specifically for political prisoners, and that the Queen Shahbanoo cut the red ribbon with her very own hand on the day of the grand opening. Those despicable images cloud my vision: the images I have seen on the German TV series of the *Coldis Detention*, the murky dungeons I have read about in Victor Hugo's novels and seen in *Papillon*.

A nauseating smell of anti-bacterial disinfectant and iodine hits my nostrils as I pass behind the heavy curtain. Before me stretches the longest corridor I have ever seen; a rising triple tier of beige railings extends the length of the corridor, with iron bars reaching from ground to ceiling. Cubical cell after cell. From behind the railing of the second tier, a few girls peer down, their fists clinging to the bars of their tier. At the sight of the *Sister*, they quickly move away. An abrupt sound of banging comes from the third tier. It sounds like there is a fight. A string of obscenities stream down. A woman shrieks. Someone screams for a cigarette as I walk by. The screaming woman has barely any of her front teeth. She reaches her thin arm through the bars and bangs a small empty pan against the railing, begging me for a Shiraz cigarette.

"Eyes on the ground! Keep on walking!" orders the *Sister*.

My eye catches a glimpse of a miserable, young-old witch, a collection of bones rotting in her own filth. Her salt-and-pepper rat tail locks fall in a clump on her shoulders. She squats down and a yellow stream finds its way under the bars' panel and down onto the cement floor. Her cell reeks from urine and vomit. "You sister-fucker bitch," she barks as she sees me pass her cell without responding to her despair. Her bold ferocity raises the hair on the back of my neck.

This is the first time I have ever heard a woman curse like that, let alone directing it at me. My grandmother would have fainted if she were to see this. And Ali would have punched the walls from rage, breaking his knuckles, knowing that his baby sister had set foot among *damaged* women. He would curse Mohammad out with the nastiest curses of the world he knew, damning him that he had drawn me into his mess, fighting for a country and the freedom of a people, as he put it, who don't have the intelligence of a donkey. I shiver at the thought of his rage. Yet, I remind myself that here, at last, I can request a visit with Mohammad now that I have come into this hovel on my own feet. I have heard gossip that he has been finally released from his solitary. The last time I saw him was twenty-two months ago, the very morning that he was arrested.

The *Sister* stops in front of a cell to my right. "Here you are," she motions coldly. As soon as they notice me, all three girls move to make room. There is only one cot against the cement wall. No one welcomes me or introduces herself. The tallest and the prettiest of them asks if I have my stuff. I shake my head.

"Where do you come from?" she asks in a southern accent.

A girl from Abadan. I know the accent well. "Sepah Detention," I reply. "I didn't know I was coming here. My things are still over there."

"They'll give them to you later," the one seated on the floor says. This one is chubby and still has her fifth-grade, round, plump face and straight bangs.

"I'm Parvin," the one standing next to the wall says. Even with the faint smile she gives me, two beautiful dimples appear. She is even skinnier than I am. Her hair is cut in a short boyish style. She, too, speaks with a southern accent.

"Are you all from Abadan?" I ask. Too late. I'm already in trouble. Personal information is the last thing one would want to learn. But, I'm intrigued by her accent.

Parvin is generous with her dimples. "I'm from Abadan. Afsaneh," she points to the tall, pretty one, "is from the neighbor city, Ahvaz. Miss Shabrang here," she bows softly as she points to the Round-Face, "is from the immaculate soil of the city of Flower-and-Nightingale, Shiraz. How about you? What's your name?"

I hesitate for a moment, but her warm, musical accent and her good humor earn my trust. "I was born in Abadan, but I grew up here in Shiraz. So, you could say that I'm a double southerner."

"Don't worry! You'll meet lots of them here," Shabrang says, amused. "Half the congenial residents of the house," she turns her index finger in a circle, "are from Khoozestan province anyway."

Shabrang is right. There are many girls here from the war-destroyed southern cities, especially from Abadan and Ahavaz. And, naturally, most are convicted as sympathizers of the leftist Tudeh and Proletariat parties, the two major organizations that have their old roots in the south where first the British Petroleum companies and then the Americans ruled until the '79 Revolution. Abadan and Khoramshahr are now almost flattened to the ground from battles between Komeini's *Hezbollah* and Iraqi soldiers. But before the war broke out, the majority of the population of these cities worked for the oil refineries or were simple, working-class people and Arab fishermen, living in the palm groves at the bank of the Persian Gulf. A handful of population consisted of the affluent high-ranking oil refinery employees and executives who lived in the posh British-style housing sections in the upper part of the city.

Of the three cellmates, Shabrang is the youngest. She is only sixteen years old and has been here ten months already, still waiting for her verdict. They arrested her from behind her desk, in her junior class, for distributing anti-government pamphlets. Her older sister, Fariba, is here on the same tier but in a different cell. She is condemned to seven years for attending anti-government demonstrations in front of her school.

The cells are meant to be solitary, but now, including me, the four of us have to share this 2 x 3 meter cubicle. Most of the time, Afsaneh sleeps on the cot. She believes that she has developed rheumatism from sleeping on the floor and her body can no longer tolerate the cold cement. She has been here nine months because she was the best friend of a sympathizer who had strewn anti-government fliers under the houses of affluent residents in the uptown district. Like most girls, she too awaits her verdict. Even in prison, she is stylish; her well-off family set up a budget for her so she could buy canned food instead of eating the stomach-turning prison food. No one really has to warn me; just from the mere fact that she gets called to the entrance behind the curtain, I figure that I have to watch my tongue before her. She is an *Eye*.

At least eighty percent of detainees in *siasi* Cell Block 4 are high school and university students under the age of twenty-five. It is practically a school unto itself. There are several married women and a handful of middle-aged mothers. Mrs. Hashimi is among those mothers whose two student sons were executed last year as sympathizers of the Mojahedeen. Her youngest son is doing life in prison at Evin, the most dreadful of Tehran's political prisons. Her daughter's been held in a solitary cell at the Sepah Detention for over six months now, and her daughter-in-law is confined to the second tier among non-repentant Mojahedeen-e Khalgh sympathizers.

There is Soosan, who is only thirteen years old and sentenced to life in prison. When a revolutionary guard bus was blown up in the middle of Zand Street last spring, they arrested whomever was in the area that day. Soosan, returning from school and curious to see what had happened, lingered. When she was searched, the revolutionary guard found a pamphlet in her backpack. She was accused of blowing up the bus and sentenced to death; but somehow, they had mercy on her. Only twelve years of age then, she received parole: life in prison. Soosan, however, has found a new fascination these days: her developing bosom that she seems very proud of. She is the Block's pet, as well as the *Sisters'*. Parvin tells me that I should never speak in front of her because she reports every detail to the *Sisters*.

The first tier is exclusive to the so-called "repentant." With the exception of several hardheaded sympathizers, almost everyone who gets arrested these days repents on the spot, regardless of whatever fashionable ideology one may have adopted in school or at the university. It does not matter if you were for the Tudeh party and have voted for Communism; if you had taken the side of the Proletariat party or the Fadaee guerrillas and wanted to see Lenin and Marx in power rather than a backward Ayatollah; or if you believed that in a country that is 97 percent Shiite Muslim, all other ideologies would be failed and outdated theories, and looked instead to seek an alternative, so you stood by the Mojaheen's opposition, convincing yourself that at least they're preaching a revolutionary and progressive version of Islam. Now, it does not matter who you were only two years ago and what slogan you shouted; today, you have only one title: the enemy. And not just the enemy, the enemy of Islam and God Himself. Rahbar Imam Khomeini announced this to a mass of devoted *Hezbollah* army in front of his house in Jamaron. Hearing his statement over their radios or on their TVs, the nation began to wonder, "Where are we heading now?"

Right after the revolution was highjacked so shrewdly by Khomeini and the newly fanatic Ayatollahs, one by one the liberals were dismissed from their emergent positions in the new interim government and soon all parties' activities, left or right, were declared banned and counter-revolutionary. The people's revolution was still fresh out of the oven when the arrests began. The same political prisoners who spent years of their lives in the Shah's prisons and gained their freedom by the uproar and pressure of the masses, now were labeled anti-revolutionary, sought after, and condemned to jail once again. The same political parties which fought and struggled to establish a liberation movement, the heroes of the people, now were deemed foreign secret agents. Barely one year had passed before the *Hezbollah* took to the streets, blasting the organization offices with grenades. These organizations fell apart, their leading members executed on the spot. The ones who managed to escape took political asylum in foreign countries. Those who had returned from France, Germany, America, or wherever in the west, with the hope of building a prosperous, proud, and independent homeland, turned around and fled the country on planes, boats, the backs of mules, or on foot, dejected and disillusioned. The Revolutionary Court arrested and executed thousands and thousands of young students all over the country without holding any trials. The violence and the executions were so unexpected and brutal that it left many no choice but to announce repentance to save themselves from the noose. Regardless, the Revolutionary Court still continued to execute on the pretext that this repentance is phony and a mind-game. Maybe it is. But can you blame them?

None of the prisoners in this Block are members of any parties, left or right. No one here has ever been involved in armed actions against the government. If they were, their remains would have been already decomposed in the New Cemetery. No members or fervent devotees are being brought to Adelabad. They are kept either at the Sepah Detention Center in solitary confinement or sent to dreadful Evin prison or other unknown places. Most girls' crimes involve selling the parties' newspapers, distributing pamphlets, reading flyers in public, and discussing current affairs in street groups.

They keep the *oldies*, the non-repentant Mojahedeen sympathizers on the second tier. Among them are a number of non-repentant *lefties* who still refuse to do the five-times daily prayers or read the Koran, and a group of *Bahai* believers whom the *Hezbollah* had announced to be non-Muslim and infidel. The *Sisters* refer to the entire second tier as "the dirty, soiled dogs" who soil the ground Muslims walk on and the air Muslims breathe. Any contact between the first and second tiers is absolutely forbidden. Some always follow the rules. Some, now and then. And some don't and pay a hefty price. If any of the *Sisters* or one of the *Eyes* catches us using body language or any sort of exchange with the ones on the second tier, we're up for a lashing, an interrogation, and solitary confinement.

There are midnights when the loudspeaker calls someone's name from the second tier, and we all know that she will never return. Even though most of them are condemned to life in prison, each one of their verdicts has gone to Tehran's Central Revolutionary Court for revision and a request for the death penalty. Sometimes, people disappear in the middle of the day and return days later limping, their faces colorless and their eyes hollow. Now, I understand the pain and suffering Mohammad must have endured in his solitary cell. I wish there was a safe place somewhere so I could cry for my brother and for all those who are held here because they wanted true freedom for this country and a democratic, liberated society.

Among the non-repentant condemned to the second tier is a group of *Bahai* whose members the new government has declared to be foreign-protégé spies, one of the many newly invented labels. They spring out daily from the magic box of the Ayatollahs who determine hell and heaven on earth. And of course, the death penalty permissions bear the very sacred signature of the *Rahbar* Imam Khomeini or his designated chief justice at the Central Revolutionary Supreme Court. Among the minority religious groups, the Bahais are the ones who really got targeted by the government and the reactionary guard *Hezbollah*. Most of their homes were either burned or taken away from them, their wealth confiscated and distributed among the government organizations as public booty. Almost every dawn, one of them gets called over the loudspeaker. They leave their cells quietly, knowing that they will be hanged an hour later. And all these despicable acts are done in the name of God, his prophet, Mohammad, and in the name of the people of this country, making us Muslims, as Bibi puts it, "black-faced." In the mornings, the *Sisters* pass by our cells and joyfully announce how the Islamic guards have glorified the planet earth, that they have served God and His people by eradicating another evil-driven soul. And, of course, we nod our heads in approval because the chill in our bones reminds us that any sign of sympathy or disagreement could send us back to the Sepah Detention where the *pasdars'* cable-whip is mighty enough to freeze our hearts into solid stone.

# CHAPTER 7

The fights and the noises hardly ever stop on the third tier where they keep the non-political, ordinary, *normal* inmates. There is always shouting and screaming of some sort. There is always something falling to the ground: the crash of a pot, the fall of a ladle, the dirty panties they want you to smell as a sign of their love and affection for you. Most of the women were arrested under the Shah's regime. Perhaps they saw glimpses of the demonstrations on the black-and-white Sony TV set on the occasional TV days, but they were too busy doing time or oblivious to the outside world to realize that the Khomeini government had taken over. They have no idea of what's going on and what it means to be a political prisoner. Either the *Sepah* guard had made them believe or they have grasped on their own, that we are afflicted with contagious, incurable diseases. None of them owns a black chador or has an idea what to do each time the loudspeaker announces: *"All tiers, complete hijab,"* before the curtains are pushed to the sides.

Never before in my life have I heard such words that the women call each other. They bite off bitter sentences. For each verb, there are two curse words. After the lights-out, the lovers chase their quarry in the dark. The muffled moaning, the giggling, the singing, the nightmares, the sleepwalking, and the howling just begin. The *Sisters* don't dare to interfere with these women, whose severe victimhood has made them predators, like packs of wild wolves. The *Sisters* save their brave faces and tortures only for us, the *siasi* prisoners. Even though these *normal* women are here in the political Block

38

section, officially they are under the jurisdiction of Criminal Justice rather than the Revolutionary Court.

Block 4 belongs to these women. They were here long before we came. They hate us, these inmates. And if the *Sepah* guard will let them, they will split our legs apart for violating their territory and shooing them off to the third tier where they're forced to share their cells, and where there's no corridor for them to walk. Not that they really move much. They will rip the hearts out of our throats for bringing the *Sepah* guard, who had banned smoking in the women's prison. And to top it off, they are forced to observe *hijab*, get up at dawn for the ablution rituals, and attend the religious commemorations on Wednesday nights.

The *Sepah* guard keep them here for one purpose only: to inflict psychological and emotional torture on the political prisoners. Now and then, they even throw one of the non-repentant, or someone who needs a little reminder of where she is, into one of the cells on the third tier. The *Sepah* use any excuse to give us a taste of what it feels like to be among professional prostitutes, once daytime-mothers-and-nighttime-whores, the drug addicts, and the heroin smugglers who come and leave in a few days on a hefty bail.

"The worst part is this bitter feeling," Parvin whispered to me the other day as the *Sisters* dragged one of the non-repentant to the third tier, "that you may have wasted your precious life. That you had torn your throat, shouting on the streets for the liberation of the masses. That you demanded a better life for the poor, underprivileged people just like these ones who dare to spit at you." Of course, they, too, are victims of circumstance, I thought to myself, only in a different way than we.

The most disturbing of the *normal* inmates are the newly-arrested, miserable opium and heroin addicts who lie down on the floor all day long behind the bars, shivering violently in pain, scratching their arms and chest to the point of bleeding, begging for a cigarette. You see them sometimes spreading their naked legs, yelling to the others: "I give you my pussy. Come and fuck it. For the love of the Prophet, somebody have a heart and give me a cigarette! Shiraz, Zar, Oshnoo, anything. Just a puff of smoke."

Then, there are the insane. There is Ashraf *khanoom*, for instance, who they say has gone mad since the day she was condemned to thirteen years of prison when the late Shah's government gave her breast-feeding child to an orphanage. In her sleep she wails: *babam, babam, babam,* my baby, my baby, my baby. They say that she had murdered her husband with rat poison because he had taken a lover in another city. Her crying is so heartrending I want to stand in the middle of the corridor and scream out loud. Within myself, I take refuge in a faraway place, a vast desert, and I run and run and run the entire night.

# CHAPTER 8

Monday is the Visit Day for the women's Block at Adelabad. Most *normal* prisoners don't have any visitors. Monday has become a sacred day for us. We wait for the fifteen-minute visit an entire week. In contrast, it is the worst day for these godforsaken women as they hear the loudspeaker calling our names and as we line up impatiently before the gate. They lament and whimper all day. It is the only time they wish to be us. "Even God Himself was not generous to grant us at least a bit of luck to be a *siasi*," they utter as they peer down through their tier's bars, thinking that being a *siasi* is something genetic and can be inherited.

This afternoon, two of my older brothers, Ebrahim and Rahim, came to visit me along with my mother. Now that I am in prison, I actually get to see my brothers. My mother kept biting her lips to stop the tears from overflowing. My brothers did not look directly at me as they handed the receiver to each other. I know they have feared this, to visit their sister too from behind the glass barrier. Rahim tried to convince me that everything is going to be all right and that soon I will be free and coming home. Ebrahim just stood there and let out frustrated sighs.

"Why did they have to bring you here?" He shook his head. "It was supposed to be a couple hours of questioning."

My mother couldn't bear it any longer. Two large tears bubbled over, but she wiped them off before the droplets trickled down her cheeks. After nearly two years of visiting Mohammad from behind the glass barrier, she knows well enough that crying would cost her weeks of visits being revoked.

"They promised me personally that they would never imprison you," she maintained. "They swore on the Holy Book that the questioning would not take even a half day. It's not like you were a murderer or a criminal. Mother, what have I done?" She sobbed as she pulled her black chador down over her face.

"It'll be all right, *Momon*," I said and tried to comfort her by putting the palm of my hand on the glass for an instant. "It's just the official procedures, I guess." I was sure I did not sound convincing.

Maybe it was because deep down I was bitter and angry at my mother and my brothers, even at Mohammad. I was angry at my mother's naïveté. I wanted to tell her that these bastards lied to you, so that you would willingly bring your own daughter and hand her to the *Sepah* guard. Instead, I covered the receiver with my hand and pronounced *Mohammad* without making a sound. My mother nodded her head slightly, and I understood that Mohammad had his visitation rights last Wednesday. The conversations are being overheard and the first interrogator made it clear that I was not allowed to know anything about Mohammad or his whereabouts. My mother motioned with her hand, asking if I had been lashed. I shook my head no. She has enough sorrows to haunt her for the rest of her life.

It is exactly two months since the day that my mother brought me to the Sepah Detention Center. And how bitterly my grandmother cried that day when my mother came with the news that I had to turn myself in. The news which shook the foundation of everything I believed in and which changed my fate.

"Are you out of your crooked mind?" Bibi yelled at her daughter that day. "Has your heart turned to stone to offer your only daughter to the open mouth of a dragon? This is the time that Ali should have been here," she howled. "Despite all his flaws, if he were not jailed himself, he would've slaughtered you this instant like a Lamb of Sacrifice for doing an ungodly thing to this innocent virgin. If her brothers were man enough," she gestured at my brothers, "they would not allow their baby sister to walk with her own feet to a dungeon run by blood-thirsty *Shemrs*. These murderers are non-Muslim. They have no fear of God."

In that week before I turned myself in, Bibi refused to eat anything except a piece of fruit or bread. She cried and prayed, prayed and cried. At night, I could not sleep because I could hear her muffled voice, praying desperately in the next room. She sat right there on her small prayer rug in the dark, her arms held high to heaven. "I am begging you, you the merciful Divine. I am but a humble slave of yours. I bow to your Moses and Jesus. I bow to the Prophet of the Prophets, Ebrahim, and to your Prophet Mohammad, may peace be upon him and his descendants. My wish was to walk in the footsteps of Hadjar in the holy city of Mecca. But now, I am asking you to please forgive me this girl as you have forgiven innocent Ismaeel to his mother, Hadjar." She cried, and I cried for her pleading. I was worried about her. With that horrible sight of hers, I feared that she would go blind.

Miserable, miserable Mother. She was baffled, heartbroken, and didn't know how to solve this new dilemma in her life. She didn't even curse that day, delivering that horrid news. I wish she had. Like the way she did when my brothers and I were much younger. When she would come home exhausted from work to witness my brothers' bloody noses after they had gotten into another fistfight with each other. "God, why didn't you bless me like the rest of the barren women," she would wail. "If you're a merciful God, you would take all my children away and plant them behind seven black mountains and let me be the loneliest woman on earth so I could breathe a moment."

God, my mother could curse. Now she commutes three days of the week to see three of her children behind the bars. There was a time when she would rush back and forth between Adelabad Prison and the Detention Center, carrying baskets of fruit and medicine for Mohammad who suffers from an ulcer, from this end of the city to the other end so she could see three of her sons from behind the glass barrier in one day. And the rest of the days she stood in line for hours among hundreds of other mothers, wives, and sisters in front of the Revolutionary Court, fighting either for a revoked visit or to find out about Mohammad's verdict. My brothers are leaving her house one by one, but she is still the most miserable mother I have ever known. She is right, my brothers and I have brought her nothing but pain.

That day was a Wednesday when my mother came to see me with four of my brothers. Bibi and I were surprised to see them all together. None of my brothers knew where I was and my mother came a little sooner than I expected. It was Mohammad's visit day and she knew that I would be waiting impatiently for her and for any fresh news, which was never good anyway. After twenty months of imprisonment, Mohammad's verdict, too, was sent to the Revolutionary Supreme Court for revision. It was a mistake, his interrogators at *Sepah* decided: he did not deserve such a light sentence as life in prison. He deserves the death penalty, they decided. When he was arrested on that summer midday, perhaps in one of the less-traveled residential neighborhoods in uptown Ghasr-e-Dasht on the pretext of the typical suspicious *siasi* student's clean-cut looks—his brown framed glasses, shaved face, and sky-blue shirt—the revolutionary guard did not know who he was or if he had any connection to the anti-government movement. I guess God was with him; the *Sepah* did not execute him right away. He turned twenty-two the same week he was transferred to Adelabad Prison.

It was 1981, barely two years after the revolution. None of the phony, staged court histrionics we go through now existed yet. Then, whoever looked suspicious of being a sympathizer of what the *Hezbollah* labels "anti-revolutionary" groups would be snatched off the street and brought into the Sepah Detention Center. If the trapped ones were lucky enough, they would be condemned to life in prison or to a lighter sentence of twenty years or so. God forbid if the *Hezbollah* actually found a banned book or any political pamphlets lying in the street, or had any hint or suspicion that one favored anti-government parties. The noose would be set up in an instant, and the suspect hanged, be it in the public street or in the hidden execution yard. The fanatic Khomeini government was not bluffing when they threatened death. They were here to stay; and if they had to eradicate the entire population of Iran in order to enforce their twisted version of Islam, then that would be it, as Khalkhali, the head of the Supreme Court shouted in one of his Friday rants.

However, not much later, those who were sentenced were considered the real anti-revolutionaries. Among the *oldies*—the title *Sepah* gives to the initial group of prisoners who still would not repent or recognize the imposed government—Mohammad was tossed back and forth from Adelabad to *Sepah* every time someone new was arrested. On and off, he spent fourteen of his twenty months in the Sepah Detention, a good portion of the time in solitary confinement. The *Sepah* claims that Mohammed has organized a secret alliance to regroup the political prisoners and prepare them for a sudden revolt against the prison guard.

At the Revolutionary Court, my mother demanded to know the reason why her son's verdict was revised to the death penalty. They told her that her son had brainwashed his cellmates, preaching that the Islamic Republic would not last more than a year. Then the *Sepah* told her that she must advise her son to repent, for she has an Islamic obligation to do so.

Once, I ran into an acquaintance at a funeral; he had been released from temporary arrest at the Detention Center. I begged him to give me any news about my brother. He told me that Mohammad was like a ball of energy and had brought the *Sepah's* guard to their knees. I was not surprised. I always knew Mohammad had secrets; I knew that at least five people lived in him. He was blessed with so much vigor and courage and guts as a little boy. I told him what *Sepah* had told my mother. He said it was partly true. "If they want to call it preaching, yes he preaches all the time. He tells everyone openly that the brave masses of Iranian people will soon throw the horrible regime into the historical garbage bin forever. That the prison's doors would be broken open just as they were in '79 and democracy and freedom would return once and for all. I saw that you are no longer allowed to talk like that in prison. This is no longer the Shah's prison, it is Khomeini's now."

Then he said that in reality Mohammad has been penalized for gathering fruit, medicine, and clothes from everyone and distributing them among those inmates who have no visitors, are from far-away provinces, or whose families have no idea of their whereabouts. And he had set up a daily workout routine, scheduled chores for sanitizing the Block to keep the contagious skin diseases in control, and had invented games so the inmates wouldn't get bored out of their minds. Since there are no books or magazines allowed in prison, he, among several others, set up a specific time for daily group prayers and reciting the Koran and had assigned each cellmate to encourage those weaker inmates to endure the *Sepah's* physical and psychological torture.

On these pretexts, the *Sepah* guard kept him mostly on a short leash but they were still not satisfied. They had requested his verdict be revised to the death penalty. Ever since then, Wednesday had become a dreadful day. The entire family would anxiously await my mother's return, expecting her to say that this had been her last visit with Mohammad.

That Wednesday, when my mother returned, I had no doubt that this was the day. My heart sank at the sight of the paleness of her face.

"We came to tell you something," Rahim said in a choked voice.

I looked at him. His large honey-brown eyes were red. *Has he been crying?*

A cold chill ran over the arch of my back; I slid down against the wall, collapsed to my knees, and burst into tears. "My innocent brother's gone," I murmured.

"No, dear. He is alive," my mother gasped. "I had a face-to-face visit with him today."

"A face-to-face visit?" I shook my head. "*Momon*, they give mothers live visits just before they hang their children."

"I know that," Mother said, irritated. "But it wasn't the reason they gave me for this visit today. It's something very important. That's why all of us are here today. It's about you."

"Me? Why does this visit have anything to do with me?" I asked, feeling the sweat escaping my palms even though my hands were frozen.

My mother looked at my two eldest brothers who looked back at her, then at me. My two other brothers followed their glances without saying a word. Bibi was getting impatient and agitated, yet surprisingly, she kept quiet, too frightened to ask anything.

"Please, *Momon*, tell me what has happened?"

"Mohammad has attempted suicide," Rahim said under his breath without looking at me. "He . . . he tried to hang himself in the solitary. . . ."

"Dear God!" I gasped. I could hardly breathe. "But . . . tell me he is well!" My voice was barely audible even in my own ears.

"Yes," Ebrahim sighed. "Fortunately, somehow, one of the guards noticed. That's why we didn't have a visit last week. They had taken him to the prison clinic because he had a severe ulcer and internal bleeding. Apparently, he used a bed sheet . . . I don't know how to tell you . . . at least, this is what they're telling us."

"My poor, poor child," Bibi slapped her cheeks, weeping. "Is that the revolution you wanted, my dear Mohammad? May I die for your sufferings, *babam*. God, what have they done to this innocent child? How? How could that be?"

I ran to the courtyard and threw up in the garden. I sat there leaning against the wall and sobbed and sobbed and sobbed. My mother and my brothers stayed frozen where they sat, crying solemnly. Minutes passed before Ebrahim came to the courtyard and offered me a glass of water.

"It is not possible," I kept shaking my head. "Mohammad wouldn't ever think of taking his life. Would he?" I asked, looking into his mournful eyes.

"He is just a human being, my sister." He squatted down next to me. "It's been two years of living in hell for him, not to mention the year before when he got arrested. Almost all of those taken in during his time have repented now. He has been real hardheaded. No TV interview, no collaboration. But all that lashing on his feet and his back, the solitary cell, day-in and day-out interrogations, his ulcer pain, the constant psychological torment, and worst of all, seeing Mother growing old visiting him behind the barrier glass; it would break any man. These bastards use emotional and mental torture."

"I always thought nothing, no hardships and no person could ever break Mohammad's spirit," I said.

"He's not made out of steel. Is he? I saw him today," Ebrahim uttered. "Believe me, it's not his spirit that's broken. It's this," he tapped his chest where his heart was, "that's broken. He's practically skin and bones. He uses an elastic band to keep his glasses from falling down. You should've seen him. He was still smiling." Ebrahim's lips quivered. Quickly, he wiped his eyes. "Sometimes I wonder what kind of people God has created. So heartless."

"I know Mohammad better than anyone. If that's true, I am certain he did it to save others," I murmured. "Everything is out in the open.

There were no secrets to begin with. One day all parties are legal, the next day they're banned. They want him to give the names of the people he had contact with. They have arrested everyone already. But Khomeini's regime knows well that these are bright minds who would not bend to their fears. They will not sleep at night until they kill them all."

Ebrahim did not say anything. He never approved of any political involvements. He believes that the superpowers have already determined Iran's destiny, and this government is no different from any other corrupt governments with corrupt power. He thinks that all the slogans of freedom, democracy, and nationality are just a bunch of empty promises. So why should one lose his life for the illusion of a never-come-true democratic system that would never be allowed, either from the inside nor the outside.

Ebrahim helped me to my feet. I washed my face and went back to my mother. She was still sobbing. My mother's crying is the most painful cry I have ever heard, a soundless, bitter sob with large droplets of tears. I used to think that she was not capable of crying, but in these past few years I have seen plenty.

"*Momon*," I said quietly. "You all came here to tell me something. What is it?"

My mother looked at me. So did my brothers.

"Mohammad has announced repentance," she said painfully.

"That can't be," I shrieked. "Saying what? That the Khomeini's regime is fair and justified? After all that torture and lashings done to him, and God knows what. . . ."

"He wants you to turn yourself in," Rahim interrupted me.

"What? Did they burn him with hot iron? *Momon*, you saw him. Was he all right? Did you touch him? Did you get to hug him? Did you feel anything unusual?"

"He was wearing his sandals," Ebrahim said.

"But he wasn't leaning in the chair," my mother cried. "So, maybe they lashed his back again. I couldn't tell. We weren't allowed to touch or hold each other. He gave me a quick hug and kissed me on the forehead, and I kissed his cheek. Don't you know him? You can't ever tell if he's in pain or not. He always keeps a good face."

"Why does he want his sister to turn herself in?" exploded Bibi suddenly. "After all this time she's been hiding here, all that misery finding her a safe place."

"I told him that," Mother replied, ignoring Bibi and facing me. "He said that sooner or later they will catch you and that you can't be in hiding forever. He said that the *Sepah* had arrested everyone and everyone had told whom they talked to, what they did, and what kind of connections they had. He said that you have not taken part in any organizations and if you had read or distributed any pamphlets at school, it was because he gave them to you, and it was at a time that they were still permitted. Am I right, Ebrahim?" she paused, obviously searching for my brother's help.

"The *Sepah* is angry mainly because you escaped that night," Ebrahim said. "Torabpoor said if you come in voluntarily and repent what you have done and admit that you are not against the Islamic Republic, they will forgive you. The last thing Mohammad said was that I should tell you this," he faltered and ran a hand through his curly hair. "He said that his fate is already determined, but he can't witness your life being ruined as well." Ebrahim's voice trembled.

It was all too much, more than my brain could process and my heart could accept. I was expecting anything but this. After all the catastrophes the entire family had gone through. My mother took me from this place to that place like a mother cat carrying her kitten at its nape.

"I guess you all are forgetting that these people executed school kids who had read a flier. Twelve-year-olds, for God's sake. What would they do to a fugitive," I said.

No one responded.

"I know I was nobody, not an active sympathizer of any organization," I said in a disappointed voice, "but I believe in justice. What about dignity? What about pride? I learned all this from Mohammad himself. By going in I will make a fool of myself. You know what kind of message I will send to others? That the regime is capable of making us bend, to make us bow to injustice, to validate them. And even if they let me go, what would I be? A traitor in the eyes of both sides. Who's going to respect me anymore? My God, this regime has figured it all out."

"You have your life ahead of you, dear," my mother said.

I looked at my mother for a moment, then leaned my head against the wall and stared at the ceiling. No one said a word, and Bibi was still crying. "If I turn myself in," this time I looked at Ebrahim, "would that improve Mohammad's verdict? Did they say anything about that?"

"Torabpoor was there himself," answered my mother instead. "After they took Mohammad away, he told me that the *Sepah* knows well that I know where my daughter is. He said that he could actually arrest me today with the charges of harboring a counter-revolutionary fugitive. But he promised that he, personally, will give his word not to imprison you if you go in voluntarily. He said there are some questions you should answer and they would let you go. And besides, by your going in, Mohammad's verdict of life imprisonment will be reinstated."

"In that case, I could actually help Mohammad?" I looked at her, a bit hopeful.

"I don't know. I don't know what to say. I have one dear-to-heart one in their claws already. I don't want to lose another one," she sobbed.

"Is there any time frame?" I asked.

"Well, Torabpoor told me the best thing is just to bring you over the next day. Or else, next week when I'm going to visit Mohammad, he said, he might have my arrest order as well."

If this wasn't psychological torture, I don't know what it was, dragging the entire family into their traps, especially the mothers. One thing I was sure of, I did not want anything to happen to her. "I'll go, *Momon*," I said.

"You don't have to decide right now," Ebrahim said. "Let's think about it more carefully."

There was nothing to think about. I would die for my brother if I had to. I knew his life in prison was a day-to-day death. Why else would he have wanted to kill himself? True or a lie? Still, who knows what would happen tomorrow. Maybe the Human Rights organizations will come to Iran one of these days. Maybe the United Nations will demand that Khomeini change his perspective towards political prisoners. Things could change; just as they did in '79. My head was full of thoughts. I was both terrified and hopeful. "I don't believe any of their promises. But I'll go, for the sake of Mohammad and the family," I said.

It is exactly two months before that day my mother brought me to the Sepah Detention, and eleven months before that horrible night of my escape when the *Sepah* guards came to arrest me. My escape stirred such turbulence that several *Sepah* guard patrols were called as backup, turning the entire neighborhood upside down, searching house by house in the heart of a night which seemed never-ending. I spent nine jittery months in hiding, confined to a small bungalow on the outskirts of the city in a new-developing, working-class area. The only view I had was a narrow alley. The entire two-bedroom place was the size of our drawing room. There was no kitchen and the shower was so tiny that you had to be careful not to hit yourself on the wall. Summer passed, and fall, then winter came, and I watched the seasons change in a treeless courtyard the size of my room in our own house. I yearned to have a glance at trendy Moshir-fatemi and Paramount Streets. I ached for the fashionable *passages* uptown where my friends and I used to meet for a cup of Turkish coffee in one of the cozy cafés after a good shouting at yet another one of the national demonstration days or for an ice-cold cherry *faloodeh* to escape from the heat, school, and the shrieking Principal Modarrasi all together. Behind the four-walls of this midget house, I knew well that those cheerful images were now just a short-lived memory and that the streets of my beautiful Shiraz are stomped by violent *Hezbollah* who knife young men in short sleeves and spray acid into young women's faces if they fail to observe the newly-imposed, mandatory *hijab*. I wondered about Principal Modarrasi and her promises: "If not anyone's, but your destiny, for sure, is in my hand. Not even in your dreams will you get to receive your high school diploma, you … you. …" And all I could hear was this last word she kept repeating as she reached to snatch the leaflets out of my squeezed hands. Her menacing voice echoing in the empty corridor, my hurried footfalls bouncing on the floor. Looking back, I wondered again whose hands will hold my destiny this time.

Bibi has been with me day and night, thinking that if she left, something dreadful would happen to me. The neighbors didn't know anything about us or that I was a runaway *siasi*. They didn't know that I've come from a big family or that I have seven brothers, two of them in prison; they simply assumed that Bibi was my only family. To them, we were just a humble, courteous grandmother and grand-daughter. I didn't mind them thinking that. It kept me safe, because nowadays, even the neighbors could turn out to be one's enemy. The *Hezbollah* and the *Sepah* guards ordered people to report any suspicious movements, or anyone who might have ties with counter-revolutionaries. The corrupt Ayatollahs have created so much terror and extreme fear that there are times now that the closest family members would report each other. A mother-in-law may accuse her daughter-in-law of being a counter-revolutionary because she did not mince the meat right. Or a neighbor could report her closest neighbor out of pure spitefulness and old resentments. Now, revenge and ignorance hang in the air, and tyranny and terror rule the country.

My mother came once or twice a week, bringing baskets of fruit, gunny sacks of rice and other necessities. Suddenly, her sense of fashion bloomed gloriously. She turned the situation to her advantage and brought me clothes of her taste. For once she liked my style. I despised them, but I wore them anyway. She brought me outdated, cliché novels and magazines my brothers gave her. The books of crossword puzzles were back in my life, but now I didn't know how to solve them. The questions were all about the Mullahs and their inventive version of Islam, making me feel like an illiterate person who had just started to read. So, I threw them in the garbage and returned to my abandoned hobbies: needlepoint, design, and sewing. She brought me wool knitting yarn, an electric sewing machine, and sewing materials in order to keep me from turning into Kal Habib the beggar who talked to his shoes as he rummaged from alley to alley. We owned no TV and the radio reported constantly from the war-torn, southern cities, promising next week's victory and the overthrow of Saddam Hussein. Music was no longer allowed, and the radio played distressing combat songs and depressing prayers in Arabic all day.

My mind now wanders to the heart of that night of my escape. It was a hot summer night, a little past midnight. My mother already had arranged my brothers' bedrolls over the rooftop and had set up the wooden double-bed along the fishpond for herself and me. She filled the larger flask with crushed ice and placed it at the edge of the fishpond and carried the smaller one to the rooftop for my brothers in case one of them felt thirsty. Three of my brothers were hanging out in the alley, conversing with their friends; a common thing the neighborhood boys did when the heat became overpowering and robbed the sleep from their eyes. Rahim was sleeping on his cot by the orange garden. He had just started working for some sort of manufacturing company and usually left when the sky was still gray so that he could beat the long commute.

Ever since I was a little girl, I had looked forward to the summer nights of sleeping on the rooftop. When I was much smaller, before my mother invaded my childhood and the entire house and gardens still belonged only to me and Bibi, I would crawl into Bibi's bedroll, and in her arms I would watch the stars play hide-and-seek with the moon above.

That night, on their rooftop adjacent to ours, our next-door neighbor, Mahboobeh, a new mother, was breastfeeding her baby under a mosquito net. I helped my mother carry the bedrolls upstairs. She did this every evening as soon as a breeze began to start so that my brothers could sleep on cool bedrolls.

The day before, at my insistence, Bibi had come, unwillingly, to visit, despite the fact that she felt uneasy stepping into a house that once belonged to her but was now legally her daughter's, who had made her hand it over so she could apply for a home loan. My grandmother left the house she had built with her own hands to live in a minuscule fifty-meter house in a far-off neighborhood. Something told me that I ought to spend as much time with my grandmother, ignoring my mother's mocking comments about her sincerity. And since Bibi's knees were bothering her again, my mother arranged her bedroll by the rose bushes so she did not have to go up the stairs. As usual, I dragged my mat next to Bibi's and brought one of the novels I had borrowed from the City Library. I used to read different types of stories to her. They were books that were banned from libraries across the country. Books by Ashraf Darvishian, Ahmad Mahmood, Simin Daneshvar, Jalal Al Ahmad, and many other great authors;

you did not see their stories in any schoolbooks or hear their names spoken above a whisper. Bibi would cry for the characters and their misery, giving constant thanks to her infinite, white-bearded God that despite all her misery, at least she did not live as hard a life as they. I always thought she too lived a hard life that deserved to be a book by itself. "Some day," I told her one night, "I will write your life story, Bibi." She shook her head bitterly. "Ah, my child's child, by then, your Bibi's bones will be a fistful of ashes in a cold grave."

There were hundreds and hundreds of books banned under the Shah's regime; then, they called them lefties, anti-Shah, and *deviated* materials, corrupting youth's minds. I read them only to Bibi and hid them in the back closet of her room, which my mother had generously turned into a storage place with a good supply of five-years of Tide detergent, cartons of Lux soap, Paveh shampoo, Colgate toothpaste, gallons of sun-flower frying oil, and gunny sacks of Basmati rice and sugar-cubes. Bibi never knew that they were forbidden books or that the Shah's secret police, the *SAVAK*, had jailed their authors at one time or another, labeling them Communists, Marxists, and terrorists. I decided to leave out a few minor details. Bibi wouldn't know what a Communist was anyway; she couldn't even pronounce the word. She enjoyed the stories so much, I had to read them to her over and over. I must have read Simin Daneshvar's *Soovashoon* at least three times to her. She shed so many tears when Yusef was murdered that it made me regret reading it again. Her sight was bad already. "Just like my *shahid* father, may I die for his pure, wound-ridden body," she would whimper, recalling the death of her own father. "Your great-grandfather was killed by the hand of merciless feudal landlords, *babam*. Those godless savages took his land, possessed his fruit gardens. Hey . . . hey . . . hey . . ."

My grandmother could not read or write, but I read to her almost everything that I had been reading so that by then she was familiar even with a handful of Russian and French novels. Although she could not pronounce their names, she would ask me to read her novels by Dostoyevsky, Victor Hugo, Charles Dickens, Mark Twain, and Hemingway. A great traditional storyteller herself, she had so insatiable a desire to hear, as she always put it, "the stories from books" that I had become her reading eyes once I began to learn how to read.

That night I dragged my bedroll next to Bibi's and read a chapter of a book to myself. The story wasn't that appealing, and I read just out of mere habit to put myself to sleep. It was a hot, breezeless night. My mother was wearing one of her flowery summer dresses. Without bothering to cover herself with a sheet, she lay down motionless on the wooden bed right next to the white *nastaran*, sweet briars, and jasmine bushes, her eyes wide open to the dark sky, perhaps thinking of her sons in prison. It was her favorite spot. In the morning I could smell the jasmine perfume on her. That same evening, Bibi had picked some of the blossoms, let them float in a bowl of water, and placed it by her bed to keep the mosquitoes away. My mother had lost her vibrant energy. Not being good at expressing her thoughts and feelings, communication has never been her forte. To make up for it, she'd put all her efforts into physical actions. She would go about the house for hours doing the chores without talking much. Sometimes, I would hear her mutter random, vague words to herself as she cooked over the stove in the quiet of the kitchen. She was not much of a sleeper either, but now insomnia seized her at night when she would just lie there in her bed, staring at the gliding moon. She was suffering from rapid weight loss; each morning, the plump half-moons under her eyes were becoming darker and the lines around her mouth deeper. When was the last time I've seen her laugh, I wondered. In our house, barely anyone laughed anymore. The thought of Mohammad behind the bars of Adelabad Prison hung over the entire house. like an invisible tent of webs.

From where I slept, I could hear my brothers and their friends talking in our small alley. No one played soccer or chess any more. These were signs of corruption and disrespect to the youth who were dying around the clock on the front line of the war with Iraq. Chess had been forbidden and everyone who had a set burned it or hid it to keep it safe from the *pasdars* who searched the houses without a warrant. Mohammad, too, broke into pieces his prized ebony chess set when the Ayatollahs announced this ancient game to be a satanic device; it had been presented to him by the very hand of Prince Reza Pahlavi when Mohammad won third place in Iran's National Youth Chess Championship. He was fourteen then.

I could hear the boys talk about war, and that so-and-so, son or brother of this person and that person they used to go to school with had died stepping on an Iraqi mine; they were *shahid* now, martyrs. This was another one of the latest words one would hear at least a hundred times a day, along with the new Arabic words like *jihad* and *kafer*.

I had barely fallen sleep when I woke up, startled. The *Sepah Pasdaran* guards had already barged into our house a few times, searching for anything to substantiate their indictment of Mohammad as a key player in the anti-government movement, so we were not surprised that they would pay us yet another surprise visit. I feared that one of these days they would come for me. I had read anti-government fliers and distributed them at school. To protest against the mass arrests, I had handed fliers to passersby on the street corner or slipped them under people's house doors until the vicious, one-hour executions started and the connections between the parties and their sympathizers were lost. After Mohammad was arrested, I was so angry that I could not just sit at home and read passively. So, to support the people's solidarity in struggle and to show my respect, I went to visit mothers and sisters whose children, brothers, or fathers were hanged or had disappeared. In doing so, I sought a bit of comfort; after all, I, myself, was the sister of an imprisoned brother whose life wavered at the blade of a rising, bloody tyranny. Soon, this sort of moral support was labeled an act of aiding and harboring terrorists and was strictly banned. Death and imprisonment were threatened and carried out openly. The way things were turning upside down, I knew that one day, sooner or later, somebody would be arrested, and somehow my name would be mentioned. I warned my mother, who thought I had been taking a fashion-and-design class all this time, to prepare her that one of these nights they might actually come to arrest me. She cursed with half the curses she knew, wondering why on earth I had not learned my lesson; the Islamic Revolution had brought us what a new revolution will bring: nothing but horrors and misery. My brothers, who were like my mother, didn't think that what I had done was something to be persecuted for. "You were giving moral support, that's all," they said, so I left it at that and hoped that they were right. Yet, every day I lived with fear in the pit of my stomach, robbing me and everyone else in the house of sleep.

That night when the *Sepah* guard came, I thought I heard my name and surname. I have not heard my surname spoken since I graduated from high school. I heard Hossein arguing with someone: "There are women sleeping in the courtyard with their hair uncovered," he was saying, blocking a man from entering the doorway. He was always the hardhead of the family. "I won't allow you inside until I tell them to cover their hair." His voice was shaky. At that very moment, I knew that this time the *Sepah* had come not to rummage around the house, but they had come for me. I sprang to my feet and instinctively ran for the rooftop. The door flung open with Hossein pushed into the courtyard. Even in the dark I recognized the *pasdar's* green uniform. The stairs were too dark for them to see me, but the empty bedroll next to Bibi's, the half-open book, and the headscarf I kept handy and forgot to snatch up, caught their attention.

I jumped from my rooftop over to the adjacent neighbor's roof, half a meter lower than ours. I squatted down for a split second and looked to see in which direction to run. All the roofs were flat, so I ran again across the short wall to the next house and to the next roof until I came across what I dreaded: a good one-and-half meter, narrow blind alley separating the two houses. I crouched along the wall. I could hear the hard footsteps of armed men running over the rooftops. I could smell the dust they kicked up saturating the air. My heart stood still in fear. I had no breath. Beneath me I could see the street sloping down. The lights of the houses had begun to come on. The wall must have been at least four meters tall. I hesitated a few moments, and then jumped. I was barefoot and came down hard on the asphalt. I felt my right ankle twist, so I limped on my good foot and rushed out of the alley. This was my childhood neighborhood and I knew each centimeter of it. Growing up with older boys hadn't allowed me the luxury of being a helpless girl, and to prove that I was as good as they were, I had climbed the trees and jumped over the walls. As a child I would come and hide in the alleys when my brothers and I played hide-and-seek. I knew so many hidden corners that they could not possibly find. This was my little corner of the world and I had discovered it well before my brothers did. *Moham-mad would have been proud of me. Tonight, I have jumped the tallest wall ever.*

I stopped beneath the awning of a house and stepped into the doorway. Most neighbors didn't lock their courtyard doors, and I knew
this one neighbor well. Luck was with me. I pushed the door slightly
open, limped inside, and went directly to the courtyard toilet. I left
the door ajar and squatted there frozen behind the toilet on the cool
tiles. My heart was in my throat, and I thought it would explode any
second. I prayed that the black cockroaches would not crawl out of
the hole. As I shivered in the quiet of the dark, I bit into the flesh
between my palm and index finger to avoid breathing hard.

Only minutes had passed when I heard footsteps in the courtyard.
I heard voices coming from the alley. A dim light came up in the
garden of the next neighbor's house. The *pasdars* were banging at the
doors, waking up everyone. There were shouts and orders: "Open
up the door! Open up the door!"

"What is happening? What do you want in our house at this
hour?" I heard a frightened, half-asleep neighbor's voice. People
had seen so many uncalled-for searches that they knew any sign of
resistance would be considered an act of complicity helping the anti-
government groups, leading to arrest and execution.

I sat there for what seemed an eternity. My entire body was turning into ice even though it was one of the hottest nights. Bibi wouldn't
approve of praying in the toilet, but I prayed to all the saints, to all
the prophets, to all the sacred Imams about whom Bibi had told me
stories. I prayed that the *pasdars* would not find me, especially since
this was a neighbor's house. I knew the *Sepah* would never believe
that these neighbors had no idea I was hiding in there.

Suddenly, the door was pushed, crushing against me. *Dear God!
They found me already. Are you deaf? Didn't you hear my prayers?* The
light came up. I shielded my eyes with my hand from the blinding
light overhead.

"My God, child! What in the name of the Prophet are you doing
here?"

*Ah! God. You did hear my prayers.* It was the old Baba Rahman.
"Please, Baba Rahman. Please, don't tell them I'm here. I beg you,
Baba Rahman."

"Don't you worry, little girl," he whispered in his kind voice.
Quickly, he turned off the light. "I heard the disturbance. It is as if

this is the very Day of Judgment. They're turning the alleys upside down. You can't stay in this hole. They'll find you. Come out, child. Hurry up!"

I ran to their parlor, not knowing what I was doing and wished he had let me hide in there. I didn't want to cause them any harm.

"What is it Masht Rahman? What is going on out there?"

"It's Nastaran," he whispered to his wife.

"What? Your mother is after you at this hour, dear?"

It had been years since I came to their house to seek refuge. The good woman perhaps didn't even know that I had already graduated from high school. "No, Fetemeh Khanoom. It's not my mother I'm hiding from. It's the *Sepah Pasdaran*."

"God, I thought so, with that poor lad in a cage. What a boy. Ah dear, what a misery. What a misery."

"Do they have a picture of you? Do they know what you look like?" the old man asked.

"I don't think so." I shook my head, dumbfounded.

"We'll set up a bedroll for you. If they come to search our house, we'll say you're our grandchild come from the province for the summer. Her name. . . ."

"I know her name, Masht Rahman. But they will kill you if they find out that you have have protected me. I can't let anything bad happen to you." I got up and limped to the door.

"Come here, child." Fetemeh Khanoom ran toward me. "You're hurt. What have you done to your ankle? Stay with us. Have faith. May God's will be with us all. Come dear, come."

"Fatemeh Khanoom," I gasped.

"That's the least we can do, dear," said Masht Rahman. "And pray that soon their evil roots will be pulled up so they will leave this country alone. Come now. Whatever God wills."

I lay in bed, pretending that I was asleep. I knew their granddaughter; she was a couple of years older than I. We never got along. When I was in middle school, I tried to be friends with her, but it didn't work. She was pretty and dumb like a moss-covered rock and hardly had the slightest desire to read any books. The only literature she had ever read in her life was whatever our Farsi book offered, a couple of short stories by Hans Christian Andersen and a few parts of Victor

Hugo's *Les Miserables,* so that she could get at least a passing grade in literature. All she thought about was meeting a boy from a well-to-do family so she'd be accepted as a suitable daughter-in-law.

But I had great respect for Masht Rahman and his wife. As a little girl I carried trays of gourmet dishes that my mother gave me to bring them at midday rest time, and I took refuge in their house when my mother chased me with the water-pipe stick and Bibi wasn't anywhere near to save me. I would hide in their guest room until my mother calmed down and Fatemeh Khanoom took me back to our house. Those days were only a memory now and it was ironic that I had to recall them at that awkward time.

A half hour or so passed before an army of green uniforms stormed into the courtyard. They jumped down from the walls and several of them stood guard with their *Kalashnikovs* pointed at us. They rummaged around the house, in and out of the small rooms. For the first time I was thankful for the chador Fatemeh Khanoom had handed to me. I covered myself from head to toe like a good, religious village girl and sat there on the bedroll. The *pasdars* asked my name and who I was. I gave them Farideh's description. I could see Masht Rahman and his wife trying hard to keep from shivering, whle I trembled under the chador. The *pasdar* looked at me hard, and called another one of the *Brothers*. He, too, looked at me for a long moment. They asked me to stand up. I did. I prayed they would not ask me to walk and see my limp. "Do you have any identification of her? Birth certificate, perhaps?" One of the *pasdars* motioned to Masht Rahman.

"She is my granddaughter," Masht Rahman's voice trembled. "There's no need for her to carry her birth certificate when she comes to see her grandparents. She's just visiting and we have nothing to show you."

"Do you have anything on you? Library card? Anything of the sort?" he asked me.

"I came to take care of my grandmother. She is not well," I said, surprisingly in a tranquil voice that almost convinced me that I was indeed Farideh. "I always come to visit them during the summer time."

"Bring one of the neighbors," the head *pasdar* ordered another one.

My heart sank. Poor, poor Masht Rahman. They'll shoot him on the spot. What have I done? Why did I come here? I have to stay calm for the sake of these people. Please God! Have mercy! I prayed as Bibi prayed in despair.

The *pasdar* came back, bringing Mr. Zamani. He was a pharmacist who worked at one of the public hospitals. He was still in his tank top and striped pajama pants. "Do you know if this girl is the grand-daughter of these old people?" he asked.

*Stupid pasdar*, I thought.

Mr. Zamani had to have a quick glance at me and at horrified Masht Rahman and Fatemeh Khanoom to grasp the entire scenario. "Yes. She comes from her province to take care of her grandmother."

Dear God, how many people are going to be hanged on my behalf tonight?

"What's her name?" the same *pasdar* asked.

"Farideh," Mr. Zamani didn't hesitate. "Farideh *Khanoom*." He swallowed hard.

"Let's go, brothers. We can't waste time." The head *pasdar* motioned for everyone to leave, including Mr. Zamani. Masht Rahman fell to his knees and Fatemeh Khanoom leaned against the wall raising her hands in prayer and thanking God.

I wanted to go and hug them both, this God-sent, kindly old man and woman who had risked their lives for me tonight, but I could not move. My pants were wet. I crumbled to my knees and thanked God from the bottom of my heart.

Next morning Mr. Zamani came and gave us the news. The *pasdars* had arrested Hossein on the pretext that he had helped me to escape. My other brothers had interfered and my mother had blocked Hossein with her body, not letting the guards take her son away. So they arrested her too. Bibi had fainted because one of the *pasdars* had pushed her to the ground as she was reaching for her glasses. No one in the family knew where I was, if I was alive or was shot, dying somewhere in the dark. Bibi must have cried and prayed all night. I told Masht Rahman and his wife that I feared my grandmother would have a heart attack and convinced them that the *Sepah* would not think I would dare to go back to the house. I reasoned that they might not come back to the neighborhood for a while.

As soon as darkness swallowed the alleys, I covered myself in the borrowed black chador and went back to my house. They had freed my mother that afternoon, keeping Hossein in custody until I turned myself in. Bibi remained mute as she fell to her knees. My mother hugged me for the first time in my life, and we both cried in each other's arms. That very night, I wanted to turn myself in so that Hossein would be freed, but my mother and my brothers did not allow me to do it. "We just have to wait and see," they convinced me.

Around midnight, my mother took me to one of her old acquaintances, a very wealthy family living in the affluent, uptown Bagh-e Eram, until she could figure out what to do with me. Before she left, she bowed as a servant would and kissed the hands of the friend and her husband. "I don't know how to thank you," she cried. "She is my only daughter. May God bless you and this house for granting my daughter shelter."

That moment, I wished the ground would open and swallow me whole; I would rather be arrested by the *pasdars* than see my mother humiliated, begging, bending low, kissing someone's hand, becuse the woman hesitantly agreed to give her runaway daughter a temporary refuge.

My mother moved me to three more places. They freed Hossein after one month. He was lashed and interrogated; but somehow the *Sepah* decided to let him go. In that month, my mother had three of her sons in prison. Mohammad was condemned to life in prison on the charges of a *siasi*; Hossein was charged with helping a counter-revolutionary sister to escape; and Ali was condemned to three years in prison in Cell Block 2.

My mother couldn't move me to any more houses, so she sold some pieces of her remaining gold jewelry, borrowed money, and bought a miniature bungalow in a newly developing working-class area. Along with a stove and a refrigerator loaded in the back of an open truck, she took me to the new place and forbade me to leave the house even for an instant. Bibi opened the door. It was the first time I'd seen her in forty-eight days. She burst into tears. I let myself fall into her arms and breathed her familiar jasmine scent.

# CHAPTER 9

Time is our most sadistic enemy. Our foremost challenge is to tear the fabric of time as painlessly as possible, while awaiting our verdicts. At night this invisible stubborn fabric stretches even longer as each minute seems like an hour and each hour an entire night; yet there is never complete darkness. As they pace the length of the corridor, the *Sisters* aim their flashlights at us to scrutinize every move we make. Right before the lights-out, everyone must lie down, frozen as a corpse, on her thin sponge mattress. We lie awake with our eyes shut, silent as statues frozen in time.

The days linger with nothing to do. In the Block, daybreak begins as all the florescent lights in the corridor go on and the loudspeaker bursts with predawn prayers. Only when the green tarpaulin curtains are drawn are we allowed to remove our head-coverings. When it is announced that Brother Torabpoor, the only man who is allowed to enter the Block, is in the entrance and wishes personally to monitor the corridor, the complete *hijab* must be observed, the black chador, that is. Almost every day, at random hours, he comes and plants his bulky trunk of a body behind his desk, talking nonstop on his wireless radio or on the phone as he instructs the *Sisters*. At these times most of us stay inside our cells to save ourselves from his distorted glances. There are times that even with the curtains drawn shut, the loudspeaker announces that we are not to enter the corridor, and we know that someone from the Revolutionary Court must be with him.

During the day, the bars to our cells are open so we roam about the corridor, walking back and forth. Even though there's no restriction against mingling with the same inmates on the same tier, I notice that the girls play it safe about which cell to go to and are cautious about whom to talk to. The *Sisters* monitor our communications and the *Eyes* report out of context everything inappropriate they determine was said. I am a new target and fresh bait, Parvin lets me know. In a nutshell, she tells me that the *Eyes* have written so many cast-off reports that as soon as someone new arrives all their focus is directed at her. She advises me not to go to the other cells so often; and, even if I come across someone whose face I remember from somewhere, had gone to the same high school with, or have seen in public gatherings, I should not acknowledge that person because the Sepah will subject both of us to a new chain of arduous interrogations ten times worse than before.

Parvin is nineteen years old and was arrested on the street for selling the Mojahed newspaper. I have seen deep cuts on her arms, which she usually hides: the brutal marks from the blades of the *Hezbollah* when they attacked the sympathizers who sold banned newspapers. Her house was one of the first to be bombed in Abadan when Iraqi missiles suddenly hit her neighborhood that early summer dawn in 1981 when the war broke out. Her sister lost one of her legs in the explosion and her entire family had no choice but to leave town in their nightshirts, holding on to the back of an open truck carrying dozens of war refugees to Dezful, the nearest city. Because of the cuts on her arms, which hinted at a struggle with the *Hezbollah* and the Basij guards, she was condemned to fifteen years in prison; but from the way things smell here, I am afraid that one of these days Torabpoor will send her to the second floor as well.

No one dares to talk about politics, about the war, which has been destroying the southern cities one by one for three years now, about freedom or the world that exists beyond the walls of the Block. Nor does anyone dare to talk about the injustice and mistreatment of the inmates on the second tier. Instead, we talk about dull, trivial subjects and troubles: the prison food or the water in the shower, which was at least lukewarm today and not freezing again as it was yesterday and the day before.

As if all the fears that attack me from every corner were not enough, now I have to confront a new fear: the skin fungus disease, the most widespread malady in the Block. The girls warn me about the brown spots that suddenly appear on the arms, in the armpits, on the thighs, between the toes, and on the back of the neck. Everyone gets only a part of the 20-minute shower twice a week. The water is hardly ever warm, and since there's no airflow or sunlight, we breathe the same recycled, mildew-filled air over and over. There's no washing machine, dryer, or place to hang the laundry, so our clothes hold the moisture at all times. Every cell has a specified hour to do the laundry and to dry the clothes in a small area in front of the showers. But the dampness clings to us and floats in the air, causing this contagious fungus to spread even more rapidly. Most girls have cut their hair boyish short to save time in the shower as well as for fear of lice. My hair comes down to my tailbone; I simply cannot bring myself to cut it. Maybe I will be released one of these days.

The Revolutionary Court has demanded a special quarter which would separate the political prisoners' yard completely from the men's section of ordinary prisoners' Block. They have knocked down the old walls in the prison yard in order to rebuild much taller walls made of stone, bricks, and cement so that even death itself would have to come down on us in some other way. The cells seemed once to have had a small window that opened into the yard. Under Khomeini's government, the Sepah guard had cemented the windows so that no one would be able to get a glimpse of the sky. With the prison yard under construction, the days are filled with the hubbub of the workers. To rebuild the walls, the Sepah is using the men from Block 2, the ordinary prisoners. They have ordered them not to get near the wall of the *siasi* Block, but we could still hear them shouting, cursing, laughing, as they go by pushing their wheelbarrows. There is a man who has the eternal voice of a lover. At midday rest time, when the workers relax, I throw my white prayer chador over my head and cover my face, pretending to recite the prayer book as I listen to the southern voice of the lover singing a sorrowful folksong:

> *Do not play with my heart,*
> *For it is caged and in love,*
> *And I fear that one day,*
> *It will die in my breast.*
> *So, do not play with my heart.*

The pinnacle of the day is at noon when lunch gets delivered. First, the *Sisters* let the designated women from the third tier come downstairs and receive their rations. Waiting behind the bars, their pot-size ladles in hand, the archaic prostitutes swarm over the huge caldrons of stew, fishing for chunks of meat. Then the *Sisters* let three women from the *soiled* tier, the second tier that is, come down and carry their share of food upstairs. Most days, the miserable inmates refuse to eat because they are on another hunger strike, sitting down solemnly in their isolated cells. At the end, the lunch gets distributed among those of the first tier.

There are no books or reading materials allowed except the Arabic or selected Farsi translated version of the holy Koran and the prayer book of *Mafatih*, the religious prayers interpreted and distorted by the Mullahs, and the Imam Khomeini's *Resaleh*, the dissertations which guide a Muslim in daily life, according to him. The guidelines are new to us, even to those who are far more religious and claim that they had done intensive research on religion. It is as if a new prophet had descended from the sky of Iran and had brought a new Islam. The *Nahj-el-Balaghe*, the speeches, exhortations and guidance written by Imam Ali, the first Shiite Imam, on the other hand, is not available in the Block and forbidden for our family to bring to us.

There are girls who at eighteen have become monks. Even in their cell, they refuse to remove their head-coverings. They hardly talk to anyone as they sit quietly for hours, reading the holy book verse by verse. They vow to complete one thousand rounds of prayer beads each day and finish the entire prayer book of *Mafatih and Komeil* that the *Sisters* bring into the Block. I, too, have already finished reciting the entire Koran. It must be years since I have last read the holy book, when I was very young, and Bibi would take me to the *Rouseh* sermons.

There's no mirror here, so someone else knows better how one looks. "Is my face too pale? Is my hair in place? Are my eyebrows too bushy?" one is always asking another. The girls had managed to snatch a lunch tray and polish it so that it can serve as a mirror. Even though it makes our faces expand and stretch in bizarre, amusing ways, revealing a much chubbier and puffier face than we would like to see, it still travels from hand to hand like the *Kuh-e-Noor* jewel, especially on Visit Day when our faces are the only uncovered body part our families get to see.

No group workout or individual physical activities of any kind are allowed. Our physical exercise is limited to walking in the fifty-meter-long, ten-meter-wide corridor, back and forth, back and forth. That could also be interpreted by the *Sisters* as a sign of strengthening body and mind. They comment that since the Islamic Republic now had mercy on us and instead of being hanged we still inhale the precious air, in return we ought to pray nonstop and ask God for absolution. They say, as women, we must focus on cleansing and restoring the virtue of our soiled souls rather than concentrating on our physical strength and beauty.

Lack of physical activity, the greasy prison food, and stress have caused most girls to look blowzier and older than they really are. Most of them complain that they have gained at least five to ten kilos since the day they've come to Adelabad. Parvin is one of the girls who still can manage to keep her slender figure. In the corridor, one can always see her and Farzaneh walking together the entire length, back and forth.

As for me, fatigue, lack of sleep, anxiety, and the hopeless waiting are my other new enemies. A thin layer of fat is the first sign I notice covering my ribs. It is not fatness, Farzaneh tells me, it's puffiness and bloating. She's a tall, slender girl and, like Parvin, hardly ever eats the prison food. Her spirit is what strikes me the most. She's been arrested as a sympathizer of the Fadaee Communist Party and condemned to life imprisonment. Despite the fact that she has formally repented, like the rest of us here, and practices her daily prayers, the *Sisters* still keep a watchful eye on her. Even though she keeps her mouth shut every time someone is taken away to solitary confinement or for execution, her cheerless face leaves no doubt for the *Sisters* to accuse her of being a false repentant. It is obvious to me and to the *Sisters* that both girls have a routine of walking, especially after each meal. I hardly ever see Parvin's face or Farzaneh's without a smile, something the *Sisters* do not approve of.

Unlike the ordinary prisoners, who get to knit handmade plastic purses and necklaces, the only artwork we are allowed to do is making beads out of the leftover toast bread, the same artwork that

Mohammad was lashed for and accused of practicing to keep his cell-mates' minds engaged. We soak the leftover bread in water, knead it into soft dough, and form it into hard beads. With the yarn the *Sisters* give us, we make strands of prayer beads.

Bibi has sent me one of her most precious prayer beads that she bought in the holy city of Mashhad a few years ago. She said that between the two of us, we should do one thousand rounds a day, five hundred rounds for Mohammad's verdict so he will receive a life sentence, and five hundred rounds for my freedom. At the beginning, I did my share, but little by little my rounds began to shrink. I convince myself that Bibi will do more than five hundred rounds anyway. So I do only round after round for Mohammad and hope that I do not miscount them.

The meals, too, are prepared by the male neighbor of Block 2 who also works in the prison kitchen; yesterday's criminals are today's cooks. The yellow half-cooked rice is either too salty or full of grits and mouse droppings. Once the girls fished a dead mouse out of the chicken stew. A shoe sole, shoelaces, a plastic comb, and even a Citizen men's watch are among the treasures that have surfaced as the ladle was withdrawn from the greasy stews. The fear of camphor, too, lingers as the gigantic pots of food are being delivered. The girls say it is used to keep the prisoners' sex urge suppressed, especially the men; the cooks are ordered to add camphor powder as one of the main ingredients. It sickens me. The substance is used in burial rituals to cleanse and fumigate the dead body before burying it in the ground. They say that the powder induces lethargy and stupor, and increases body hair growth in women. No wonder the hair on my arms is growing darker and thicker. Subsequently, I try most of the time to walk away from the pots and stuff myself with Lavash bread, cheese, and dates instead.

The puffy steamed rice smeared with butter and the mouthwatering lamb kabob that they fed us in the Sepah Detention are now a thing of the past. The food at the Detention Center was restaurant-prepared and the same as the food served to the Sepah's staff. The distance between the prison and the Sepah Detention isn't the reason that they do not feed the detainees the prison's food. It is rather part of the interrogators having been trained to use psychosomatic techniques. Their gesture took us off guard. The Khomeini regime arrested so many so suddenly that the anti-government parties did not know how to prepare their sympathizers for the prison's tortures. What the sympathizers expected were the horrible torture techniques used by the Shah's secret police, the infamous SAVAK, specifically trained by the American CIA. All those Made in the USA nail-pulling machines and electric shocks, the cigarette burning on the freshly cable-lashed backs and feet, now are the techniques which failed both regimes, the Shah's and Khomeini's. The old techniques are being replaced now by much different, unfamiliar methods. If the torturing machines failed the Shah, the Khomeini's government may as well put that valuable experience to use. The solution: catch and kill.

That failed too: the more the Ayatollahs executed, the more they ignited the fire of people's anger. The *Sepah's* latest strategy is nothing like what they used a year or two ago. This time, the Revolutionary Guard did not hang the political detainees in public the minute they were arrested. That was a mistake, they soon realized. Why make martyrs of these young university students and high school kids when they can make traitors of them in the eyes of the public? Why make more martyrs like Golsorkhi or Rabiaa-Zadeh, whose names and faces are carved in the hearts of young and old for decades to come. Better that they would lose everything: their peers, the love and support of a people who admire them, and their dignity. The Islamic Republic has decided to make sure that these "traitors" lose both heaven and earth. The Sepah's interrogators promise amnesty, that our repentance will be accepted by them and by God himself. Suddenly, these interrogators, cable-in-hand, were the big brothers; their only intention: to guide us back onto the righteous path in life. To prove it, they fed us delicious kabob for lunch and whispered in our ears with their trained, falsely-kind voices. If this method did not work, then they revealed their true selves in the cellar: it was time to brandish their cable-lashes and show us what it means to live like a filthy dog for days and months on end in a dark solitary cell. *They* whip us, and at the same time they blame the anti-government organizations for us being whipped and kept in prison. After all, it was because of your own comrades that your names and whereabouts were revealed, the very traitors, the Sepah guard would tell us; "*They* are the real enemies." Under torture, the interrogators convince you that you are in safe hands, that you are protected under their wings; and when you repent, as they force you to, they hang you one miserable dawn, laughing at your childish notions. If they got you with a plate of lamb kabob, they sneer, so would any of the anti-government parties. Bibi used to tell a proverb which I think elucidates the Islamic government's torture approach: "The devious enemy slits his opponent's throat with a cotton ball instead of a sharp knife." So, unlike the Shah's SAVAK, first they kill your soul, then your body. And if you survive their twisted mind games; and you happen to grow old and become a grandmother or a grandfather, you would not dare tell your grandchildren that you had fought for this land, for the freedom of its people and for justice. Instead, they would make you ashamed of your own guilt, which would haunt you for the rest of your life.

# CHAPTER 10

Three months have already passed, and still I have no verdict. This is the longest time I've ever spent without seeing Bibi. I can't help wondering about her health. My heart aches for her and to hear her voice. I know she must be staring at the door, waiting for me to enter her courtyard again. By now, she must have miserably pleaded to all the dead saints for my release. Every Monday, I beg my mother to bring her to see me.

She came today, lost in a cluster of dismal men and women, old and young, swarming toward the glass barriers. She even had her glasses on. For the first time in her entire life, she was wearing a black chador. Black was never a color she would choose to wear. Her face was flushed and tiny beads of sweat sprinkled her forehead.

I pinched my cheeks a few times to bring some color to them before I walked up to the designated cubicle.

The moment she saw me, tears filled her eyes and her lips began to quiver. My mother gave her a good nudge in the arm. Bibi gasped and adjusted her chador, bringing it closer to her face. She seemed frightened and couldn't understand why she was not allowed to hug me or touch my face, all the while peering and touching the hard glass. Prison and glass cubicles are foreign objects to her, existing only in horror stories, not in real life. I knew she now felt as if she'd been led to a sinful place. Clumsily, she took the receiver my mother handed her, yet she failed to control her choked voice. "I have never harmed a soul in my life," she said bitterly. "Dear God! Is that your reward to keep me alive to come and see this precious piece of my heart from behind glass?" Her voice broke and she gasped so hard that my brother had to take her outside for fresh air.

"Don't ever ask me to bring her here again," said my mother, frustrated. "I have so much on my mind that her funeral is the last thing I want to deal with right now."

I nodded.

Back in my cell, I add another hundred rounds of prayer beads, this time for Bibi's health. As I sit in a corner, I take refuge in memories; I let my mind float like a stream of molten tar back to the alleys of my childhood. I fill my ears with the melodious callings of the fruit vendors bringing a different kind of fruit, the first fruit of the season.

In my grandmother's house, time shifted under my feet as seasons changed like a transparent fabric dancing over a canvas of colors, trancelike and tangible. And in our alley a new fruit, a new taste, and a new smell meant a new season.

Spring was Bibi's favorite season, summer was mine. So, when the sparrows began to hatch their eggs somewhere between the high branches of the white mulberry tree, and when the black grapes' molasses stained the saffron color-glazed tiles of the front porch, I knew it was summer again. Bibi called it the season of date-killers for the dates were ready to be picked in the palm groves of the tropical south. I knew it was summer, and summer meant honey-sweet grapes and hungry sparrows, chunks of ice, Bibi's bamboo hand-fans, and heat. Running under the arbors, I would wave one of Bibi's head scarves to shoo away the chirping birds who dared come near my ripening grapes.

I remember one summer specifically, the chill waterfall-taste of the crunching ice still in my mouth and my memory. The heat was such that even Bibi could remember only a handful of summers like it among all the summers she had seen. Each day the weather grew hotter than the day before until it got too hot for anyone to sleep in the bedrooms. Right before the sunset, Bibi would sprinkle water on the short cement walls enclosing the rooftop. Sometimes, she'd even hose the entire roof to cool it before she spread out the straw-mat runner or the colorful Qashghaee rug. Having done that, she would set up the white mosquito net, carrying the bedrolls upstairs, and placing the cushions and pillows under it. She'd fill her special canary-flower-painted china bowl with water and the most fragrant orange blossoms picked from the garden, placing it in a corner to keep the mosquitoes away.

Finally, at nightfall, when the courtyard was swallowed by shadows and filled with the smell of breeze-kissed white jasmines and the sound of garden crickets, the air would begin to grow cool. Gracefully, the sky put on her nightgown of dark crushed velvet, black hair falling around her shoulders. On these summer nights Bibi let me stay up late and choose any stars I wanted and name them as I wished. Over our rooftop, Bibi would kneel on her Mashhad silk prayer rug. We played the moon-and-star game; she would be the moon and I would be the circle of stars, twinkling around her.

The first summer we moved into the house, we had to sleep in the courtyard because the roof wasn't finished yet. Only the master bedroom had a temporary roof, so that the rain would not pour inside and Bibi and I could sleep there. Right before going to bed, she'd prop a heavy copper tray against the door to warn us just in case, as she put it, an ungodly burglar made the mistake of visiting the wrong house. One night, I woke to the vibrating sound of the copper tray whirling on the cement floor while Bibi stood in the middle of the room, a mighty wooden bludgeon in her hands, shouting "Thief! Thief!" and threatening that she'd bring the bludgeon down on the crown of his head if he took another step. When she turned on the kerosene lamp, the thief was only a white stray cat, looking for the leftover chicken stew in the ice-chest.

The house didn't have electricity yet; so the next day, Bibi held my hand and together we went to Masht Nader the Mason. She begged him for the sake of this orphan child to demand that his workers finish the roof before winter came with the pouring rain. Masht Nader suggested that Bibi rent a room in one of the neighbors' houses and wait until her house was completely finished. But she shook her head, glanced at me, and said that she would not pay another *shahi* for rent in someone's house where her child was not allowed to run around and play in the courtyard. Vehemently, the mason gave her his solemn word that he would start the work even if he had to do it himself.

On the way home, Bibi stopped at the Kolbeh ice-cream store, bought me a wafer cone of Shirazi saffron *faloodeh* and promised that

I would soon have my own room, my own garden, and the entire two-hundred-meter house to myself. I could run around in our own private garden without any stranger ordering me, an orphan child, to be quiet.

"God bless his heart," Bibi prayed for Masht Nader the first night we slept on the rooftop. "He's done such a fine job, smearing and covering the roof with heavy layers of molten tar. Not only that, he tiled the entire roof, so not even a seven-meter snow could break the tile and leak onto the ceilings." For all this, Bibi said contentedly, the mason had charged her only two thousand *tumans* extra, which he let her pay in installments. "I still owe him money," she sighed, "but who is alive, who is dead tomorrow? God willing, I'd take more jobs spinning wool and weave more *giveh*—cotton summer shoes—to pay off the remaining six-hundred *tumans*." She thanked God now that the entire four rooms were covered with a solid roof.

I didn't know what an orphan was, but I noticed that people caressed my hair whenever Bibi talked about me. Under their breath, they murmured a prayer for Bibi for doing such a blessed job, raising an orphan.

"What's an orphan, Bibi?" I asked her one night.

Bibi held her prayer beads in her palm, looked at me for a moment, then she pointed to her breast with the finger in which she wore an agate-ring. "I am an orphan, *babam*," she said, "never saw the shadow of a father over my head or sucked the nipple of a mother. My brave young father got killed by the merciless feudal landlord when I was still in my mother's womb. I never caught a glimpse of him, but what a body he had, my aunts told me. What height! Chest as wide as an Arab stallion. He was a rifleman for the *Khan* of our village. Only twenty-four years old when he was murdered. And my mother died, giving birth to me. What can I say? God gave me a big head. I was fat as a baby lamb. My bride-mother died before even holding me in her arms. She had lived on this earth to see only fifteen springs."

Bibi's eyes always turned watery whenever she talked about her family and her life in the village. She wiped the tears away with the hem of her muslin scarf and kept braiding the fringes at the base of the rug. Swaying her body back and forth, she glared at the red flowers and motifs in the rug.

"And myself, I too was raised by my mother's mother," Bibi went on. "May her grave be covered with the rain of lights. Ah, what a world! She raised me on goat's milk. You can say my mother was a goat. You know, I grew up with little baby lambs. Two of them. That's why I never eat lamb meat. How could I?" Bibi baaed then, just like a lamb. "When I was three years old, worse luck, my Bibi died too. Just like that. Her head lay in my lap. After her, I was given to this uncle and that aunt. I worked on their farms, in their rice paddy, herded their animals."

"Am I an orphan, Bibi?" I asked.

"*Ha, babam.* Yes, my baby. Your Baba's gone. Let's hope he's in heaven. He was a good man, though he didn't do his Islamic obligations right. Hardly prayed once a day, let alone five times a day. He saved all his lapsed prayers for the whole week and did them all in one Friday from sunrise to sunset at the worship place. Now, how could you say that to his folks when the man's heart happened to stop on his prayer rug, right where his forehead touched the *mohr*, the holy prayer stone? How lucky can a soul get? All his sins are forgiven now. It runs in that family. Their hearts stop right when they bow to Allah. Because of how he died, his family likes to say he was a holy man. But God forbid. It's not like I'm jealous or something. I hope that he walks with golden-haired *houris* of Paradise, one on each arm. He was a helpless man. If it wasn't for his mother's money, he'd never have made it in this world. He didn't have to shovel or to plough the land. God forgive me for saying it, it was the smoke and the oil refinery that killed them all. But if you dare tell that to his almighty family . . .

"And your *Momon*. What can I say? It's my own damn fault. I should never have given my baby to that gypsy woman. She was such a beautiful baby, her face like a bunch of flowers. Everyone wanted to hold her and kiss her cheeks. I was scared that she would die like my little boy I'd had before her. What a baby he was, only God knows. White as untangled cottons. He weighed five kilos when he was born. People said that someone cast an evil eye on him. My poor baby died and flapped under my breast like a little dove. Well. There was this old woman, Qamar the Tale-teller. She would wander in the alleys at night, chasing the moon overhead, saying it was her face.

She came to the house one day and said to me, if I wanted to save this girl, I should give her to a gypsy for a couple of days to drink the gypsy's milk so she'd live a long life. That's why she has a gypsy soul. I shouldn't say that. She's my baby and came from my own belly. But she became a naughty girl from that day on. When she was a little girl, let me tell you, she'd gather the neighbor girls and rub pink marvel flowers and rose petals into their cheeks and make their lips red. She'd steal barnacle powder from Maherah the Face-maker to make up the girls' faces. Barely six years old, she stomped her feet on the ground, demanding a tambourine. She'd invite the gypsy girls to the house to play bride-and-groom. That fire-torn girl never wanted to learn a line of the holy Koran or say a prayer. All she wanted to do was dance and prance in front of the mirror or rear-range the furniture. It's the gypsy's milk, what can I say?"

Bibi was still on her prayer rug as I closed my eyes to the blinking stars above. She kissed me and hugged me and thanked God for giving her such an innocent girl, though I was her daughter's daughter and didn't come from her own belly. She whispered and thanked the Creator of the universe that I loved to listen to the Koran stories and was as well behaved as a little girl could be, even though my skin was as dark as a gray kitten, and she had to smear soaked henna on my entire body when she bathed me, hoping that my skin would turn a milky white.

# CHAPTER 11

One morning, right before sunrise, I woke to the sound of Bibi's praying, whispering in my ears. Kneeling on her knees and facing the direction of the holy House of God, she told me to get up and go to God's Empire and ask whatever I wanted from him, because this was the best and the quietest time of all, she said, and He would be listening much better to His slaves. She reminded me again that I should be like the birds, going to sleep early at night and getting up early in the morning, not like dogs that stay up all night, for they are the night-watchers and sleep all morning. She told me that I should pray: given that I was just an innocent child the doors of heaven would open to me much wider.

I didn't know where heaven was or the House of God, but Bibi's eyes always sparkled and moistened at these names. It seemed to me that they must be pleasant places to visit. Bibi wished to make a pilgrimage to the House of God some day. I asked her if she would take me along if she ever went there. "Ah, *babam*," she said, "that's not a place for children, for they have small hands and feet and they'll be stomped by grown-ups."

It puzzled me. I couldn't understand why Bibi liked such places where grown-ups could hurt people with small hands and feet.

To answer my question where heaven was, Bibi responded with a smile: "*Voy, voy, babam*. What a curious child you are," she chuckled. Whenever she did that, her cheeks rose, each forming into one round peach beneath her small brown eyes. She said that Heaven was a grand place in the Seventh Sky, far, far away where all the good people go once they had washed their hands of this world.

"There you could see garden after garden with ample trees of all kinds, emeralds, rubies, and sapphires hanging from their branches instead of fruit; whenever you pick them, new jewels will grow in their place."

Bibi's eyes smiled in amusement as if she could imagine Heaven in her mind's eye. Lowering her voice to a whisper, she waved her hands, in the air. "There are peacocks and hoopoe swaggering gracefully under the trees or drinking from *Zam Zam* and *Kosar* springs and the Fountain of Life. Waterfalls stream from the green hills. There are brooks of milk and honey turning and twisting between the gardens. And wherever you look, you'll see golden-haired *houris* of Paradise and guardian angels accompanying and serving the good slaves of God. It's a place like no other place," she sighed. "An immortal Eden. It's the reward and compensation for those who've done good and avoided sins in this mortal life." I was overwhelmed by Bibi's description of Heaven. I clapped my hands and asked,"Would you take me with you, Bibi, when you go to heaven?"

Bumping the crown of her head with both hands, she said: "Alas for me. May Heaven's soil be upon my head! I am only a sinner." She wiped her ever-moistened eyes as if they were burning, and sighed again. "Who knows, maybe God will forgive all my sins and I'll be blessed with His infinite compassion and go to Heaven. Only He Himself knows, I have done no harm to any of His creatures. Ask any neighbor, anyone who knows me. Then again, who am I to say that? Let Him and His angels be the judge of that."

Bibi was always worried about the two angels on her shoulders, though I never saw them. She said the angel on the right shoulder writes all the good things one does, and the angel on the left shoulder writes all the bad things. At the end, on Resurrection Day, all the dead would be called to come forward with their action reports in their hands. "*Voy, voy*, what a day!" she smacked her thigh with the palm of her hand. "Let's hope that your good actions outweigh your bad," she moaned, "for that day, you'd be asked to walk on a line between purgatory and Paradise, a string thinner than a hair. Off you go with your report card in your hands. Now, whichever side is heavier," Bibi spread her hands in the shape of two-pan scales, "you fall down on that side. If you fall on your right, you'll go to Heaven.

God forbid, if you fall on your left, you'll go to purgatory where an eternal fire burns you until all your sins are forgiven."

I have never heard anyone make an unkind remark about Bibi, or wish upon her the burning fires of purgatory and hell, so I didn't want to think about any of that. Instead, I imagined Heaven, which was magical like the places in the fairy tales. Ever since that day, wherever Bibi took me, I searched for the signs to find Heaven, until that shady afternoon when I crawled under the canopy of vine branches to feed lettuce to my bunny. That day, suddenly, it occurred to me that my own yard could be Heaven. The trees weren't as tall as those in Bibi's descriptions and there were no peacocks or animals, except for a few red fish in the pond and the neighbors' cats. Yet somehow it did not matter; I had found Heaven in my very own garden.

My heaven lasted until the day Bibi took me along to her heaven, Deh, her native village out in the country. It was only a few days into summer, but the grapes were already sweet and succulent like the moist baghlavas. Bibi had plans; she wanted to take me to Deh.

The night before we left, she gave me a much longer bath than usual in the zinc washing basin and sent me to bed early so that I would not be tired on the long drive the next day; three hours, Bibi said.

The dew was still embracing the rose petals when I woke up, as always, to the sound of Bibi's prayers. That morning, I drank the entire cup of boiled goat's milk, as Bibi insisted, to have good stamina. In front of the silver-framed mirror on the mantelpiece, Bibi gathered her auburn hair in a ponytail and fastened the ivory muslin-scarf neatly under her chin. After she dressed me in my New Year's outfits she went to her walnut chest and took out her own clothes. She changed into a flower-print georgette dress, the one she wore only on special occasions, and threw her white cotton chador over her head.

We took a taxi to Valiahd Square.

There, by the lines of buses, *taxi-bar* trucks, and sedans, Bibi and I paced baffled, looking for any minibus that went to the city of Jahrom. Shielding her eyes from the sunlight with her hand, Bibi waved at a green-and-red minibus as it disappeared before our eyes, drowning us in its gray puffs of exhaust smoke and dust. A man with a cane in his hand approached us. Pointing to a man leaning over the edge of a blue *taxi-bar*, he told Bibi that his truck was heading for Jahrom in a few minutes. Disappointed, Bibi shook her head. She hesitated, but followed the man without letting go of my hand. "We have no choice but to take the *taxi-bar*."

Bibi fought with other passengers over the front seats, reasoning that she had to protect her grandchild, just a delicate twig, from the strong draft in the back of the truck. She pleaded with the man with the cane, "Brother Driver, my little girl goes deaf sitting out there in the back. Have a heart and let us sit in front."

The driver groaned and told Bibi that he'd have to charge her a higher fare because not only did she have a heavy bundle, but she also had a companion. Bibi bargained with him that I was only a child and could sit on her lap, and her bundle could be placed in front of her feet. But the driver said that he could easily fit two or three grown-up men in front, who could pay him a nice fare. "I know, I know: they smell like sheep-dung, but hey, they pay more," he argued with Bibi. Nevertheless, Bibi's pleading and sweet tongue won the heart of the driver. He told the other passengers: "Let the woman with the child come in front!" The others were mostly construction workers who came to the city for work, or villagers who came to sell their fruit, or to buy the staples they needed. Bibi explained that to me when she saw me gawking at them.

On the red shiny vinyl front seats, Bibi sat me next to the window so I could watch the road. I tried to count the trees along the road-side, but they raced by the window so fast, leaving only the tips of their high branches in my view. Bibi taught me all the trees' names: sycamore, creeping willow, cypress, evergreen, palm. She promised that she'd show me even more trees as soon as we got to her village, for she was a child-of-the-garden and knew all the trees, plants, and flowers.

Regardless of how hard I tried to count and recount the trees, I kept losing track of them and fell asleep. I woke to the sound of Bibi's re-bargaining and blessing with the driver at the bus stop.

There, at the fork of a dirt road, Bibi and I sat on the cumbersome boulders and waited again, this time for any of the villagers who might commute on their donkeys, horses or whatever four-legged animals they had to take us along into the village.

It must've been around noon, because I felt hungry. Bibi gave me a piece of *Sangak* bread wrapped with cheese and basil. I looked up as I chewed my midday meal. A big orange sun glowed in the middle of the belly of a blue sky, burning even the rocks beneath us. A villager on the back of his mule stomped the dirt road. He stopped before us, greeted Bibi, and helped us onto the back of his mule; he himself began walking ahead.

As we neared the river-stone frontier wall of the village, we were ringed by a pack of shepherd dogs warning the villagers of the new-comers. Women and girls in their native tribal dress approached us in groups. Our hostess, Mash Zoleikha, welcomed us with her two sons, Rasool and Bahram, the fattest of the villagers. "*Silam, silam . . .,*" people greeted us loudly in their country dialect, as if we weren't only dusty, but also deaf. Their accent made me chuckle. Bibi scolded me and forbade my laughing. "People from different places tend to have different accents and dialects," she whispered to me. But, when I said *salam*, and not *silam*, the villagers laughed at *my* accent and said, "*Voy, voy . . . afarin.* Listen to that island-girl's accent."

Island accent? What's that? I asked Bibi. But she was too busy greeting the villagers who reached to kiss her hands and to carry her bundle.

The villagers fought with each other over who was going to have us for the night. Since there were so many of them, Bibi decided to rotate the nights and stay only one night at each person's house; though she would have preferred to stay with Mash Zoleikha whose house was the cleanest and most spacious of them all, not to mention the least infested with fleas.

In the afternoon, our hostess, knife in hand, chased a speckled, red-feather hen, clucking about the dusty yard, and beheaded the poor bird in honor of our arrival. The women brought large black pots and put them over fires in the open kitchen in the corner of the courtyard. Mash Zoleikha boiled water to cook the rice. At din-ner time, when the delicious scent of cooked rice and chicken stew wafted through the yard, the women spread an extensive *sofreh* on the ground, as the men returned from the rice paddy and everyone, old and young, gathered around to eat. At first, I hesitated to eat my meal with pieces of that red hen buried in the buttery rice mixed with green, baby almonds and figs, but Bibi said it was impolite not to eat. She promised me that she'd let me go to the chicken coop the next day so that I could pick the eggs with my own hands.

I finally got to see it with my own eyes; this was the heaven everyone prayed for Bibi to go to. In the village, there were trees so high and growing together from all sides that I could see only broken pieces of the sky through the stray branches. All kinds of fruit trees: oranges, pomegranates, peaches, nectarines, grapes, even walnuts, almonds, olives, and so many others whose names I didn't know yet. Brooks bubbled underneath the trees, and waterfalls poured out from the lush green hilltops surrounding the village. I looked around for peacocks, but all I could see were sheep and goats, lots of chickens and roosters. There were also goldfish in the river, though much bigger than the ones in my small pond at home. Still, there was no milk or honey running in those brooks. But one could milk the goats and cows, and bees were everywhere anyway, I told myself. I really didn't like the taste of that rich creamy milk and I drank it only because of Bibi's pleading, who wanted me to develop some flesh under my skin. No matter how much honey she added to my cup, I still saw the mother goat, kneeling before me, staring with those innocent eyes, claiming her milk.

The houses were adjacent to each other with the yards separated by a low, straw-mud wall. The neighbors would swing over the short wall to borrow tea, sugar-cubes, tobacco, or other necessities from each other. A narrow, crystal-clear brook ran through everyone's courtyard. Women sat at the edge of it and washed their clothes, dishes, or even bathed their babies in a small basin. For their drinking water, however, the women went to the spring in the mountains every dawn and carried the water back home in their large goatskin *mashk*, a leather container. Mostly they walked there, because even their donkeys could not climb the rocky, winding way up to the stream.

In the morning Bahareh, Mash Zoleykha's youngest daughter, took me along to the chicken coop. Together we collected the white and brown eggs. I didn't understand; this was a village, but they called the eggs here "city eggs." When Mash Zoleikha scrambled the eggs for us in the pan over the outdoor stove, mine was an egg with two yolks. Bibi said it was because of the fresh air in the country and the good grain fed to the hens that made them lay such quality eggs. They were truly delicious, especially when eaten with the thin village bread fresh off the hot tray over the clay oven.

As she promised, Bibi let me go to the spring along with Bahareh who was bringing back the drinking water. Bahareh was ten years old and engaged to be married to her cousin, Sohrab. She told me that their marriage was arranged from the day she was born. She showed me the Seiko watch on her wrist, which Sohrab's parents had bought for her as a sign of engagement. "A family friend who works in Kuwait City sold my fiancé this Seiko watch," Bahareh said proudly. The two families exchanged sweets and delicacies at the New Year. Bahareh was to be married the day she turned fourteen.

The entire village was just a large family, all related to each other, cousin of this cousin, or aunt or uncle of that one. Most girls knew which of the village boys they were going to marry. They talked about their future husbands as they wove carpets and hummed love songs.

At night, villagers gathered shyly at the hostess's house one by one or in a group to show their respect: "*silam, silam, silam . . . ,*" until the guest room was filled with people and the newly arrived had to sit outside on the hard earthen yard, sprinkled with water. The floors were covered with handmade, colorful *Qashghaee* rugs and matching cushions. They asked Bibi to sit in the center-end of the room, the most honored place for a dear guest. The eldest sat next to her and after that the younger ones. Children sat at the end of the room. But they made an exception for me, because I was the guest's grandchild and connected to her like a flea to a cat.

Everyone was eager to listen to Bibi's elaborate memories from the old days, tales from ancient legends, or stories from the holy Koran. These were actually Bibi's deceased husband's relatives, my grandfather's family, Bibi told me. "In my time, there used to be two villages, the Upper Village and the Lower Village. Your grandfather lived here, in the Upper Village. When I married him, I was only seven years old, and he was nearly sixty. He didn't have a tooth left in his mouth or a strand of dark hair on his head. While I lived in this village, I never returned to my own. I had tons of family still back there. But I had a bad experience; there was fighting over the land and over my share of the plantation; the relatives had taken it from me and cultivated it for themselves. After your grandfather died, I took my only child, your mother, and headed out for the big city, Shiraz. I had hardly any money, or any place to go. My relatives thought that I had done a rebellious thing; it was improper for a young widow to leave her own village."

Unlike back at home, now in the morning I couldn't wait to get up early. I even did my morning prayers with Bibi, so she'd let me go along with the village girls to the fruit gardens. Bibi had told me many stories about her Deh, and that there everyone—men, women, old, young, even children, everyone—always works hard in and around the village. Now, looking at them, with their quick pace, they reminded me of the black ants in my own yard, always searching hastily for the leftover crumbs in the corners, carrying bits of grain. A dusty, bumpy path sloped down sharply between the houses and gardens, just like the pathway to their nest of a nonstop army of ants. From above, I could see women walking by, carrying a pile of washed dishes, clothes, or their water jugs on their heads.

The entire village yawned, waking up as the sun rose behind the green hills. There was no sound of *Izan*, the call for morning prayers, for there was not even a single mosque anywhere in the village. Instead, all at once, from every courtyard roosters crowed harmoniously, announcing a new day. It occurred to me that like Bibi, people here used the rotation of the sun to measure time. Some even propped a long stick against the wall and by looking at its shadow on the ground, guessed the approximate hour.

I was enchanted by all the commotion around me; I had never seen that many people before. I liked to listen to their dialects and watch them as they worked. The village was so broad and the land so open that people communicated in a loud voice, as if everyone was like the deaf Mash Banoo who scrubbed Bibi's body whenever she went to the public bath. Soon I realized that men worked in the gardens, plowed and furrowed the land. Narrow brooks ran throughout their gardens. It was the men's responsibility to guide the course of the water's passage, a tedious but important task, they said, for the fruit trees had to be watered before the morning haze burned off. All the landowners had a share of two hours of watering in the early morning and early evenings.

There was always some sort of negotiation and concern over the water among the gardeners: whose turn was first and whose last; if there was a problem somewhere or someone's son forgot to close the water gateway on time; or if someone had fallen sleep and the water had overflowed into the neighbor's garden and ruined his fruit trees.

Herding the animals was the boys' job; they shepherded the sheep and ploughed the land when their fathers called out to them.

There were times when women helped their men in the gardens, though their main job was to pick the fruit and stack them in the wooden crates, so their sons or a delivery man could take them to the city and sell them to the markets and grocery stores.

*Shalizar*, the rice paddy, was the women's territory, Bibi explained to me. Sometimes, even ten-year-old girls worked in the field if their mothers were sick that day or needed an extra hand. Bibi wouldn't allow me to enter the wet ground of the rice paddy. She warned me about the leeches, which cling to one's ankles and suck the blood until the creature itself is dead. Not to mention those sneaky, long, black water snakes, the women warned me, laughing.

Away from the gardens, back in the houses, young women and girls sat at their horizontal nomadic looms and wove colorful scorpion and tarantula figures and star motifs into their *Qashghaee* nomadic carpets. The weaving girls sat together in a straight line, hunching close to the vertical weft strands, as they looped the strings of wool around their fingers. At the end of each woven row, one of the girls used a wooden beating comb to press the weft strands into place, pushing each new row against the next one.

Sometimes they let me sit next to them; I watched them in awe. Setarah, Mash Zoleikha's eldest daughter-in-law, showed me how to loop the string. I couldn't loop as fast as she, but she said that my city-fingers were too delicate and too weak to knot and twist tightly. Instead, she made me a small rectangular wooden loom to weave a bag for Bibi. This was a little girl's job, Bahareh told me, for the weaving required thin, fine fingers to easily loop the strings in and out of the rows of the weft strands. The girls chuckled at my clumsiness, but asked me to keep talking so they could hear my city accent. They reminded me of Marmar, who thought I had a different accent from the rest of the neighbor girls.

Wearing a white or a gold-plated watch on their left wrist as a sign of their engagement, the weaving girls chanted together, singing mostly sad songs about a man, a lover who'd gone to a faraway place, while the beloved impatiently awaited his return. "The songs may sound sad," Bibi said, "but it is a bittersweet joy that you can see on their faces." The married women teased the soon-to-be-married girls whenever their young fiancés walked by or looked at them shyly from behind the low river-stone walls or from under the shadow of the trees.

I couldn't believe the women's hands. They were brown, dry, cracked, and much older than their pink, peachy faces. Even though Bahareh was only ten years old, her hands looked like an old woman's, wide and wrinkled , her nails all chipped. It reminded me of the fruit-lady who compared me to the village girls. I glanced at my own hands and looked hard at theirs. They didn't look the same to me. In complete awe, the girls would hold my hands in theirs, "They're so soft, so pretty," they'd sigh. Their hands were the first part of their body to age, they said, because of all the harsh work they did. The fruit-lady is definitely wrong, I thought. Maybe my hands weren't as white as Marmar's, but, for sure they were nothing like these village girls' either. All at once, I did not want to hide my hands any more.

It was the girls' faces that made me want to gaze at them: their pinkish, plump cheeks, just like Bibi's, and their enormous, honey-brown eyes which sparkled like two stars beneath their arched eyebrows. Bibi's daughter could be right about my cheeks after all, I decided. She said that there was no color in my face and that I had round, black eyes. Round, black eyes? Isn't that how a chicken's eye looks? I wondered. Mash Zoleikha kept saying that I had Bibi's eyes, not my mother's almond-shaped eyes.

Children and toddlers were all over the place. They looked bashful around grownups. Sneaking in the yard or by the brooks, they sat quietly near their mothers or older sisters. Bibi brought many differ-

ent types of *klucheh*, cookies, candies, and sweets to give each child
as a keepsake from the city. She reached often into her canvas sack,
handing colorful candies to children whenever they approached her
so that soon she was encircled and followed by a cluster of small, shy,
and noiseless children.

As much as the village kids liked Bibi's candies, I liked their
unshelled fresh almonds. Usually, after Bahareh was finished helping her mother with the house chores, she handed me a basket and
together we headed for the gardens, yards away from the houses. I
picked as many almonds and green baby figs as I wanted. We'd soak
the almonds in a bowl of water and eat them sprinkled with salt. We
did the same thing to the white baby walnuts. I couldn't believe how
many kinds of apples there were in the gardens: rose-water apples,
Egyptian apples, red apples, and a kind of hard-skin green apple
which the gardeners fed only to their cows and donkeys.

The sour apples, small as a walnut, were my favorite. Bahareh
taught me how to *bride* them. First, she fished out a smooth, shiny
river stone from the bottom of the brook, hammered the apples with
it softly all around until they turned brown, then she split them in
half, sprinkled them with dry crushed peppermint and salt, let them
simmer on the fire for a few minutes and once the apples were juicy
all over, she told me that they were *bride*, ready to eat. Just looking at them made my mouth water. I ate so many of them that my
belly began to growl. I felt nauseous and drowsy. The pain grew
stronger. Bahareh took me back to the house as she talked nonstop
about the home remedies she saw her mother use to calm an upset
stomach. "My mother will make you black tea with orange blossoms
and a dash of cardamoms," she said hastily. "You'll be well by the
first gulp."

As I entered the earthy yard, the smell of fresh-baked village bread
surrounded me. The courtyard was swept and drizzled with cool
water from the brook and a gentle, damp, dusty straw aroma filled
the air. For a moment I forgot the ache in my belly. I walked toward
Setareh who sat in the open kitchen and baked bread on a large black
frying pan. At the same time, she was breast-feeding her baby who
pulled at her nipple, playing with a loop of hair that had fallen out
of her see-through head covering. Setareh moved her face toward

the baby in a swaying motion, letting him play with the strand of
her hair. Another woman, whom I didn't recognize, sat across from
Setareh, spreading frosty dough over a wooden round tray. She took
a handful of dough, placed it on the surface, sprinkled a good dash
of flour over it, and with a long wooden stick, stretched the chunk
into a round large thin section, which she spread over the black frying pan. Red and orange flames rose from the logs beneath. Setareh
removed the baked ones from the top and placed them one by one in
a basket next to her. Both women's faces were red as pomegranates,
tiny droplets of sweat forming at the edge of their hair. Their long,
multiple layers of brightly colored petticoats were gathered around
their legs.

By the chicken coop, a neighbor woman was beating sour milk
in a leathern *mashk* on a wooden tripod, I knew that later she would
churn butter and yogurt from the white sour liquid and pour it into a
tin container to be served with the fresh-baked bread.

Bahareh wrenched off a piece of bread and stuffed it in her mouth.
Still eating, and with a bucket in her hand, she chased a black goat to
milk as her sister-in-law had asked her to. The scent of bread moved
like a breeze, filling the entire yard; it made me even dizzier. Setareh
rolled a piece of bread and handed it to me. I wanted to eat it, but I
simply could not.

Clutching my belly, I moved toward the guestroom. I pushed the
door ajar and heard Bibi crying softly. For a moment, I hesitated to
enter the room, but I pushed the door a little further. Through the
slant of the doorway, I could hear the humming sound of a bubbling
waterpipe and Bibi talking to Mash Zoleikha. The smell of tobacco
filled my nostrils. There was something about Bibi's crying that startled me. I stayed frozen. It wasn't like Bibi, being upset, or crying
in the presence of other people, unless it had to do with her daughter. And even so, her crying was different from the times she talked
about Heaven or the angels. Now she seemed bitter and moody. I
turned to move away, but my hand stiffened on the doorknob. Their
conversation was so muffled that it made me want to stay and listen.
Besides, I found the sound of the bubbling waterpipe hypnotic and
soothing. I peeked again through a space between the two doors.
Bibi would never approve of me snooping.

"May God keep your children safe from the evil eye, sister," Bibi was saying. "It breaks my heart to see those boys. Imagine that. The sons of Agha Bashi, with all that name and fame." Bibi paused, wiping her tears with a handkerchief, and took a long drag from the pipe. My eyes moved to the tiny plastic gold fish bouncing around in the flint glass jug of the waterpipe as Bibi puffed the gray smoke into the air.

"When I gave my little girl to him, everyone envied her for marrying into such a substantial family. A family with a name."

"Where's she now?" Mash Zoleikha asked Bibi. "Is she still back on the Island?"

"No," Bibi replied. "She's in Shiraz, living with Agha Bashi's uncle and aunts as if they're still her family. They live in Sar-e Dozak neighborhood, not even half an hour drive from me. From all of that so-called fortune, all that's left is a shabby house. Even now, she has to share it with Agha Bashi's relatives. Now that I look back I wish that I'd burned the back of my hand that day Agha Bashi's aunt set foot in my house. It's my own fault. I still can't forgive myself for giving my daughter away, marrying her off to a complete stranger in such a faraway province. I didn't know any better then. I was young myself, I had no money, no shadow of a man over my head. I took all kinds of jobs. The other women stayed at home and their men came to them every night with money in hand. But, I, I had to work in the cotton factory. At night, I would burn an entire candle so I could spin wool until dawn. That's why my eyes suffer now. I did needlepoint, anything to put a bite of food in my girl's mouth. I just wanted to live with honor, to hold my head up in the face of friends and enemies."

The sound of Bibi's sobbing became muffled. My belly cramped and I thought of that black tea Bahareh had promised me. I wanted to enter the room and sit next to Bibi. I knew if I put my arms around her, I would cheer her up; it always made her happy when I did that. But I was afraid if I went in, she'd tell me to go outside and play with the other girls, as she always did when she was engaged in grownup conversations, especially now that she was crying. So I just squatted on the earthen floor behind the blue door. I curled my arms around my knees and tried to bear the pain. But my curiosity took over my stomachache as I listened more carefully, even though I knew Bibi wouldn't like my doing it.

"You're like my sister. More dear than the pupil of my eye," Bibi said. "You're like the sister I wished to have. Nowadays, you can't tell your troubles to no soul; they buy you cheap, and sell you expensive. God only knows the fire that's burning in my heart for those innocent boys, and that little girl."

"Whatever comes to you, sister," Mash Zoleikha sympathized with her, putting her hand on Bibi's shoulder, "it's because of your good heart and your simple spirit. How else would you have known?"

"I guess you're right, sister," Bibi muttered. "You never know who people are behind their masks." She sighed and fanned herself with the handmade bamboo fan.

"What can I say? Whatever I say about my bad luck, it's not enough." Bibi said bitterly. "One day, this neighbor woman dropped by with this tall, dark-skinned lady. They had name, fame, money, the Lady Aunt said. She buttered me up 'First see the mother, then select and approve of the daughter!' I told her, don't look at my girl sweet-talking like a nightingale. Well, she was always a nimble and agile child, that's for sure. Even did chores for the neighbors. Washed the dishes, organized and tidied the house. Mash Namaki, the aunt, coming and going to the house a few times, saw it all. She said that her nephew is employed at the Abadan oil refinery. That he was born into money, born after eleven dead children. His dead mother was a rich woman, I was told. She had everything her heart desired, except children. All her children died before they could even walk. So, she made a vow that if God let her keep a child after age five, she'd dedicate that child to God, just like the dear Prophet Ebrahim did with his son Ismael. And to show her appreciation, she would do charity; she'd give away half her wealth to the poor, she vowed. That's why she named her twelfth son, *Agha Bashi*, Forever Alive Lad. And she did as she promised. Went to the houses of the poor and left food and clothes and money at their doors. God bless her soul and her ancestors who were from the holy city of Karbala. I wish that for a day I could reach and touch the holy shrine of my lord, Imam Hossein."

At this point, Bibi looked up with her arms extended above her head. "May my soul be sacrificed for your innocence," she grieved; her crying, as always, heartbreaking when she talked about the saints. She took a sugarcube and put it in her mouth as if to sweeten her bitterness, and went on talking to Mash Zoleikha.

"The aunts said that the groom was harmless as a lamb. Never disturbed any of God's creatures, not even a fly sitting on his nose. Mash Namaki talked and talked. Promised and promised, that she, herself, would be a servant to my daughter, not letting her touch black and white of anything until she'd grown up. She said Agha Bashi lived in a respectable, full-size house. So big, that I should move in with them. She'd treat my little girl like her own daughter. And I'd be her crown jewel. I could live with Golrokh as long as I wanted. I told her, this is the only child I have. My only girl. It's not a close commute. It's not the nearby alley or the next block. It's another city, far away in the Persian Gulf. God knows, I even had difficulty pronouncing the name, A ba dan, let alone go live there. One whole day of travel on that road. I said this girl is more delicate than a flower's petal. How could I give her away to live in that heat, like the fire in hell, in that stifling humidity.

"But before I knew it, a bunch of gypsy musicians with *tar* and tambourine had swarmed into the house, *kililili . . . kililili . . . kililili . . .* Dancers made everyone clap and sing. The neighbors threw sugarplums and coins over the groom's head. His relatives brought a white dress, twice the bride's size, and put *trick-lights* in her hair. All the neighbors gathered to watch that crown of colored lights. My poor little girl was so happy with the lights twinkling in her hair. She would click on the switch in her hand and giggle with the girls her age, proud of getting all the attention. She was a bride now, but like me, she had no clue who the groom was. When I saw him that night for the first time, tears filled my eyes. He was well into his thirties. I choked. I said, I hadn't meant for the mother's scarf to be worn by her daughter. That was my destiny. I didn't want my child to have my bad luck. But the neighbors and the groom's relatives circled around the bride and sang to her:

> *Our bride has cardamoms,*
> *Our bride has salt and pepper,*
> *The bottle of rosewater next to her,*
> *Praise to her eyes and her arched eyebrows.*

As the bridal chamber, they furnished and decorated the five-window room upstairs with colorful fabrics and tapestries. When the Mullah finished eating a tray of sweets, drinking a pot of tea, and pronouncing them husband and wife, Mash Namaki turned around. The very next day, she took my little girl and went to Abadan. Without me! As if you see the camel, but say you don't see it. I cried and cried. I begged Mash Namaki not to let Agha Bashi touch her until she was a little older. She was only nine years old then, just looked fuller than the other girls her age. Mash Namaki said, 'It's better for you not to join us on this voyage. Maybe a few months later, when she has become used to us and her husband. We'll send you a letter and a bus ticket when the time is right.'"

Bibi grew quiet for a long while. She was still moping when I rose to my feet and pushed the door open. I peeped inside with my body in the door way.

"My belly aches, Bibi," I said quietly, my hands on my stomach. "Bahareh said I should drink black tea."

"*Voy, voy*," muttered Mash Zoleikha. "Come in, child!"

"Did you eat too many Egyptian apples again?" Bibi asked, quickly wiping the tears from her cheeks. "I told you to eat the rosewater apples," she scolded me. "They're sweet and won't upset your stomach."

I nodded my head, but stood still like a statue. Bibi motioned with her hand for me to come in and sit next to her. Mash Zoleikha took a crystal cup from the silver tray, poured tea from the pot next to her, and handed it to me with a chunk of honey candy in the saucer. Bibi blew on the hot tea while caressing my hair.

I finished my tea. Bibi let me lie down on the folded Turkish blanket in the corner of the room. "Go to sleep! You'll feel much better when you wake up."

The dizziness and sleep had almost overcome me, but as the two women started to whisper again, I shifted my body and my entire attention to Bibi as if she was telling me another bedtime story. Bibi's story was interrupted by Bijan, Setareh's toddler, crawling in through the doorway with Bahareh chasing him. Mash Zoleikha hugged the baby and showered him with noisy kisses all over his persimmon face and chubby arms. Bahareh sat next to her mother, her eyes on the tray of sweets and honey candies. I sat up on the blanket as if waiting for Bibi's approval, gawking at all of them.

"Are you feeling any better, *babam*?" Bibi asked in a motherly way. And without waiting for an answer, she tapped her thigh with the palm of her hand, gesturing for me to sit on her lap. I moved toward her on my knees and plopped myself into her arms.

"Ah . . . my chest . . . *babam*. Don't hurt Bibi like that." She protected her enormous bosom with her free hand while pushing me softly to sit upright. "Sit down like a good girl next to Bibi, my pretty one."

Bahareh laughed quietly. I walked toward her and sat between her and Mash Zoleikha with Bijan struggling in her arms. Bahareh and I tickled the baby's foot until he made chirping sounds.

"I never could imagine, that of all people, Golrokh could live like that," Mash Zoleikha said to Bibi. "We heard so much good news from relatives coming from the city that we thought she was printing money , that she lived like a grand city lady."

"Well, that fooled me too," replied Bibi. She cried silently. Mash Zoleikha poured her another cup of tea, but Bibi did not touch it.

Sitting on the coarse goat-hair blanket, I was hearing yet another of Bibi's tales; this one was her daughter's life story. Now that I had heard it from Bibi's mouth, I knew that Marmar was right. The fruit-lady was my mother after all. Something inside me did not welcome this knowledge.

We returned home to the warm welcome of the villagers, who gathered around us, each bringing us a keepsake for our way home. At first, Bibi refused to accept their gifts, but they were so insistent that Bibi gave in. We were given many different kinds of fruit from their gardens to take home; someone gave us a rooster, another a pair of speckled hens and a family of chicks for me. A small hand-made tapestry came from someone in the crowd. Butter, syrup, and dates in tin containers got passed along to us hand by hand. Mash Zoleikha's husband, Uncle Safar, came running up at the last minute carrying a baaing black lamb, its legs dangling around his shoulders. Our *taxi-bar*, the only village truck, was ready to take off. Bibi wiped her moist eyes and kept thanking the villagers: "I'm embarrassed for all your kindness and your hospitality," she told everyone, kissing their cheeks. "May it be soon that I can return this generosity to each of you."

At Valiahd Square, across from the bus station, Bibi bought a straw knitted chicken coop, the shape of a big upside-down cone. At home, she set it in a far corner of the courtyard under the shade of the sweet lemon trees.

In the mornings, now, I looked for the eggs under the coop so that Bibi could scramble them for breakfast. The little black lamb baaed so much in the dark that one night Bibi had to bring it inside our bedroom because she was afraid it would disturb the neighbors. She shook her head and said that I should not get too attached to the little lamb. "*Babam*, we live in the city," she reasoned with me. "We can't keep this animal too long. It needs grazing grass in a real pasture, like the one in the village. Here, it'll eat all the grape vines in the garden and end up dying from stomach pain."

But when I cried, she relented and said that I could keep it until it grew a little older and fatter before she sold it to the alley butcher.

# CHAPTER 12

Summer is approaching fast, and the heat in the Cell Block is murderous. There are no fans, no air conditioning, no vent, no windows, and no fresh air. Lack of airflow exacerbates the skin fungus diseases. I am among those fortunate ones still immune to any of the widespread infections or the Block's maladies, yet not resilient enough to defeat one major snag: the excessive growth of body hair. I fear that if I ever get out of this hole, I will leave as a furry zoo monkey for I have never seen so much dark fuzz growing on my arms and legs. Bibi used to say that I was so skinny that she could count my ribs just by looking at them. Now, my daily meals consist of eating mainly bread, cheese, and occasional dates, so that my belly bulges out like the malnourished African children in the UNICEF documentaries I used to watch in my history and geography classes. The craving for starch attacked me so often at odd hours, leaving me feeling hungry at all times, that I too began nibbling now and then at the prison food. Even though I remove the chunks of meat from the stew, the camphor still does its job.

This Monday, my mother brought me black grapes from our own garden, and apricots and peaches which the village people gave us to take home as parting gifts. If I ever get free from this repugnant hole, the first place I want to go is to Deh. To visit all those beautiful peach gardens. I would want to run again like a child in that luscious green village where Bahareh and I used to skinny dip in its cool bubbling brooks streaming in and out of the palm groves and orange orchids.

As the days pass, I sit on my prayer rug and stare at the wall for hours just as my mother used to do after Mohammad was arrested. I try not to think of freedom and to be strong in case I am given a sentence. Instead, I turn to my new addiction of taking refuge in memories and let my mind wander off to a not-so-distant past. I think and marvel about our house more often, especially in those sacred hours when the lobby's radio plays the soothing *Iftar* prayers in Arabic: *Rabana, atena va zonobena* . . . I think about my mother and all the preparations she blissfully might be planning for this holy month.

Last Monday, she did not come to visit me. Ebrahim came alone. In an artificial, casual tone, he said that Mother was not feeling too well and that she had fainted on a public bus on her way to the market. She'd been taken to a nearby clinic, and the doctor had advised bed rest for a few days. "She's just stressed out," Ebrahim said, trying awkwardly to reassure me that there was nothing I should be concerned about. Knowing my mother, the things she would not tolerate for herself are being passive and being ill. She does not believe in things like bed rest and relaxation. The last thing she has on her mind these days is her own well-being.

When I saw her during her visit yesterday, there was no color in her face. Her lips looked dry and cracked, and her voice was barely audible. An invisible heaviness oppressed my heart and pressed against my chest the moment I saw her like that. As if someone had drained all the life out of her overnight, packaged it and shipped it generously to those bodies who don't have a clue about what it means to be alive. I begged her not to come visit me until she recovered. It's summer and I know that the heat in the uncovered prison waiting area is unbearable, especially now that it is Ramadan and she would be fasting, not eating any *sahari* meal at predawn. She commutes to Adelabad three days out of the week to see Ali, Mohammad, and me. For the first time I fear for her, I fear for her health, and for her loneliness.

My mother has never been a religious person. I have hardly ever heard her praying, and I doubt that she has ever attended a *Rouseh* sermon in her entire life. Nor does she know how to read the holy Koran, or to cover herself properly as a traditional Muslim woman is required to do. Yet ever since Mohammad was arrested, she has turned virtuous, begging even Bibi to pray more often and much harder. She has even visited the dead saints who are buried all over the city, even though she does not know their proper names or who they are exactly. For the first time in ages, she has gone to the Shrine of Saint Shah-e Cheragh. Now, she visits the shrine every Thursday evening and lights several candles, and gives charity to the poor in return for a prayer for the release of her imprisoned son.

The day the Shah left the country, she cried; and the day that Ayatollah Khomeini's airplane landed at the International Mehrabad Airport, she cried for a country gone astray. That day, Mohammad, beside himself with joy and out of breath, barged into the courtyard and turned on the TV so that the entire household could watch the spectacle live. Mother sighed and said to her overwhelmed agate-eyed son: "Since I can remember, the Mullahs' place was either at the mosque or at the graveyard, reciting prayers for the dead and eating the halva offering, not governing the country." Mohammad ignored her comment and said that Mother did not know much about the world she lived in. A year later he sat before the pile of his precious once-again-forbidden books and burned them to ashes; that very day *he* cried. God, how bitterly he cried. Mother bit her lower lip and didn't repeat to her forlorn son her legendary phrase, "I told you so," but Mohammad swallowed his pride. "Mother," he said without taking his eyes off the burning books, "I owe you an apology. No one can lie as shamelessly as the Mullahs."

It is the holy fasting month of Ramadan. I have never felt as I feel now in prison about this sacred and spiritual month; the girls say they feel the same. Maybe it's because there's something poignant about the locked-away fasting people. These past days, at predawn I wake to the sound of heartrending Ramadan prayers, a mournful sound that raises the hair on the back of my neck and hardens the lump in my throat. It is as if everyone in the Block has turned her back on the ephemeral world, shifting into a different dimension in a faraway galaxy, where no human is condemned to such suffering and cruelty. Even the *Sisters* seem to pretend to act kind and gentle in their own way. During the night and a good portion of the day, the corridor's loudspeaker plays the soothing voice of Abdolvaset to which the girls, holding their Koran before their faces, recite the verses solemnly in the corner of their cells. My vow is to pray alone and complete another round of Koran recitation so that Mohammad's verdict will reject his death penalty; it is after all the holy month and the doors of Heaven are said to be wide open. *God is listening*, Bibi's voice echoes in my cell. So, if I pray more wholeheartedly, maybe He will answer my prayers. I hope that this year Bibi will not be fasting. At her age and with her bad health, the faith does not require her to fast. My ears are filled with her warm voice, responding to the sound of predawn prayers from her transit radio: *Rabana, atena va ʒonobana* . . . like those dawns when I was still a little girl, before our house went through stages of transformation.

That summer, too, coincided with Ramadan. I remember the first thing Bibi did, as soon as she returned home from her almond-picking job, was to shed all her clothes and soak herself in the fishpond for a good half hour. Then, she'd lie on her back under the arbor, letting her enormous bare breasts fall to her sides as she fanned herself with another one of her souvenirs, a handmade Abadani palm-leaf fan, waiting for the sun to set so she could break her fast at *Iftar*. That summer, Bibi intended to fast the entire thirty days and hoped that she would have the stamina to bear the hunger and thirst.

As the sun began to sink behind the horizon and the sky was filled with the colors of orange and pomegranate, Bibi brought out her transistor radio and her round vintage clock from the bedroom and settled them in the open spot right between the gillyflower and verbena bushes. While she did the ritual prayer ablution and listened for the counting seconds before the *Iʒan*, I waited impatiently, staring at the colorful, long-feather rooster in the bottom corner of the clock; the bird moved its head up and down seeking the grains he could never reach. I watched the second hand as I listened to the radio's simultaneous ticking sound.

With the sound of a dropping cannon ball, indicating *Iftar*, Bibi began her rounds of prayer beads, praying for the whole world. When she was finished, we sat together at *sofreh* and she broke her fast with a glass of rosewater syrup *sharbat* or cold lemonade from the tin pitcher, treats she had made before sunset. She fetched a watermelon from underneath the shrubs and let it float among the goldfish in the small fishpond under the arbor, to be chilled for *Sahari*, the last meal before sunrise.

Ramadan may have been a holy month to Bibi, but to me it was the month of sweets, *zoolbia* and *bamieh*. Usually, Bibi wouldn't let me eat any sweets or *baghlava* unless she stood right there next to me, toothbrush in hand, so I could clean my teeth as soon as I swallowed the treats she gave me. "I don't want you to end up like me with rotten teeth and premature toothlessness," she'd say. But it was Ramadan and the neighbors brought us so many sweets that Bibi let me eat as much as I wanted. The neighbor women gathered together every day at one of their homes and cooked sweetened saffron rice pudding and honeyed *tarhalva*, as if they were cooking for the entire city of Shiraz. Right before *Iftar*, Masht Reza, the greengrocer, made a huge copper pot of lemonade and the alley's butcher set up tin bins so large that my hands never reached their faucet. He'd filled them with drinking water and big chunks of ice as an offering to the thirsty passers-by who wished to break their fast. Since kids are exempted from fasting, the neighborhood children and I brought our sweets and shared them with each other. As she saw me once eating sweet *halva* with Marmar in their entryway, Bibi forbade me to eat in the alley where others passed before us even if they themselves were not fasting. "You may be too young to fast, but you're not too young to respect others," Bibi scolded me that day. "It's the holy month of respect and reflection."

Each time a neighbor brought us sweet *halva* or any other offerings, in return Bibi blessed their faces with a sprinkle of rosewater. Later, when she sent me to return a clean dish to the neighbor, Bibi added vine leaves or orange blossoms to their bowls as a sign of gratitude. "It is not polite to send a dish back empty," she'd tell me as she reached for the very green and shiny leaves. "Tell the neighbor politely, May your entire family be blessed as the evergreen gardens!" Bibi asked me to recite the phrase a few times, making sure I got it right. I would omit this part of her blessing and simply thank the neighbors, "Bibi said *merci*," I would say instead. The neighbors didn't seem to mind my version of blessing and still were happy to see the green vine leaves. I decided the phrase was too long and Bibi wasn't with me anyway, although it made me a bit antsy, because she said it so light-heartedly that I thought the neighbor women ought to hear it. I convinced myself that they knew Bibi would thank them in long phrases.

Unlike the neighbor women, Bibi never prepared much food and said that she had a small stomach. I didn't mind her saying that, though I thought her belly looked like a slab of rising dough. She said that this was, after all, the holy month, month of worship and praise to Allah—a month that one should eat less and give more to the needy, for the purpose of fasting is to feel what hunger and poverty is, so one would make a habit of feeding the famished and helping the destitute. I thought a while about what she told me and I understood why she kept nourishing me with all kinds of food. I was neither a famished nor a gourmand girl, as she put it, but she still wondered why all that nourishing food did not put any meat on my ribs and I was still just skin and bones.

Some of our neighbor women cooked many kinds of rice dishes, stews, sweets and *halvas*, and threw down a big *sofreh*, inviting family and relatives at each *Iftar*. But Bibi said that a body should not have a colorful *sofreh* like that, for fasting all day does not serve the purpose of purification when one stuffs her stomach with all kinds of food at *Iftar*. "It's the month of serious practices," she emphasized over and over. She sat me on her lap and told me that I should not lie then, not that lying was acceptable at any other time, and reminded me that I should not hurt others' feelings or say disrespectful words. "And don't forget!" Bibi said, "Be kind and polite to the neighbors!"

I was not even allowed to hurt animals, Bibi reminded me, not even to kill a fly itching the top of my nose. So I had to tell Marmar to put off the battle between the red and black rider ants. It was a thing we did, messing up the separate highway of red and black ants carrying leftover crumbs off the warm mosaic tiles. These were not the tiny kinds of ants like those in the rest of the world. These were the size of baby spiders, had long legs like a horse, and knew how to inflict worse pain than a bumblebee. Marmar and I had had the taste of their sting many times. With the help of a stick, Marmar usually messed up the red ants' line while I caught the black ones and dumped them into the line of red ants. There, instead of searching for food, the ants fought with each other, making us laugh for hours. We did this when Bibi was not around, because if she were to see that, she'd scold me that she had not fed me to become a bully, hurting the tiniest of God's creatures who served such a useful purpose of acting as a sweeper for the human race.

I wanted to fast as well, but Bibi disagreed and said that I had to wait until I was nine years old, the obligatory fasting age for girls. Good thing I was not a boy, because then I would have to wait until I was fifteen, since boys mature more slowly than girls, Bibi supposed. "You still have a few years left to feed yourself so you can grow solid bones," she said.

Despite my age, I pleaded with Bibi to wake me up for *Sahari*, because I wanted to play with Marmar and eat more *zoolbia*. But when I felt the dew tiptoeing on my cheek, and I woke up to the sound of *Izan* coming from the mosque's turquoise minaret—*Allah-o-Akbar, Allah-o-Akbar*, God is the greatest—I knew that I had missed another *Sahari* again. As Bibi kissed my forehead and caressed my hair, rocking me back to sleep, I knew I could eat as much watermelon as I wanted all day.

# CHAPTER 14

That same summer, before Ramadan ended, I was struck by the chicken pox. It was one of those idle and indolent summer days, as Bibi put it. I had just begun to recover from that terrible virus. Bibi had found another seasonal job at the Sour-Pickle factory, skinning and cleaning eggplants and cucumbers. Some days, she took me along. Other days, she let me stay home, either asking a neighbor to keep an eye on me, or instructing me to stay in and not to open the door to any strangers. I wandered between Marmar's house and mine, engaging myself by fidgeting around the vegetable garden, playing with my bunny, chasing the hens or the little lamb.

I looked down to see how many more baby tomatoes had sprouted again when I heard the sound of the knocker breaking the quiet of the courtyard. I knew I was not allowed to open the door. I listened carefully. There it was again: *Tagh . . . tagh . . . tagh. . . .* I peeped. A man's head appeared from the iron bars above the house door. "Is Bibi home?" he asked. I ran and hid behind the chicken coop, my forehead barely above it, and hoped he would go away if I didn't answer.

"Girl! Open the door!" he said, irritated.

"I'm not allowed to," I said quietly. "Come back when Bibi's home!"

"Don't you know me? Open the door, Nastaran!"

*The man knows my name. How strange. Who could he be?*

"I'm Ali. It's quite all right. Just open the door, or else I'll have to open it myself." The little lamb began to baa; the hens wriggled around the coop. Startled, I peeked. The man's hand was reaching for the door's top-latch. There was a thumping against my chest. The door flung open and a tall young man entered the courtyard, slamming the door shut behind him.

"Where's Bibi?" he asked as he walked past me hastily. "Where's your *salam* to your older brother?" he shot me a sidelong glance. "Has the cat eaten your tongue?"

Things happened so quickly, his breaking into the house like that. I just stood there and gawked. Speechless. Bibi always said that it was not good to stare at people, so I looked down at my toes. This time it was even harder, now that a strange man was claiming he was my brother. "She's at work," I forced myself to say, still looking down.

"Working at that factory?"

I nodded my head. Surprised. He paced around, looking under the vine branches.

"They're *askari* grapes. Very sweet," I mumbled.

"I have eyes myself," he mumbled back.

My eyes traced his steps. He was as tall as the arbor. He could have picked any bunch of grapes he wanted. By and by, I was less spooked and more curious. *He's my brother?* I held my bunny tighter. Again, he shot me another glance. He had the hugest honey-brown eyes I have ever seen. He walked in my direction, passed me, then paused by the fishpond, turned on the faucet, and splashed his black hair, pushing it back from his forehead. He rubbed his hands on his slacks, fixed the creases so the lines fell straight on his shiny black, pointy shoes. "What's that thing you got there in your hand?" he asked, combing his hair.

"It's a bu . . ."

"I can see that." He looked around. "What's all this? Is this a house or an animal husbandry? What is it? Did Bibi open a cattle-yard?"

I could not make up my mind whether to like him or not. Usually, the neighbor girls liked their brothers. Even if they were not handsome. This one was. He looked like that man in the poster Roaya had hanging in her room. Marmar kept kissing his dimples, saying that she'd marry him when she grew up. Roaya always laughed at her sister and said, "By the time you grow up, Elvis's bones will be a fistful of ashes."

"You do know how to talk, don't you?" Ali said.

"They're keepsakes," I said hesitantly, "Bibi's relatives gave them to us. From her village."

"That's Bibi, all right. The village-woman."

It was then that I heard it, the same strange tone I had heard in Bibi's daughter's voice, the same wavy, chic accent. Suddenly, his voice didn't sound good to me.

"Do you go to school yet?" he asked, sitting at the edge of the fishpond.

"No. Bibi says it's too soon."

"Do you know the alphabet?"

I kept quiet.

"Talk!"

"Bibi can't teach me to read. She doesn't know how."

He rose and looked around some more. "Why are you home alone?" His tone changed suddenly.

"I have chicken pox. She'll come back soon. The neighbor isn't home today."

"I'll stick around."

With that, he went up the stairs, heading for the rooftop. Coming back down, he paced the yard again, the gardens, the rooms, barging in and out of the house the entire afternoon until Bibi arrived. As soon as she saw him, she reached out to kiss him. He moved away. "My hair, Bibi. You're messing up the hair."

"Let Bibi kiss you, my brother-father. You're the pupil of my eye, *babam*." Bibi reached excitedly for his face again.

Since that day, Ali continued to come to the house unexpectedly. Most of the time, as soon as he arrived, he went up to the rooftop, to meet with one of the neighbor boys whose hobby was flying pigeons. Bibi didn't approve of Ali associating with this new friend, saying that the pigeon-boy was not good company for someone like him. She said that flying pigeons was not the kind of thing a proper kid from a good family would want to do. Ali was annoyed with Bibi's advice and ignored it. Now and then, he quarreled with Bibi over her cooking, saying that her dishes were inedible and he preferred his mother's cooking.

One day Ali came with a brown ball under his arm, a basketball, he called it. He nailed a basket onto the storage wall. Jumping up and down, he'd shoot the ball into the basket. Bibi told me once that in his school back in Abadan, he used to be a very good basketball player. Occasionally, he brought a large white pad with him, and drew all kinds of pretty pictures: faces, noses, lips, ears, hands. If he was in a good mood, he'd let me look at his drawings.

One day he brought me a small binder, a book, pencils, and erasers. "Come here!" he motioned to me. "Today, you will learn the alphabet."

He put a pencil between his thumb and index finger, showing me how to hold it. Then he drew strange patterns on a piece of paper. "See . . . that's your name . . . n a s t a r a N," he sounded it out. "nas taa rrrraN. Now you do it!"

I scribbled the pattern the way he showed me.

"Good, good," he praised me. "Now, look here. There are thirty-two letters. I wrote them all here for you. It starts with 'A' and it ends with 'Y'. Each letter has a small and a big form. Now write A^B, water. You have to write 'A' with *hat*, and big 'B' A^B."

Again I copied the word the way he instructed me. He seemed pleased. And I liked the way the alphabet sounded and looked on the paper. He told me I had to practice the alphabet every day, writing the letters each ten times, and show them to him next time he came back. I was so overjoyed that I even wrote more than he asked me to. I even spelled (bY bY). When I showed Bibi her name, she cried with joy and clapped her hands: "My little girl's growing up. Look at you!" She kissed my entire face a million times.

Sometimes Ali stayed for the night, other times only for a few hours. As always, he hurried upstairs to the rooftop. This had become his routine until one day he quarreled and fought with Abu, the pigeon-boy. When he came downstairs, his nose was bleeding. He pushed me out of his way and rinsed off the blood at the fishpond. When he saw me looking at him, he asked me to bring my homework. He seldom praised me, but I was hoping he'd be happy this time, because I'd practiced a lot of new words. He looked at my work and yelled, "You've done everything wrong. You misspelled 'a' with '*A with hat*.'"

I looked at the words and compared them with the ones he wrote on the top line; to me, they looked identical. But he said that I chattered too much and should repeat them again. I just stared at the pages. He held my hand, placed the pencil between two of my fingers, and squeezed them so hard I almost fainted. Tears trickled down my cheeks. I clutched my fingers with my left hand, but the pain didn't go away. He repeated his demand, jamming the pencil between my fingers, yelling, "Write it! Write it now! You idiot, you brat." I tried, but my fingers felt numb. My eyes burned with tears, making the lines blurry. He slapped the back of my neck and left the house as I fell to the ground, writhing in pain.

When Bibi returned home, I told her what had happened. She kissed my hand. "He's out of hand, that boy," she cried. She told me if he ever hurt me again, she would not allow him in the house.

A few days later, Ali came back again. This time Bibi was home. I hid behind her, because I was terrified that he would ask me about the homework. Bibi was bitter. She criticized him, saying that this wasn't the way to teach a little girl how to write, squeezing a pencil between her fingers. He told her that my head was stuffed with hay and that I was as stubborn as a donkey. I'd never had anyone call me names or hit me. Bibi protested that she would never tolerate this kind of behavior in her house, and that she would not allow anyone to talk to her granddaughter in such a manner. Ali countered that he was my older brother and had the right to discipline me, even if it requird some good slaps on the back of the neck.

"Is that right?" Bibi said furiously, holding her arms akimbo.

"That's right," Ali shouted back.

"Well. We'll just have to see about that," Bibi said, turning her back to him.

Ali hung around for a while. Later, I heard Bibi pleading with him to be more sympathetic to his only sister. That he was seventeen years old, and I was only a child of five, not even ready for any schooling; he should treat me in such a way that I would look up to him as an older brother; and he should never, ever raise his hand to me, an innocent girl, or any other female for that matter. He nodded his head.

A few days later, when Bibi was not around, Ali repeated his routine, so that Bibi became afraid to leave me home alone. She pleaded with the neighbors that for the love of God they should watch over me when she was at work. She told me that I should shout as loud as I could and ask the neighbors for help if he ever hit me again.

One afternoon I was in Marmar's courtyard when I heard Ali knocking at my friend's door, asking me to come home. Marmar's mother and her older sister had gone to the market; forbidding us to leave the house. Her father, as always, was dozing in the back room and the two of us were playing guests, serving each other tiny cups of pond water pretending it was sweetened tea. Ali's voice grew louder, ordering me to leave. Even though he was outside the locked door, I began to shiver. "It's your mean brother again," Marmar said, looking at me. There was something in her look that made me leave her house. I didn't want my playmate to know that I had a mean brother, so I followed him.

The minute I walked in our courtyard, he slapped my face and twisted my ear. I began to cry. He said that I misbehaved and was being donkey stubborn again because I didn't obey his order imediately. Then he asked me to begin my writing. This time, he gave me long sentences. I couldn't copy everything properly. He slapped me some more, pushed me to the ground, and left the house.

When Bibi came home and heard my story, she went mad. This time, she was even angry with me. For the first time I could remember, she yelled at me. Grabbing my shoulders, she said: "Didn't I forbid you to leave Marmar's house? I'm not putting food in that mouth of yours, raising you to become another Golrokh. Don't you dare turn into your *Momon*, gutless and chicken-hearted. Couldn't you shout? Couldn't you bite? Why did you leave Marmar's house in the first place? Huh?"

"I was afraid he'd come inside." I began to cry. "I didn't want him to hit me in front of Marmar, Bibi."

"What is it with you? What is it that we all have to be helpless and some ungodly man has to bash us on the head?" Bibi broke into tears. She waved her hands in the air. "I am not my father's daughter to let that happen to me again. I won't allow that. Open up your ears real good. Don't you ever let a man raise his hand to you! Look at the other girls! They have a tongue this long," she held her elbow, drawing an invisible line up to her wrist. "They're brave. Why can't you be like them? I won't always be around to guard you, you know! You should learn that *now*. Do you hear me? Put your shoes on!" she commanded. When she saw me standing right there motionless, she yelled, "I SAID, put your shoes on!" Holding my hand, she dragged me behind her.

In the taxi, she talked to herself the entire way, mumbling and whimpering.

We passed through the narrow shady damp alleys with walls all mildewed a good half-meter from their bases up. Bibi stopped at an old rustic wooden door. She knocked and without waiting for an answer, pushed the door open. We entered a small treeless court-yard. A woman in a short skirt and sleeveless top was gathering clothes from the laundry line. She approached Bibi, "Good day," she greeted. Bibi, red, sweaty, and in tears, kissed the woman on both cheeks as she mumbled nonstop. Stepping out of a room, the same fruit-lady appeared on the porch, leaning against a white column, her hand on her waist; a little boy peeped behind her legs. She glanced at me, her familiar ominous glare. I crept behind Bibi.

"What is it? What's all this fuss about?" she asked Bibi, her eyes still on me.

"Why don't you ask your dear son?" Bibi stepped toward the porch. "Isn't that bad enough now that you have forsaken this tongueless child so that you have to send your spoiled son to torture her?"

"Good, good," Golrokh walked down a step. For a moment, I thought she was going to walk over to me. But she sat on the bottom step, pulling the little boy to her lap. "Since when is the pot hotter than the soup?" She waved at Bibi. "Now you're more Catholic than the Pope? If that girl is your grandchild, so is Ali. He's only a high school kid. And in case you're forgetting, they're siblings."

"He's seventeen years old, not a child any more. Soon, it will be time for him to serve in the army," Bibi bellowed. "If she's his sister, he should treat her like a sister, play with her, teach her something good, not hurt her." She gasped for air. "Do you know what he does to her? He comes and squeezes a pencil between her fingers!" She raised my arm, showing my hand to her daughter.

"Well. He doesn't mean any harm," Golrokh said without pay-ing much attention to my fingers. "Don't tell me you've come all the way here to tell me you're worrying about some sort of silly quarrel between siblings."

"I'm not just worried about this girl, I'm worried about him too. Don't you see? That boy of yours is getting out of hand. The boy, Agha Bashi's sweetheart, is already carrying a knife in his pocket, like a penniless peasant boy, and plays marbles with bad company in the back-alleys. He flies pigeons over the rooftops. I'm ashamed when neighbors tell me all that. I don't want to lose face in my neighborhood. I'm warning you now, before it's too late. You already put the rest of your kids in that boarding school. And I have to earn a morsel of food to raise this child. If he keeps acting like that, I don't want him to come to my house any more. You hear me? I'm not saying he's not welcome in my house. Just tell your son never again to raise his hands to this innocent female."

Bibi was out of breath as we stepped back into the alley. "Who was that little boy, Bibi?"

"You poor little thing," she shook her head and looked at me with her watery eyes. "That was your baby brother, Amir."

# CHAPTER 13

Leaves turned yellow, orange, red, and brown.

The gardens were filled with fallen leaves. Bibi was tired from her sweeping, so she let the scattered dying vine leaves cover the courtyard. I wondered and asked Bibi why they fell and crumbled into tiny particles like that.

"You hear that?" Bibi whispered, cradling her hand against her ear. "It's autumn's footsteps." Gingerly moving under the wooden arbor, she scooped up the amber red leaves with her hands. "Here! Can you smell the *orangey* air, *babam*? All kinds of fall scents, putting a spell on the air, making the leaves dance to the ground."

The grapes were long gone. The ones saved from sparrows' bruises, Bibi gave away to the neighbors. The persimmons, on the other hand, green and tiny like buttoned chickpeas, began to bloom in the garden on the left, the fall-season side of the courtyard, as Bibi called it. As soon as the grapes were gone, taking the summer with them, the fall side of the yard would come into bud. The oranges, as small and green as still-in-husk walnuts, began to shed their white blossoms on the glazed tiles, scenting the air. The pomegranate tree didn't survive this fall. Bibi blamed it on Ali Akbar, the city gardener, who brought her an unusual type of fertilizer. Sure enough, the instant she added a pail of it on the garden soil, the poor tree shed all its pink blossoms and its shiny green leaves. Later she found out that the gardener had forgotten to tell her that it was some sort of chemical fertilizer. When Masht Akbar cut the tree from its trunk, Bibi sobbed as if he were cutting off her own fingers. She did a pilgrimage around the leftover trunk, mumbling to herself that nowadays you sleep at night, and wake up next morning to some new fabrications mushrooming in the market. "I should've known better when plastic and melamine came and replaced the crystal mugs and copper dishes," she said sadly. "Hey, hey, hey," she huffed, "whatever happened to those natural things. Those were the good old days, the days when you fed your garden sheep-dung and everything was just fine and dandy."

The black lamb we brought from the village, as Bibi predicted, got a stomachache and died at the end of the summer. We kept bringing it to Bibi's bedroom at nightfall so often that it became family. Most of the time, it cuddled next to Bibi or lay on her lap. "This tongueless animal thinks I'm its mother," Bibi would say.

One day when Bibi was taking her afternoon nap on the front porch, the little lamb chewed her bangs, forming a zigzag pattern on her forehead. I laughed so hard, my stomach ached, but Bibi said this was a sign that God was not delighted with her uncovering her hair, although no man was in our house. The next day, the little lamb died, its head on Bibi's lap. I cried and wished I had never laughed the day before.

Even though half the trees were leafless, Bibi and I cherished the autumn's *orangey* air. I filled up my hands with the most crimson colored leaves and tossed them high in the air. Crunching and crushing the leaves under my bare feet, I ran around the yard, chasing my bunny. The moist-dry leaves tickled my feet. Bibi cranked her rickety gramophone. The silvery music filled the autumn air. Dancing to the music, Bibi held my hands. We spun round and round, singing and dancing around the fishpond and in and out of the arbors.

It was in the midst of our dancing that Darya, the butcher's wife, entered the courtyard. As always she came to seek Bibi's advice on some sort of medicine for her husband, Mash Gholam, whose loose back was troubling her. I wondered how a man's back could be loose, especially someone like Mash Gholam who was the largest creature in the alley and didn't need a ladder to climb up the mulberry tree in front of his butcher's shop. He would simply reach and fill his fist with black mulberry and didn't even offer it to anyone. Good thing he didn't, because who in his right mind would want those bloody mulberries anyway? And why would his back trouble Darya, who only thought of having a child? The two women whispered in my presence. "It's really not my fault, Bibi," Darya said to Bibi, as if she'd done something bad. "Poor Mash Gholam . . . he really tries hard, but as soon as he gets near me . . . well. . . ."

Minutes later, Bibi, reaching for her flowery chador, motioned for me. I followed the women.

On the street, Darya waved her hand at a green-and-white taxi, calling out: "Bazaar Vakil, Mr. Driver. Bazaar Vakil." Her golden bangles jingled and shone in the noon sun.

On the way to Bazaar Vakil, Bibi said to Darya, that only Sayyed Attar could resolve her problems and cure her husband; and that Sayyed Attar is a far more competent druggist than any *Farang* educated doctors.

Sayyed Attar the Druggist was a tall lean man with a bristly salt-and-pepper beard. A gold tooth shone when he smiled at Bibi. He wore a small green cap on his head. "He's a *Sayyed*," Bibi explained to me. "A direct descendant of the Prophet Mohammad."

The counter of Sayyed Attar's chamber in Bazaar Vakil was covered with containers of all kinds of colorful spices and relishes heaped in pyramids. The pungent scents permeated the atmosphere. I could see a rainbow of red, yellow, brown, gold, and green everywhere, on the ground, around the counters, on the shelves. There were black powder and henna to color hair, ground cedar, saffron, and many other spices I didn't know the names of or what they were good for. Full sacks of roasted seeds of watermelon, pumpkin, pistachio, almonds, and *moshgel-gosha* mixed nuts were stacked against each other. Bibi whispered something to Sayyed Attar that I could not hear. He glanced at Darya who stood next to Bibi quietly, looking down. Sayyed Attar pointed his finger at some of the spices and talked rapidly to Bibi in a high-pitched voice. Bibi kept nodding her head and saying that she understood Sayyed's instructions. She bought a little of almost everything, handing them to Darya.

I watched Sayyed Attar's animated motions: with a silver scoop in his right hand, he measured out a small quantity of the spices and herbs he had pointed out to Bibi, poured them onto a sheet of newspaper or some sort of colored wax-paper. He then weighed each item separately on one side of the copper scale, placing iron cylinder weights on the other side until both sides were in balance. He rolled the filled papers into a cone, handed them to Bibi, took Darya's money, and scribbled something in a thick old binder.

When we were ready to leave, Bibi bought me dried fruit *lavashak* and crunchy white mulberry. For herself, she bought henna and hair-washing cedar powder. We left Sayyed Atar and the singsong sound of copper workers in the adjacent chambers, hammering and shaping new pans and pots. For several days, my ears buzzed with the wheezing noises and commotion coming from those rooms, and the sound of busy people bargaining with the merchants as they bought all kinds of colorful fabrics and carpets.

On the way home, Bibi advised Darya to give her husband, for seven consecutive mornings, a blend of goat-milk, egg yolk, and honey mixed with the powders they had just bought from Sayyed Attar. She reassured the woman that her husband would be good as new, and soon she'd bear fat boys.

At home, Bibi let me eat my share of dried *lavashak* while she prepared the remedy for Darya's husband. The two women talked nonstop about children and family. Darya told Bibi again how much she wished to have a daughter for herself and a son for Mash Gholam.

"Whatever you don't have, you wish for," Bibi responded to Darya's grievances. "God granted me only one child, my only daughter, but alas," she paused for a moment, "it's not like I'm being ungrateful—- whatever God wishes. But what's the point of having a child who doesn't appreciate you? When you don't have children, you have only one concern, yourself, but when you do have them, their pain is your pain, their worries, your worries." Bibi took a piece of paper from the pile of medicine, folded it in half, and fanned herself with it. "My daughter . . ." she paused again, facing Darya. "You haven't met her. Have you?"

Darya shook her head. "No. But I have seen her son a few times hanging out with Abu. Well. It's really none of my business." Darya hesitated. "But that Abu boy is bad news. It's a pity. Your grandson is such a lad, with that handsome face. Tall too. These boys around here are not his kind of breed, you know!"

"He's a handsome lad all right," Bibi sighed. "Well, I don't see my daughter's face from month to month, but her troubles are always here. Ali is my oldest grandson." Bibi sighed. "What can I expect? He's fatherless. He's here in Shiraz for a couple of months and a few months over there in Abadan. He's not only handsome, he has a head on his shoulders, too. Yet, what a pity. You should've seen him when his father was still alive. You know, a chauffeur used to come to the house, to take him to school. Such a cushy life. What can I say about those darling boys? God only knows, my heart bleeds for them, my child's children, Agha Bashi's sons. With all his passivity, while he was alive, who could dare to say that there was a curved eyebrow over his child's eye? When they were babies, his aunts wouldn't allow their bottoms to touch the ground. Now look at them living in that boarding school." Bibi swept away a teardrop with the back of her hand. "And you want children? I don't mean to dishearten you, dear. You're young; it's only natural, you should have children. But as they say, whatever glitters is not gold. My daughter . . . well . . . her husband's relatives filled her up with lies, and she still doesn't know left from right."

Bibi grew quiet. Darya gave her a glass of water from the clay jug, comforting her.

I knew Bibi was heart-sick again.

"What is it, girl? Why are you so quiet?" Darya asked me. "She's such a reserved child."

"No. She's not. She's just a good listener. She thinks I'm telling a story," said Bibi, looking at me. "What is it, *babam*?"

"Nothing," I shook my head.

"Don't eat all your *lavashak* at once!" Bibi said again.

I watched the two women as they continued talking about the remedies. Darya thanked Bibi over and over, saying that her final place was surely to be in heaven. When the remedy was ready, Bibi left with Darya. She said to me, "My bunch of flowers, this is a private matter and you can't go along." She locked the door, reassuring me that she'd be back before I finished eating my snack.

So I went about the garden, feeding the bunny. For a second, I thought I saw a tall shadow creep over my head. I looked up. I froze. Leaning against the arbor, Ali was looking at me. I felt a chill. *Bibi said she locked the door.*

"Now, since when have you learned to be so good at telling tales?"

he said in an odd voice. He motioned toward me, a strange smell radiated from him. I hadn't seen him for some weeks now.

My feet felt as if they were planted in the ground. I just stood there and stared at him. He grabbed the bunny, which was leaping around my feet. Suddenly, I felt something; I snatched back the animal, remembering Bibi's advice to be brave. "That's mine!" I shrieked.

"Let go of it, you stupid village girl," he barked, pulling the animal out my hands. "Why does she let you play with things like this? Doesn't she know they carry diseases?"

I ran after the bunny. Ali chased me. He reached for my arm, holding it firmly in his fist.

"Let go of it!" I cried.

This time he shook me harder, knocking me onto the damp ground. The hens clabbered around the yard; their brown feathers cluttered the air.

"Stop whining, you stubborn idiot!" His slap burned the side of my face.

A light passed before my eyes. No sound escaped my lips. Mute. Startled. Frozen. I felt the droplets of tears falling down my cheeks. I feared his fist, so I tried to hold the tears back. But they kept rolling down. *Where are you Bibi?* My own voice whispered in my head. Ali stood above me with his fist ready to come down. I heard the door pushed in. Bibi was in the courtyard. She looked perplexed for a moment, seeing me lying on the ground. I escaped from between Ali's legs, running to Bibi. I looped my arms around her legs, "He hit me Bibi," I sobbed. "He hit me again."

Bibi's face turned the color of sugar beets. "You boil my blood. Enough is enough," she roared. Walking toward Ali, she pointed her index finger at his face. "*Bah, bah! Bah, bah!* May your mother's eye be bright to see her son in such a delightful condition. How charming," Bibi smacked the back of her own hand. "Since when did you start drinking the snake-poison? Your mouth still smells of mother's milk. Your face has hardly grown a beard. Since when do you dare to drink *arrack*?" Bibi stepped back, shielding me with her body. I was hurt. Scared. Confused. I couldn't understand Bibi's words. How could someone drink snake-poison and still be alive? Maybe he'll die, I thought.

"That's the eternity water . . . my pretty . . . gorgeous Bibi," said Ali, now lurching.

"Well. This is not your father's house. You'd better take these theatrics to your precious father's aunts. I'm sure they'll be proud of you. I won't allow you to come here, tormenting this girl. This is the last time, I tell you. Don't you ever again raise your hand to this orphan child," she yelled, her breath choppy, her voice vibrating. Chasing him around the yard, she told him to leave immediately. He staggered around, laughing, walking on the edge of the fishpond.

"If you don't leave this minute, I'd call the *Adjan*."

"To say what? That I'm an older brother, trying to discipline my own sister," he sneered.

Bibi took my hand, heading for the door. Quickly, Ali jumped down and grabbed her from behind. He took a knife out of his pants pocket and pointed it at Bibi's throat. I shrieked.

"Shut your mouth!" he barked at me.

Holding Bibi, he threatened that if she took another breath, he'd plunge the blade into her body. Bibi fell silent, and so did I. My breath choked in my chest. Bibi and I exchanged silent glances. My entire body was shaking. That very moment, I understood why the leaves fall and crumble. I forced myself not to cry, for I didn't want anything to happen to Bibi.

With Ali's arm locked around her neck Bibi tried to wrest herself free. He yanked Bibi by her armpits and dragged her over the dusty ground. He led her to the garden's edge, pretending to cut her throat as if she was a hen. He laughed and laughed. Bibi moaned and cursed, calling out to God and all the saints, asking for help. "God, where are you? Show me your supremacy! Show me your power! Prophet Mohammad, help! Imam Ali, help! . . . Somebody help!" She choked, her voice sounded hoarse, her breath was short, her scarf came undone, and her auburn hair covered her muddy face. But help didn't come.

I darted toward Ali, hitting him with my fists. "Let go of my Bibi . . . let go of my Bibi!" I cried. He pushed me away with his arm, but he let go of Bibi. "Her place is in that orphanage," he said, stepping away from Bibi. "I'll make sure that'll happen, dear Bibi. You can count on that!"

Spitting on the ground, he stumbled out of the garden.

I threw myself over Bibi's body, pulling her to sit up. She refused. She lay on the ground for a long while, sobbing quietly, her breasts rising and falling with each heavy gasp of air. I had never seen her this helpless. I had never seen anyone disrespect her, let alone hurt her like this. No one ever talked to Bibi this way. She covered her face with her undone scarf, wiping the tears away and pulled me toward her, holding me in her arms. I couldn't see her face, but her quivering body told me that she was still sobbing. I lay there next to her, my shaking body cradled in a bed of crimson enchanted autumn leaves, listening to her breathe. "I have always lived with dignity," she said between sobs.

# CHAPTER 14

Roaya begged Bibi to let me go along with the girls to the popular Bagh-e Melli Gardens. Bibi finally gave in, though I could still see a wave of unwillingness in her ever-moist eyes. "Well, you must promise to hold her hand at all times," she said to Roaya. "I don't have to remind you that she wanders off easily. You take your eyes off her a second, sure enough she's lost in that sea of people at Melli Gardens."

Roaya made all kinds of promises that she thought would melt Bibi's heart. My grandmother kissed my forehead, instructing me for the hundredth time not to let go of Roaya's hand. After all, it was the first time ever she would have let her five-year-old granddaughter step out of the alley without her, and even worse, in the company of a couple of ready-to-be-brides sixteen-year-old girls whose feet, Bibi thought, may be on the ground but whose heads were surely in the clouds.

The moment we got away from our neighborhood, in one of the back alleys, Roaya changed into a *mini-joop* skirt and white high-heel boots. Her cousin, Mitra, wore a pair of bright orange bell-bottoms and a shirt which she knotted above her belly button. Her pants were so tight, you could see the exact shape of her buttocks. The two girls brushed their long black hair and let it fall wild on their shoulders. Marmar and I giggled as we watched them redden their lips and blacken their eyebrows and eyelids with a pencil. Roaya patted her sister's cheeks and mine with a powder which smelled pretty, like Bibi's daughter's smell. Mitra laughed and said that I was lucky that I already had black long eyelashes and didn't need any mascara; she, too, patted some more red powder on my cheeks.

The Melli Gardens was a very long way from our alley. We had to change a few different rounds of yogurt-and-cucumber colored taxies, which drove us through so many streets and boulevards that I thought soon I would fall sleep.

When we returned home, Bibi was sitting in the doorway, peering anxiously into the alley. I thought she would be upset with Roaya for returning after dark, but she thanked her instead, and hugged me. "Your *Momon* came right after you left," she said. "She came with your younger brothers. What a pity you missed them." She said that her daughter was angry with her, because she had to pay a hefty fare for the taxi. "I told her," Bibi went on, "have I smelled the palm of my hand to know you were coming? Had you said something ahead of time, I would've kept the girl at home. It's not like every day she'd get a golden chance to go to Bagh-e Melli."

In her room, Bibi handed me a box of Zoo-cookies to eat the next day. "It's from your brothers," she said. Then she said that my mother would come back next Friday, bringing my brothers along. And that day I was not allowed to leave the house at any time. "I do not fancy your mother's temper again," she added.

I was not all that enthusiastic to see my brothers with the exception of Mohammad, who kept running away. Secretly, I was glad Ali had been sent to the military, serving far away in the Capitol. Bibi thought that army life would make a man of him. "He'll realize how hard it is to make ten loaves of bread out of one kilo of flour," she said, using a favorite expression. At the same time, she cried for him and said that he was just a young lad who had lost his father and a warm home, all at once.

Bibi, noticing my lack of enthusiasm, waved her hand in my face and said that not all five fingers are the same length. "Not all your brothers are like Ali, dear. Look at that green-eyed Mohammad," she said joyfully. "What a boy, sharp as a knife. He's so clever that his school principal told your mother, he can skip grades and study two years in one year. The man suggested your mother send the boy to a special school, but where's her money to do such a thing?" Bibi sighed. "Maybe Golrokh's smart boys make up for all her struggles, now that all she has in this world are her sons."

Friday came. Bibi woke me up early; determined to turn my skin a milky white. She gave me a good hour-long torturous scrub-bath, until my skin burned red and she gave up. "What's the use? Your skin is the color of wheat, it will never turn white, *babam*!" She scrubbed under my nails and my feet, and made sure my ears shone. She was in the mood to let my hair fall free on my shoulders. "No braids today," she said. With a white ribbon head-band, she pushed my hair clumsily back from my face. She let me wear my black shiny shoes and my daisy flowers dress which were to be worn only on special occasions. That day I was not allowed to play in the garden, so as not to get my hands and dress muddy. I didn't know what it was with Bibi that whenever her daughter came to visit, she got all fancy and ordered me to sit like a good girl and not run around in the garden.

I waited and waited for my brothers, but they never arrived. Bibi and I went to the end of the alley, looking for a taxi which would stop. Finally, when the lantern at the head of our alley spread its yellow powdery light on the ground, Bibi told me it was all right to go inside and take off my dress. She emptied the bowls of mixed nuts and dry figs she had put aside for my brothers, and asked me to pray for their health, because God would listen to a small girl more patiently than to a grown woman. She braided my hair again, folded my dress and put it back in the walnut chest for the next occasion.

# CHAPTER 15

By and by, Bibi managed to educate me about many aspects of religion, which she considered her obligation. She taught me all the sacred titles, from the highest rank of *Hadji* to the lowest order *Mashhadi*. She said that every Muslim believer is required, at least once in a lifetime, to do a pilgrimage to the divine city of Mecca. Bibi herself had never been to Mecca, but it was her wish to walk in Hadjar's footsteps and to do the seven circumambulations around the *Kaabe*. She said this voyage needs a certain amount of wealth. If one was substantial enough to visit the House of God, one would earn the title of *Hadji*. "The title, however, comes with specific responsibilities and obligations," Bibi maintained. "For instance, a Hadji must feed many hungry people each day and give away one-fifth of his income to the poor and needy in order to eliminate poverty in society. He must sacrifice a lamb each year on *Eid-e Ghorban*, the Day of Sacrifice, in memory of Prophet Ebrahim, the founder of the House of God. Also, a Hadji must practice an act of virtue and purity in everyday life in order to set a dignified example as a true Muslim."

Bibi sighed as she went on: "Nowadays, everything is doable. It's not like the old times when people had to travel on the backs of camels and donkeys. Now, the flying machines take you from this place to another place in the blink of an eye. So, some Hadjis let the virtue part slide by. They kill the lamb only to have a feast with their relatives instead of feeding the poor, give away two barrels of lemonade to the neighbors and the passersby at the corner street, and keep the title which gains status for them in the community, a sign of wealth and power."

*Karbala-e*, is the next best title. One would earn this title by visiting the mausoleum of the third Imam, Hossein, Prophet Mohammad's second grandson who died in the battle of Karbala, a holy city in Iraq.

And then there is the title of *Mashhad-e*, for those who had the fortune to travel to Mashhad and visit the crypt of the eighth Imam, Reza, who is buried in the city of Mashhad and is another one of the Prophet Mohammad's great great great grandsons. "He was poisoned by Haroon Rashid, the Khalifeh at the time, who feared he would lose his throne to the love of the people for the young Imam," Bibi said bitterly.

However, the townspeople and villagers from around Shiraz, who usually don't have the means to travel too far, settle for less conspicuous titles and places, something more suitable for their intent; for instance, visiting the shrine of Shah-e Cheragh, the brother of the eighth Imam, Reza. These people arrive dusty and bewildered in their native village attire at the bus station in the District Square around the Shrine. Their bundles on their heads, they carry their colorful roosters and chickens with the legs tightly roped and ready to sell at the open market. They bargain with the vendors over the cheap bottles of Shah-e Cheragh rosewater perfume to take to their families as souvenirs. Pushing through the crowd of fleshy, sweaty men and veiled women, they are content that their hands have reached the gold railing façade to the shrine, and that their souls have become pure again, and their sins absolved.

# CHAPTER 16

Wednesday nights are the night of *Komeil* prayer with mandatory attendance for the entire Block, including the *normal* prisoners. It does not matter what kind of ideology you believed or still believe in: if you're an unrepentant lefty; if you don't believe in God or prayers; if you're a Bahai; or if you have your menstrual period and are exempt from the daily prayers and reading the Koran for an entire week, the time of the month that once again we are reminded of being a woman with a soiled body, and that the doors of heaven are closed to us and we are shunned by the very One, the Creature. It is also the night of search, the night that the *Sisters* and their backup Basiji drop in unexpectedly, rummaging through the cells, looking for anything suspicious—sharp objects, nail clippers, tweezers, scissors, mirrors—anything that may have been smuggled inside the Block through the fruit ration, even though by the time the guards distribute them, they are practically smashed to a pulp.

After every major search, the loudspeaker calls out names. The *Sisters* come and send us to a different cell; someone disappears; another is sent to the second tier, or to the Sepah Detention. This is the third month since I was transferred to Adelabad, but already my cell has been changed twice. Some days and at odd hours, the loudspeaker announces, "Aeration yard." We are not allowed to take anything with us. At the door, the *Sisters* line us up and search our bodies and clothes thoroughly. The entire time, we are ordered to sit still in groups of five. The search could take up to half a day or more. They rummage around, tier-by-tier, cell-to-cell. They poke sharp sticks into the sponge mattresses, open even the seams of our cloth-

ing, and take out all our belongings. When they're done, they dump
everything into a pile in the middle of the corridor. We return to the
Block that looks as f it was just shaken by an earthquake. Without a
word, we kneel trying to separate our things. Most of us have mas-
tered the art of living with the bare necessities. I own only three sets
of clothing. No family pictures, or any pictures for that matter, are
allowed, and the dishes we use are all made out of plastic which the
*Sisters* have given us.

The night of mandatory prayers and commemorations is not the
only craze in prison; the blood drive is another ritual. It is the only
time we get to see the prison clinic, even though we suffer from
ulcers, skin fungus, and other microscopic bacteria and viruses,
which attack us incessantly. Every month or so, the *Sisters* line us
up to give blood. A plastic cup of milk in exchange for a 100cc bag
of blood; the only time we drink milk. The blood is drawn for the
injured soldiers who are fighting in the war with Iraq. They call us
traitors, worse than criminals, below the filthiest animals, yet it is
quite all right for our blood to flow in the veins of *pasdars*, our *enemies*. The inmates who have been sentenced to death are forced to
give blood even more often.

Like any other Wednesday night, at eight sharp, the entire Block
is lined up at the gate, starting with the *normal* prisoners, the second
tier, and at last, the first tier. With the exception of the third tier
residents, who still wear their ragged floral chadors, the rest of us are
covered from head to toe in black chadors. We follow the *Sisters* as
they assign each tier's seating in the big lecture hall, perhaps used as
a theater under the Shah's regime to show occasional movies on the
big screen. The heat of summer is already unbearable. As always, the
*Sepah* guard has divided the entire salon with thick tarpaulin curtains to separate men and women. They situate the *normal* prisoners
between the first-tier and the second. I am assigned to take a seat in
the first row right behind the last row of the prostitutes. Soon, the
elegies will begin and we'll be required to pray out loud in unison,
wishing a long life for Imam Khomeini and victory for the Iranian
Muslim army in conquering Iraq's holy city of Karbala.

Most girls who have a male family member at Adelabad, try to sit
alongside the curtain, though they can't see through to the other side.

Once in a while a man's cough can be heard during the prayers; a brother might be sitting alongside the curtain, and a husband, or a son worrying about his mother in the prison. If only this curtain would fall. I still don't know if Mohammad is back in Adelabad Prison, or if he's being tormented in his solitary cell even though he was given visitation rights at Adelabad; the *Sepah* always misleads families.

The prostitutes still hold on to their ancient tradition of bringing mixed-nuts *moshgel-gosha*; their vow is to give each other sweets in the hope that their wish for release or parole will come true. Listening to the prayers is not exactly their idea of a celebration; fighting over the green raisins and the salted almonds, on the other hand, is something to look forward to. The last thing they imagined would happen to them in prison is having to pray on their hands and knees, while falsely wailing for the martyrs. The prayers are in Arabic and most of these women are probably hearing them for the first time in their lives, so they mistake them for a new national anthem. Accustomed to the Shah's regime and the callous behavior of the police, the moment they hear the speaker's greeting, they rise to their feet and sing the old national anthem as they wait for the portrait of the Shah to appear on the wall. Regardless of how many Wednesdays they are brought to the prayers, still the *Sisters* have to berate them, ordering them to sit down.

Wednesday nights are the only time we are allowed and even encouraged to cry. In fact, most of us look forward to Wednesday nights, relishing this privilege of a good sob. Even the men, seated on the other side of the curtain, cry bitterly, a sound that makes my heart sink for them.

The elegies begin with Ahangaran's audiotape, reciting an ever-mournful prayer. With that voice of his, Ahangaran could have been a popular singer, if he'd only had the good fortune to surface just a few years back under the Shah's regime. His face would have been printed on the cover of *Entertainment Magazine* as a new pop star along with the famous Sattar the Singer and Mazyar. But now, his grief-stricken elegies promise an eternal life in heaven, pumping up the blood of fifteen-year-olds, snatched from behind their school desks in far-off villages, to be used as martyrs in the frontlines, clearing up the way for the *pasdar* fighters.

The prayers have barely started when the former prostitutes-and-now-secret-lesbians begin their phony wails. They rock their bodies back and forth and slap their thighs and chests noisily as they stuff their mouths with mixed nuts. We're supposed to be crying, but their theatrical animation is so amusing that naturally all heads turn to them. We bring our chadors to our faces, trying hard not to burst out laughing, and hope that our shaking shoulders will give the illusion of genuine weeping. Even the *Sisters* can't resist grinning on the sly.

With the command of the prayer leader, the male inmates from the neighbor *siasi* Block begin to beat their chests and heads. The leader himself wails and directs everyone to repeat "*Hossein, Hossein, Shahid Hossein, martyr Hossein.*" The men respond in unison, commemorating the Shiite third Imam, Hossein. Under the Shah's regime, people used to mourn the anniversary of his death on the two days of Ashura; now the entire three-hundred-sixty-five days of the year have turned into Ashura as the *Hezbollah* imposes mourning for the war martyrs on everyone. The prayer leader compares the dead *pasdars* to Imam Hossein and proudly claims that soon every Iranian man and woman will visit his mausoleum in Karbala. Three years into the war, the *Hezbollah* still promises victory and the defeat of Sadam Hossein.

The prayer leader is still on his way to Karbala, and Ahangaran's voice is heated with promises of a holy victory, when Mastaneh the Flab sinks her chubby hand in the plastic bag of mixed nuts that is being handed down from the lower rows. She takes her time and digs deeper into the plastic bag to withdraw a fist full of almonds. Before she is able to put her goodies in her mouth, the hand of Akhtar the White-eyed comes down hard on her head, making the half-chewed almonds sprinkle over the heads of her cellmates. Like a cat in ambush, Mastaneh throws herself on Akhtar, biting and pulling, crushing the entire woman's body under the layers of fat. Her shrunken chador falls down to her enormous buttocks. Before the *Sisters* realize what has happened, the two women are entangled, wrestling like two enraged samurai, showering each other with the most vulgar curses as Ahangaran howls at the top of his lungs: "Martyrs! Martyrs! Our brothers are drowned in their blood in the strange land." The voice of Mastaneh the Flab rises louder, swallowing Ahangaran's lamenting elegy. "You whore, you damn cheap pussy-seller. I'll rip your crotch open and pull that stinky pussy of yours out of your mouth. I'll give you a lesson never to forget that no one, let alone a cheap sister-fucker like you, can raise a hand over Mastaneh."

"*Salavat, salavat*, women!" one of the guards scolds from behind the curtain. "Somebody shut this dirty mouth, for crying out loud. Men are sitting here." Then he sticks his head inside and yells: "*Sisters, Sisters*, what is all these nonsense? It is the Komeil's night, for God's sake."

"Please, brother," pleads *Sister* Marsieh. "You know that we don't dare get near these shameless women. Please send immediate help to separate these devils."

"Here we go again," mumbles Mina, her shoulders quivering. I bring my chador lower, covering my entire face, barely managing to choke back my laughter.

Ahangaran wails: "*Shahid* on the way to Karbala! Thirsty brother, just like Imam Hossein. Do not sorrow! Heaven awaits you. Alas! There's no water in Karbala."

"There is Pepsi Cola," says Mohtaram the drug-smuggler hairdresser, giggling; a few of the other women join in. "Why do you have to send the martyrs to heaven when we're here?" Mahvash the Tattoo-maker whispers to Mohataram. "Give them our dripping pussy instead." Women laugh and lightly punch her. The girls' shoulders, now, quiver badly.

*We are all in for big trouble tonight.*

"You think I'm wrong? No sugar-cube," Mahvash mumbles amusingly. "All men at war have one thing in common. You know what that is, ah ha! You guessed it right. Lack of a juicy pussy. Hear it from me. It's like a bone to a dog. You take it away from them, they'll be a fucking, bloodthirsty dog-man."

"Shut your filthy mouth!" shouts a *pasdar* guard over the women's heads. The women shoot him a dirty look, but at the sight of the Kalashnikov in his hand, they look away. "This one has an itsy bitsy one," Mahvash mumbles to the others, measuring her index finger. "I bet he can't even satisfy a pigeon, let alone a woman!" The inmates fall into a frenzy of giggles. The *Sisters* are able to handle the women, but usually in much lighter situations. Actually, they're afraid to get too near these criminals and murderers, especially the prostitutes who are daily entangled in arms and legs, capable of turning into the violent beasts that the *Sisters* don't even dare dream of. The prostitutes know well that the *Sisters* are not here to monitor them, that their torture power is only directed towards the political prisoners, and that they are not trained to handle women like these.

Finally help arrives. "They know each other's language better than we do," the *Sisters* remark; they murmur that both sides are the remainders of the Shah's regime The two women begin to beg and cry miserably as they are dragged away from the mass by four sturdy police guards sent from the men's Block 2. The others turn mute, as they know what kind of beating awaits their inmates. Now they truly pray for Mastaneh and Akhtar; if they're lucky, they'll save the rest of their teeth and will not have their ribs broken by the batons of the police guards who are trained specifically for this purpose.

I take a tissue from the Kleenex box, which is being passed on. The girls begin to pray solemnly. In my heart, I pray that the two godforsaken women will survive this night, their sin of disturbing the prayers forgiven, a sin unforgivable even if done by a lunatic like Banafsheh the Brainless who has lost the ability to talk and barks like a dog instead and pees on herself. Most of the time, the guards keep her in the solitary cell on the first tier because they fear that her peers may actually choke her in the quiet of the night, for the women, regardless of their crimes, still have enough heart to believe that not even a stray dog deserves to live like that. They can't stand her misery and her crying to heaven all night long much longer.

A quiet sob envelops the entire mass, all of us, the political and criminal prisoners; after all, this is the crying night.

*above*: The author at age fourteen with Bibi

*left*: The author at sixteen

Bibi reciting Hafiz's poetry

A High School picture (the Author is second from the right)

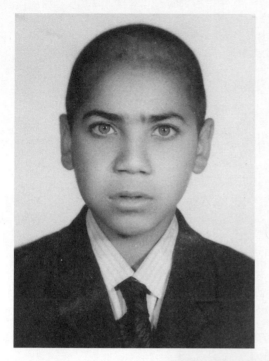

Mohammad, age ten

Mohammad, age twenty

*left*: Ali, age eighteen

*below*: Almond Trees, Deh,
spring 1986

A view of the gate of the Koran, Shiraz

A traditional bazaar

# CHAPTER 17

One day out of the week, Torabpoor has set a morning for those of us who want to have an appointment with him so we can discuss our *issues*. Issues! That's his exact word. I wonder what kind of issues he hopes we would want to discuss with him? What kind of dialogue could there be between a captor and his captive? Typically, the girls stand in line, pleading for a visit with their brothers or husbands. I see mothers go to him to request a brief visit with their sons, or in some cases, their daughters, who are kept in the solitary cells at the Sepah Detention.

During my visit today, my mother made it clear, using her inventive sign language, that Mohammad has been sent back to Adelabad. For the first time, I gather whatever courage is still left to me, swallow my pride, and stand in line. I, too, begin to learn how to beg. It is two years since I have seen Mohammad and with his case being revised to a death penalty, I think it is worth my begging. I have got to see him. I have got to hear his voice.

Mrs. Hashimi is ahead of me. She stands tall and proud. Most days I see her sitting in a corner of her cell in an all-day stupefied daze, the prayer beads hanging between her fingers. I don't see her pray or pretend to pray; with her eyes dry and tearless, she stares at the walls. She has been at Adelabad over a year now, still waiting for a verdict. Her crime is giving birth to Mojahed children, the Hakem-e Sharae judge had told her, as well as harboring two sympathizers in her house. The two boys were her son's friends who grew up together; Mrs. Hashimi, perhaps, had served them many meals as they returned home from school or a soccer match. The Selah guard

keeps her on the first tier not because she is a 54-year-old mother of
five, two of them already hanged, or because she suffers from dia-
betes, but because her daughter-in-law is among the unrepentant on
the second tier and her nineteen-year-old daughter is kept at Sepah
Detention. Naturally, the first tier would be a better choice because
her contact with her family members would be zero. I know well
that she is one person the *Sisters* don't approve of having contact
with or expressing sympathy for. She herself avoids talking to the
girls so as not to jeopardize their situations. There are nights that
she wakes from another nightmare, crying out her children's name:
"Afshin. Shahram. Bahram. Shohreh. Sohrab. Parvaneh. Where are
you? Take me with you!" The *Sisters* rush quickly to shut her up.
Her daughter-in-law materializes behind the bars of the second tier
and calls out to her, "Mother, it's all right, Mother. I'm right here."
And the rest of the *Sisters*, this time, rush upstairs to push her back
into her cell, warning her that they'll call for a *Brother* who would
gladly drive her to the Sepah Detention where she really belongs.
Her mother-in-law pleads with her in a shaking voice, "I just had a
nightmare, dearest. That's all. For my sake, Parvaneh, please don't
disobey them." Finally, both of them become as quiet as rocks. Still
and soundless.

At these moments, under my blanket, I sob freely for Mrs. Hashimi
and her broken family. They are among those reverential Shirazi
families whose names always commanded respect and admiration,
and are now stomped ruthlessly under the feet of a gang of power-
hungry barbarians. Every so often, while pacing in the corridor, I
greet her with a quick nod as I pass before her cell. She gives me a
faint smile.

Last Tuesday morning it was my turn to clean the tier's corridor
and distribute the fruit and watermelons our families had brought
us the day before. My mother brought me fresh-picked black figs. I
chose several less bruised ones and inhaled the forgotten sweet smell
of Deh. The good-natured, gentle villagers must have come to visit
my grandmother and brought along the season's first-picked figs. I
could envision children shaking the branches as their mothers picked
the fruit dropping to the ground. Mrs. Hashimi does not have any
visitors so I left the figs next to her cellmates' fruit ration behind the

bars of her cell. "These are for you," I whispered.

"Any news from your brother, dear?" she asked in a voice barely above a whisper. I shook my head no. "I pray for him. You do the same, dear," she said. I nodded and quickly moved away, wondering how God will answer my prayers when He has failed to listen to the tearful prayers of a mother, an honorable woman, when He has not saved at least her last son for her.

I stand aside so Mrs. Hashimi can talk to Torabpoor in private. But there's hardly any space; even though she speaks in a very low voice, I can still hear her. She does not plead or beg. Just a simple request. "My daughter has no one to visit her," she tells Torabpoor. "As you know, her entire family is either dead or in prison. As a mother, I have the right to visit my daughter. I would like to see my daughter as any other mother would want to."

She does not look at Torabpoor, neither does she bend over far enough to reach him when he does not bother to stand up.

"Of course as a mother you have the right to see your daughter," Torabpoor says in his dry, scratchy voice, "but not as a mother in misdeed herself." He seems amused with his own answer.

"I am not here to discuss my wrongs or rights with you. Let God be the judge of that. I am asking you to please grant me a visit with my daughter, if even forr five minutes."

"She has not repented her transgression, at least not yet," Torabpoor counters, motioning for me for me to come forward. He is done with her. I don't budge. He darts a glance at me and waves his hand at Mrs. Hashimi. "Maybe next time," he says.

"I thank God that I have not raised criminals," Mrs. Hashimi says firmly. "I thank God that I am not the mother of a criminal." She looks sharply at her captor and walks away.

I step forward. Torabpoor signals for me to stop and whispers something to Sister Zahra. She nods and walks toward the corridor, following Mrs. Hashimi. He motions to me.

"My name is . . ."

"I know. You're Mohammad's sister," he interrupts me. "What can I do for you?" he says softly.

I am surprised by his sudden change of tone. His trained gentle tongue is back in his mouth.

There must be at least a few dozens detainees and prisoners whose names are Mohammad. But in prison, every time the *pasdar* guards, the interrogators, even in most cases, the inmates, use the name *Mohammad*, I know that they refer to my brother. They hardly ever address me by my name or surname; I am simply Mohammad's sister. Even the day that the two *pasdars* took me to see the Hakem-e Sharae, they, too, referred to me as "Mohammad's sister."

"I am here to request a visit with my brother," I say under my breath. I am not nearly as audacious as Mrs. Hashimi. This is the first time I have come to him and with him in uniform and the line behind me, I feel that this is the true commission of a crime, bending low, begging my captor for my rights. I should turn away. Mohammad wouldn't want me to beg this man, his enemy. But aren't I here because he asked me to?

"Are you a genuine repentant?" he asks, giving me another one of his many sour looks.

"Pardon me?" I pretend I did not understand his question.

"At this moment, I don't think it's a good idea to visit *him*. For your own protection."

Protection? Look what this world has come to: my captor wants to protect me from my own brother.

"He has announced repentance. If that's what you're referring to," I say hesitantly.

"I recommend that you come to see me again. Maybe next time," he says and motions to the next person in line.

So, it is true that they have not accepted his repentance. Right before I arrived at Sepah Detention, Mohammad and his eleven other inmates had just done a prison TV interview. From the little I had heard and the fact that the *Sisters* proudly claimed that the *Sepah* had broken down the entire prison network conspiracy, I gathered that these were the last of the *oldies*, the ones who were arrested two years ago, including Mohammad. Every one of their verdicts is being revised to a death penalty. In the past three months, the *Sepah* has launched a huge massacre, hanging at least four groups of seventy-five people each, besides hundreds of individual executions. In the morning, the loudspeaker announces that the executed ones were the

major ranks involved in armed actions. After two years of imprisonment, their ghosts, it seems, have somehow managed to escape last
week, and shoot one of *Hezbollah*'s precious members.

In the interview they were seated at a rectangular table; all had
announced repentance. The news had exploded in the prison like a
bomb. I had never gotten to see the interview, but I was told that the
*oldies* on the second tier moped for the entire day. To them, these
twelve were the symbol of courage and their last hope. Suddenly,
the TV program had been cut short and billions of gray dots had
filled the screen. The inmates saw only a brief introduction, the condemned men's background information, and opening speeches by
only two of them. Mohammad never got to deliver his speech. The
inmates who were forced to gather in front of the black-and-white
TV, remained frozen, mouths open, wondering why the program
had been cut short. The next day, the *Sisters* started a rumor that the
*oldies* were trying to use their interview to convey a message to the
rest of the inmates, to tell them how much information *Sepah* actually had. The second tier began to celebrate again, walking proudly
behind the tier's bars. The Selah never accepted the *oldies*' repentance; to this day, they still claim that it was a tactic they used, finding a new way to communicate "covert operations." And of course,
all twelve inmates, along with several others, were transferred from
Adelabad to solitary cells, and harshly beaten. The crazed *Sepah* had
announced this openly, warning those who still wished to emulate
their tactics to expect much crueler punishment. It was right after
this that Mohammad attempted suicide in the loneliness of his solitary cell. He had lost his last hope, perhaps the last straw to hold on
to. I knew there must have been something more to the story. With
Mohammad, one always wonders, as Torabpoor wonders , and as I
wonder myself.

I wondered if Mohammed would ever make up his mind who he
wanted to be, like Ali, who came home one day and told Mother that
he had found his dream job; he would be a bus driver, roving all the
roads of Iran from south to north and from west to east. He'd be in
the Persian Gulf one day, eating succulent dates from the hands of
the southern palm growers, only to find himself a week later walk-

ing along the shores of the Caspian Sea, eating smoked fish with the
northern fishermen. "Nothing gives a man as much satisfaction as
the breeze stroking his face as he steers the wheel, the earth beneath
his feet and the sky above his head," he said proudly, blowing gray
smoke ring after ring from his Winston cigarette, oblivious to Mother
and her astonished look.

For a while Mohammad was Bruce Lee. Barely thirteen years old
with hardly any substantial pocket money, he managed to save several tumans to sign himself up for Karate and Taekwondo, buying
different sets of uniforms in black and white for the two classes he
took in the evenings. Every month or so he came home proud of yet
another of his brand new belts. "Once I earn black, I would have the
last belt," he'd tell me. He kept snatching Ebrahim's precious sports
magazines and secretly cutting out the centerfold pictures of Bruce
Lee with that dreadful look of rage in his Chinese eyes and those
polished scar lines on his cheeks. On a brown grocery bag, he'd
cut out small holes for the eyes and mouth and paste the head of the
Karate champion on it. Placing the Black Dragon's head on his neck,
he would chase Bibi around the fishpond, daring her to fight him,
this undefeated new champion. He would jump out from the small
entryway right in front of Mother as she returned from the market,
her arms laden with baskets bursting with fruits and groceries. Once
he jumped up so high, he almost gave Mother a heart attack. My
other brothers joined him in those frenzied masquerades, yelling
their guts out, kicking an imaginary army of enemies. That lasted
only until the following winter when a new champion arrived in our
living room, Mohammad Ali the Boxer. As he followed the Dancing
Feet fight on our very own very black-and-white Shob Laurence TV
screen, my brother rolled up all his Karate belts, including the brown
one, gathered his medallions, stored them in a box, and kissed the
Chinese champion goodbye.

Somehow he realized that the disguise of being Mohammad Ali
would be much harder to defeat. This time, with a promise of a cotton candy stick and endless punching, he hired my brothers, Hossein
and Amir, and me to fill up a punching bag with tons of sawdust.
Well, mostly the boys did the filling. They sneered and said, "Let's

be *realistic*; you're a girl and the last thing you would know on the face of the planet is how to punch a bag." They handed me the dustpan instead and made me sweep the ground before Mother returned home and saw the mess and yelled her guts out. The sawdust got in my eye. "You made the mess," I told them, "you clean it up yourself too, now that you won't let me punch." I dropped the dustpan and took my jump rope instead. Pretending to ignore them, I watched as they hung the bag from the arbor under the shade of the black grape vines.

Doing his foot-dance, Mohammad began punching the air and reaching for his jump rope.

There, that's something he can't do as well as I can, I thought, jump rope. I may not punch like these bullyboys, but I beat the hell out of them with my jump rope.

"Ready?" I shouted.

"No stopping up to one hundred. And no cheating. I do the counting," Mohammad yelled back, his voice bouncing on the tiled ground. "One, two. . . ."

I knew I could do it. I just had to listen carefully to the lashing sound against the tiles. It always made me jump faster. *I will beat him again.*

In the mornings, my brothers punched the bag even before they used the courtyard toilet; so did their friends as they came in. First, they sank a good punch into the bag, then greeted the household. Mohammad bought a pair of bizarre-looking, fat red gloves in order to punch harder, and a set of fake teeth that made his mouth swollen and his lips look like a trout's.

"I am Mohammad Ali Clay." He bounced around Bibi once again. "Dare fight me, so I will knock your teeth in your palm," he boasted, his fists guarding his face.

"Enough, enough!" Bibi scolded him. "Haven't you found any shorter wall than mine to jump from? Thank God I have no teeth left in my mouth. Had I known that you were such an expert at pulling out teeth, I wouldn't have spent all my hard-earned money on that young dentist, Abadehi." She shook her head and started to walk away.

"I'm just pretending," Mohammad laughed, hugging Bibi, kissing her face. "Just like Mohammad Ali. You know, the American boxer."

"Well, I'll be damned. How come he has a Muslim name then?" Bibi was in awe.

"He was a Christian at first, but he converted to Islam. He's a Muslim now, like us."

"*Allah-o-akbar*. God bless his soul. He must pray, too."

"I guess. But you know, he's fighting for the black people in America. He's a champion, Bibi. A very brave man."

"Why is he fighting for black people?" I asked.

"I guess so they could have the same rights as the other Americans." He shrugged. "Our history teacher says that the blacks were Africans, but the Americans snatched them away and brought them to America to use them as slaves. Now, they're fighting to have equal rights like the rest of the people in America."

I couldn't imagine how grownups could be snatched away. And I had never seen a black person in my entire life. The closest I had ever seen was this boy from a bunch of gypsies who came in the summer and raised their tents in that empty field at the far end of our alley. Bibi said they were dark like that because they always roved around under the hot burning sun. Neither had I ever seen a slave. "Slaves in America?" I asked again, astonished. "How could anyone be black and a slave? I thought in America everyone has blue eyes and white skin, like the Walton family."

"There are all kinds of people in America," Mohammad said. "And black people too. Like the black slave in *Tom Sawyer*, who people thought killed another man, remember? Next time we go to the library, I'll get you the book. People have different skin colors and genes."

Despite those enormous green eyes, his skin the color of sugar, and his body, which in size seemed more like Bruce Lee's than the steely, coffee-colored Mohammad Ali, my brother and the American champion had a lot in common: their name, the punching bag, and a desire to scuffle with people. Mohammad was fascinated with the champion who roared like a king in the ring. "He fights like that for black people's equality in America, and I will fight for the people of the shanty town of Halabiabad," Mohammad said. People whom he had seen only on TV, he now called *brothers*. They were his brothers he said, even though they lived at the end of the world where each day the sun sat in the blue water of the Pacific Ocean only to rise up from behind Dena Mountain in the heart of our city, Shiraz.

Suddenly one cloudy afternoon, the punching bag stood still on its hook in the wooden arbor. The bloated red gloves began to crack between the vine branches. When Mohammad no longer wanted to greet any one who entered the courtyard with a friendly punch in the stomach instead of a *salam*, he recalled his never-forgotten passion for books. He headed out for the city library and far away bookstores again only to return weighed down with books without any illustrations and heavy as bricks.

He'd retire to the small storage room, now become his secluded cozy room, and bury himself in books loaded onto the high shelves, on the floors, and in the corners, leaving him only a patch of Turkish rug to sit on. He read page after page, word by word, over the whizzing sound of the casket-size freezer.

With this new character occupying his body and soul, the sounds of the *hee-haa* and the dancing feet around the punching bag faded away. After hours of confining himself to the closed room, a new Mohammad would emerge, holy as Jesus himself, calm yet disturbed. Soon, he decided that Christianity was the religion for the entire world. And to see things better and cleaer as he saw them now, he put on his newly purchased glasses one afternoon and invited me with a nudge of his elbow to noiselessly follow him to Bibi's prayer room. I shut the door behind me and tiptoed to the mantel where Mohammad knelt, staring at the pictures before him; in his eyes was the look of a horrified eagle. He took one glance at Prophet Jesus and one glance at Prophet Mohammad, back and forth. I followed his glances from picture to picture and had to wonder when Mohammad asked, "Do you see what I see?"

As always, I had to stare hard to see things that were clear in his mind. I got closer, even asked Mohammad's permission to borrow his glasses—maybe my eyes would see what Mohammad wanted me to see, but things got even blurrier. Embarrassed, I shook my head no. "Give me those." He reached for his glasses and placed them back over his enormous eyes. It's so unfair, I thought. It's not like he needed any bigger eyes, when those green eyes of his were already like two bright lanterns. Maybe I ought to butter Bibi up, an idea came to me at that moment, so she would buy me a pair of glasses; then I might double the size of my eyes and have long eyelashes just like his.

"Look harder. This is what I'm trying to tell you." He handed me the picture he had found in some old books. An almost naked, very thin man gazed at me, with the palm of his hands and his soles nailed to a wooden cross, blood springing out from the holes that seemed perfectly clean. The poor man's head leaning to one side, he stared down at his feet with two large sad puppy eyes. His disheveled hair and beard were long and fell wild about his shoulders. On his head nested a robin. The sight of that scrawny man with his bones and ribs sticking out, and just a green shawl hanging from between his legs, made me pinch my cheek. A river of pain streamed in my heart.

"Who is this poor man?" I asked. "Why is he nailed to a cross?"

"He's Messiah Jesus," he said in a hushed voice. "His enemies crucified him and carried his body from alley to alley. But he rose and went to Heaven."

*Ah! Now I remember.* Bibi had told me stories about him, that his mother was the Blessed soul, the immaculate blessed Maryam who by God's will gave birth to a child even though she was a virgin. She went out to the mountains and there she coiled in pain, holding to the trunk of an olive tree until her baby was born. I had seen a portrait of her carved on the beautiful gold talisman hung next to the rows of necklaces and cross pendants in the glass displays in the gold market. Once, Bibi accompanied the neighbor's daughter, a bride-to-be. Her mother came to our house, in her hand a plate of sugar-cubes and assorted cookies, inviting Bibi to give them the honor of going to the gold market, for she believed Bibi would bring blessing to the union.

In one of the gold chambers, Bibi unfolded a few tumans from the small leather purse she clutched in her hand and browsed to find an affordable chain for her grandchild who stared at the shiny gold necklaces. I pointed to the gold portrait of a sad angelic face, "That one, Bibi. I want that necklace, the angel-face." Bibi took the necklace from the hand of the gold merchant, kissed the gold surface, and put it back on the glass counter. "This is the portrait of the blessed Maryam, dear, the Mother of Prophet Jesus, may I die for his tortured and hole-ridden body. The Armenians believe in Jesus as their prophet. They wear these necklaces and the cross in the memory of what those godless people had done to him, nailing his sacred body to a wooden board. You're a Muslim girl. And Prophet Mohammad is our prophet. You could have an *Allah* necklace, instead, if you'd like." So she bought me a tiny pendant with *Allah* written in beautiful Arabic calligraphy. All the way home, she told me stories from the Koran, about Jesus growing up, and that he was betrayed by his most trusted man, Yahuda, at his last supper.

"Why didn't he run away if he knew he was going to be nailed to a cross, Bibi?" I was not convinced that someone who knew he was going to be hurt like that, would stay and have dinner instead of running away. But Bibi reasoned that in the way of God a body has no value to be sacrificed, much less if it is the body of a prophet chosen by God.

In the quiet of the prayer room Mohammad was staring at the picture of the same man he held carefully with the tip of his fingers, for we were taught that the saints' pictures are holy and may not be touched with unwashed hands. It was the same man nailed to the golden cross that hung in the display of the gold chamber. Mohammed stared at the portrait of the Prophet Mohammad who had chubby cheeks as red as an apple, as if he had just finished a good portion of lamb kabob. His eyes, brown and large, his skin, smooth as velvet, a perfectly trimmed beard, and a beautiful green turban around his head. Raising his left index finger to heaven, he held the magnificent holy book of the Koran in his right hand; at his feet rested a gold-maned lion, protecting his famous razor-sharp sword. Next to the Prophet's picture was another portrait of his son-in-law, his cousin and chosen successor, Imam Ali. He, too, had chubby red cheeks. He, too, held his famous mighty sword. Even though his eyes seemed kind, they radiated a certain fear, piercing through you, making you feel guilty as if you had just committed a sin which could consign you to Hell.

That day I left the prayer room, thinking that the Islamic saints were well-fed and nicely clothed, whereas the Christian saints were poor, naked, and starved, even though they ate their dinner. For once, I saw what Mohammad saw in his head: one ought to do something good for hungry Christians.

Mohammad wondered more, and I wondered even more with him. I also wondered about remarks, hushed words, whispers, and the cut-off phrases my brothers spoke from time to time. Like that time I entered the courtyard and Ali was talking oddly with Mother as she gathered the dry clothes off the laundry line. *Mohammad is Jesus!* I heard him say. What? What is Ali talking about, I wondered as I unbuttoned the top of my school uniform in Bibi's room.

Mohammad wondered about everything. Most of the time I found him sitting cross-legged before his mountain of books, reading and thinking, thinking and reading, sometimes reading out loud, sometimes thinking out loud. At dusk, when he returned home, he went straight to his mountain and to his new-found friend, Solitude.

His passion for Christianity boiled in his blood for a while. The sense of superiority, the feeling of peace and harmony lasted until the day he took me to the movies. It was my first visit to any movie theater, let alone the very Pahlavi Shiraz University Theater.

At the entrance, we waited for our cousins to join us; the two brothers were the recent talk of family and relatives. Not only were they popular because they were tall and good-looking, they were also well turned-out boys who studied chemical engineering at one of the most prominent universities in the nation. They were only in the first and second year of their studies, but already the relatives addressed them as *Mr. Mohandas*, Engineer. A few minutes later, they arrived with a group of their friends and friends of friends. These were boys much older than Mohammad, but he was blessed with the gift of blending in so that nothing he did would surprise anyone who knew him, let alone bringing his eight-year-old sister with him. Maybe it was because of his curse and blessing of being born the fifth of seven boys, which made him take quickly to both younger and older groups. Bibi believed that an old man's soul possessed his young body, because even when he was a small boy, she said, he had a head and a mind that ached to know the mysteries of this world.

During the movie, which was called *Fahrenheit 451*, I wiggled so much that he warned me that if I did not stop moving, it would be the last time I would go to any movies with him. I couldn't see too well because the man in front of me had a big head with pushed-up hair. I tried to tell Mohammad, but every time I looked his way, I found him deeply absorbed in the film. With his famous philosophical habit of squeezing his chin between his index finger and thumb, he gazed at the screen, his mouth, as always, half-open. I sometimes reached out to close his lips, a gesture he did not find amusing and that has even earned me a smack on the back of my hand. I was too young to understand most of the movie, but I remember I kept asking my brother why the firemen were burning the books. He whispered to me that in that city books were banned and people were not allowed to read them. That's why people had to run away and hide in the woods where they memorized entire books so that they could return to the city, and retell the stories they knew by heart. "They have become the book themselves," he told me in awe.

Later that night, as Mohammad and I waited for a taxi, our cousin, Nasser, called out to him. He whispered something in Mohammad's ear and gave him a small packet, which he shoved quickly into the inner pocket of his jacket.

"What's that?" I asked once Nasser was gone.

"Do you have to know everything?" he said coldly.

I did not say another word, but a few moments later, embarrassed by my silence, he said in a very low voice, "It's just a book. I'll let you read it if you promise not to tell anyone."

I nodded mutely.

"It's a banned book," he whispered.

"Do you think the firemen would burn it if they find it?" I said, startled.

He looked at me for a moment, "You haven't heard a word of what I just said. Do you hear me?" He bent over and put his hands on my shoulders. "You do not talk to anyone, no one, not even Bibi, about what I just told you. Promise me!"

A sudden look flashed in his face; there was something in the tone of his voice which frightened me. "Not even Bibi?" I murmured.

"Not even Bibi. Tell me that you understand."

I nodded again.

Since that day, Mohammad extended his range of reading. He talked about the Dark Ages, and how the Church had suppressed people all over Europe. When he found out that the Church, in the past, had collected money from the poor in the name of religion and, instead of helping them, had built bigger churches, he was disenchanted. As he read on, he shared his new discovery: the Crusades, where the Christians had murdered thousands and thousands of Muslims. The day of this one discovery, I saw another kind of flicker in his eyes. He wiped off his glasses and told me that he ought to study Islam; after all it was his faith, and he did not know a thing about it. He began with *Nahj-ol-Balagheh*, the instructions written by Imam Ali to guide Muslim devotees to follow in daily life. Then, he started reading the translated version of the holy book of the Koran, so he could understand the verses in Farsi rather than in Arabic. Soon, he was reading book after book on Islam. One night, he entered Bibi's room and asked her to wake him before sunrise. And that milky dawn I heard my brother as he faced the direction of the House of God, responding to the Muezzin's call for dawn prayers:

> *Allah-o-Akbar!*
> *God is supreme!*
> *The Lord of the universe*
> *I bow to You, You the One, the most*
> *merciful, compassionate of all!*

From that day on, I could not imagine another day passing in which he would miss his daily five-times prayers. That year, and in years to come, he fasted the entire month of Ramadan. It was the holy month and people must give charity, he said. To Mother's astonishment, he went to the neighbors' houses, gathered food and clothing and hauled them on the back of his bike to the godforsaken people of Halabiabad in the shanty town. In his room, he took off the posters of the Chinese Dragon and pinned up a large poster of a black man he called *brother* Malcolm X. "Islam is the religion of equality, it fights poverty, frees the slaves, and empowers the poor and the deprived," he announced to the entire family. His voice had a new ring to it. Ali cautioned Mother, but what she heard was the changing voice of her fourteen-year-old son. "Like any of his other fascinations, this too will pass. It will only mesmerize him for a short while," she said calmly and went about her chores.

# CHAPTER 18

The sun must be in the belly of the sky. Cramped inside our cells, we continually dab wet towels on our necks and arms. I have learned from the girls to soak a hand towel in running water and keep it near me at all times, the best way to keep cool. With the temperature rising, it's almost unbearable to walk in the corridor after the midday meal. Walking means more sweat, and more sweat means the eruption of new spots of skin fungus disease.

I hear my name called through the loudspeaker. At first, I think I misheard but when it was announced a second time, my doubts melt away. *What could it be?* My cellmates and I look at each other.

"Torabpoor is in the lobby," Mina says as she hands me my black chador. "Maybe he's giving you a visit with your brother."

I spring to my feet. Finally he must have thought things over and found it in his heart to give me a visit with Mohammad. All covered in black, I rush to the lobby. *Sister* Marsieh motions for me to follow her outside the gate. *Dear God, thank you! Thank you! I am going to see my brother.*

In the small cubical entry, right before the massive prison gate, the *Sister* asks me to turn around so she can blindfold me. My body begins to tremble at the sight of the black cloth. It has been four months since I wore one. *Why do I have to be blindfolded again?*

"Is she ready?" asks a male's voice behind me.

"Yes, Brother," answers *Sister* Marsieh. She gives me a piece of thick string to hold on to and hands me over to the male *pasdar* who leads me to a car. "Watch your step!" he says.

Not again. They're taking me back to Sepah Detention. I turn into a lump of ice at once. The hot-chill, wet sweats return, hardening my body. *Maybe they're taking me to Sepah to see Mohammad. Maybe he's kept over there. That's it! I am going to see him after all. But wait, you mean they go out of their way to drive me all the way up to Sepah so I could have a visit? No. That's not possible. Why not? It is Ramadan. It's the month of worship and pardon. Maybe it is the Sepah's way of showing kindness in this holy month.* I begin to pray to calm myself down. A minute later stray thoughts attack me again. *What if this is Mohammad's Last Visit? Ah! Dear God, he's going to be executed tonight. No! No! Please, God, don't allow that to happen. No visit. Just keep him alive. I wish I could yell. I wish I could beg. Please, driver! Turn around! Take me back to Adelabad. My brother is not going to be hanged tonight. He will get up tomorrow morning, and the morning after, and thousands and thousands of mornings still to come. Please, God, keep him alive even if it is going to be in the prison. Soon, things will change. The regime will fall and the mullahs will run for their lives, searching for a hole to hide in. God, you're merciful and compassionate. How can you bear witnessing all the injustices done by these barbarians, done in your name? Do you not want to send your miracles down on this forlorn place? To free all the wretched young people kept behind these ruthless bars?*

The thirty-something-minute ride to Sepah Detention seems like thirty hours. I die and come back to life until I am told to remove the blindfold. Right before Hadji, the *Hakem-e Sharae*, a *pasdar* orders me to sit on a chair across from the table. *Hakem* has removed his white turban; his copper-colored, half-bald head glows like a polished tray in the copper chamber. His long black *aba* hangs from a hook behind the door; seated, he is wearing only his gray, thin summer robe. A floor fan, kept fixed in *Hakem's* direction, blows full blast. The *Hakem* stretches his sock-covered feet over the desk before him and reaches for a brown folder on top of a stack of files. Scratching his trimmed salt-and-pepper beard, he glances at the pages. Then he sets down the folder and reaches for the small sidearm pistol resting on the desk. Moving the pistol from one hand to the other, he points it at me. I look at the two armed *pasdars* leaning against the wall. They exchange a quick smirk. I look down.

"I see you have turned yourself in!" the *Hakem* says in a rural accent. He must be from one of the remote villages around Shiraz.

"Yes. I have," I say without looking up.

"Now, are you a true repentant or just a conventional one like your brother?"

"No *Hadj Agha*. I am a true repentant," I say with a bit of hesitation; his pistol is still pointing at me. "My brother is a true repentant too; I have turned myself in because he wanted me to."

"So, you're telling me that you believe that the Islamic Republic is just and righteous, correct?" he says, putting the pistol down on his desk.

"Yes, *Agha*. That's what I believe."

"Then, if you're a true believer you should prove it."

"Prove it? How so?" My voice shakes.

He sits upright and leans forward. "Have you ever held a gun? Or used it or carried it?"

"No, *Agha*. This is the first time I have ever seen a gun in my life."

"You have never seen a gun before?"

"On TV. In American movies. But not in real life."

"Your brother is a traitor. A high-rank hypocrite."

"My brother has been in prison for more than two years now. He was arrested only a little over a year after the revolution. Back then every school kid was drawn to the political parties. It was not illegal to be involved in political activities. My brother is becoming a man behind the bars. He is . . ." I pause. I know I shouldn't be talking like this. He is the *Hakem Sharae*, and an armed one at that. Mohammad would not want me to jeopardize my verdict and perhaps his own. I should think of my unfortunate mother. Enough is enough. Somebody please shut me up. I should hold my tongue. "He has no fault. He is only a good-hearted, principled person, that's all," I say quietly.

"I see you still defend your br . . . , a *traitor* brother."

*My brother is not a traitor. You are. You uneducated, fanatic crook. You who have stolen a people's revolution and put its children behind bars. If it wasn't for people like my brothers who risked their lives, went to prison, took to the streets, shouting for justice, liberation, reform, and a regime change, you would still be begging for a piece of halva in the graveyard.*

I don't say any of this, I don't have enough courage to stand up and shout these words. I have come in voluntarily.

"If you're a true repentant as you claim," he fondles his pistol again, "you should stand up for the Islamic Republic and destroy the traitors. What if I give an order to bring your brother here and have you shoot him? Then, I'd believe your true intentions. What do you say to that?"

"I am not a murderer," I say, looking into his menacing eyes. "I have never touched a gun in my life and I'd rather shoot myself before shooting anyone else."

The two *pasdars* whisper something to each other and the *Hakem* looks at me for a good while. "So you believe your brother's acts are justified?"

"As I said before, I have not seen my brother for over two years. I don't know what his stand is and what is on his mind. But I am sure of one thing, he has not harmed anyone in his life. He lost his job under the Shah's regime because he distributed Imam Khomeini's flyers. And right after the revolution, he gave 100,000 tumans, all his hard-earned saved money of five years, to Friday Preacher, Imam Jomeh Dastgheib, so he would use it for the improvement of the deprived villages." I bring my chador closer to my face and try hard not to shed a tear. My entire body is shaking violently and I don't know how to stop it. I wish I was as courageous as Mrs. Hashimi. I wish I could stand up tall and proud, and shout that my brother does not deserve to spend his days behind bars. No twenty-four-year-old man deserves to spend any minute of his precious life behind these brutal bars you have created. He ought to be a scientist now, an inventor, a designer working on big projects in some prosperous company. He ought to live in a country where they would value his talents and his bright mind, his sense of justice and honor, instead of killing him day by day because he had enough courage to raise his voice against the injustice and corruption, and to demand the basic human right: freedom.

"So, you would not shoot Mohammad?"

This time, I do not hesitate. It is an act of immodesty, but I stare straight into his eyes. "No, *Agha*. I would not shoot my brother."

He leans back in his chair as he reaches for the file he has set down a while ago. Then he motions to one of the *pasdars* and says, "You can take her now."

I have no idea what it means to "take her now." I am so filled with rage that if they hanged me this very moment, I would not object. I am outraged with myself. I should turn and spit in his face, telling him that he and his kind are a disgrace to humanity. They have manipulated my brother and fooled my mother. They can take my life, but I would walk out of this door with my head held high. They have succeeded in making me come down to this hole on my own feet, but they can't break my dignity. Let them hang me. My miserable mother and my poor Bibi. I never meant to cause them any pain.

A *Sister* pushes me, blindfolded again, into a car, perhaps the same car which drove me to the Sepah Detention. *No solitary?* An hour later, the *Sister* removes the blindfold and walks me back to Cell Block 4.

I let out a deep breath and enter the floor. During the entire ride, I thought over and over about the conversation with the fat-bellied *Hakem*. At this point all my thoughts are on Mohammad. *Is he still alive? Is he going to be hanged tonight?*

This is my fifth month at Adelabad, and still no verdict. After what happened today, whatever hope I kept clinging to simply melted away. I'll never be released. I walk directly to Mitra's cell. Since no sharp objects are allowed in the Block, the *Sisters* let her use a pair of scissors while one of them stands right next to her so she can cut the girls' hair. Mitra is tall and rather forlorn. I can read poems of Fooroogh in her mute, melancholic gaze each time she blinks. Going from page to page. Poem to poem: The Wind Will Carry Us; I Pity The Garden; The Bird Is Mortal; I Will Salute The Sun Again; It's Only Sound That Remains. It's Only Sound That remains. It's only SOUND that remains . . . remains . . . remains . . . remains. She has the shortest boyish hair ever and the easiest laughter when the *Sisters* are not watching, and when her spirits are high again. She is condemned to ten years in prison for being a sympathizer of the Proletariat Party, as are many girls from the south. If she ever gets released, she says she would want to become a hairdresser.

I kneel in front of Mitra and ask her to cut all my hair as short as her own Googoosh-e hairdo. A group of girls surround us, trying to convince me that soon I will be free. What's the use, the voice in me hisses. My hair will never see a ray of sun again. Even *Sister*

Zahra sighs as the clicking scissors chop through my hair. I swallow hard when Mitra holds a section of half-a-meter of brown hair before my eyes. My grandmother would have kissed this hair. For my wedding, she wanted to make a garland of fragrant *nastaran* flowers from her garden and place it on the crown of my head with her very own hands. I close my eyes. Cross-legged, I sit before my grandmother. She braids my hair and tells me stories of the good fairies with long, golden hair. It is hot, so Bibi pins up my braids and twists them into a tomato, kissing the back of my neck. "What a breezeless day, *babam*," her sweet dialect fills my ears.

One of the last days of summer. A hot *Shahrivar* day. One of those days that made Bibi hunt for the coolest spot under the arbor where she would lie on her back, fanning her bare breasts. "I can't wait for the summer to puff out its last breath and make way for autumn," she lamented. If I looked at the courtyard's tiles roasting under the heat of the afternoon, I could see them shimmering wet and slippery. The air was hot and dry, so not even the ants dared to crawl out and construct their highways. As always, Bibi filled the large china bird-flower bowl with chilled water and a chunk of ice floating in it, and placed it nearby.

Uncle Engineer came to our house on this hot day, bringing me boxes of lemon-wafer cookies, bonbons, and *Smarteese* chocolates. If Masht Ismal was the tallest, Uncle Engineer was the cleanest, most well-groomed old man ever. His hair was as white as the snow I have seen in the pictures. His plump cheeks glowed like the waxy rose-apples on the store-counter of Masht Mahmood the greengrocer. A handsome golden pen poked out of his white shirt pocket.

Quickly, Bibi sent me to Marmar's house to borrow a chair. With the help of Marmar, I carried a folding chair and placed it on the porch for Uncle Engineer to sit on. Bibi whispered to me that he was not used to sitting on the floor, especially with the sharp, ironed crease of his trousers. He pulled me up and settled me on his lap. He smelled like the shampoo *Paveh*. "You're a big girl now," he said, stroking my hair. He spoke so soft and low, I had to listen carefully.

As he and Bibi began to talk more and more about the house, work, and money, I went to the vegetable garden, busying myself with the pumpkin flowers and measuring the honeydew melons.

When he was about to leave, I heard him saying to Bibi, "The girl is talking to the tomatoes."

"Ah, no, Mr. Fekri," chuckled Bibi. "She just reads to herself out loud."

"What do you mean she reads?" he asked Bibi. "Does she go to school yet?"

Bibi shook her head in disappointment.

"Kindergarten?"

"No. We're not some rich people, Mr. Fekri, to afford those fancy schools. Of all the people, you should know that by now."

"Come, child!" Uncle Engineer gestured with his fingers.

He glanced at the book in my hand. Turning the pages, he looked at me. "It's the Farsi book all right. First-grade-reading workbook. Where did you get it from, little one?"

Before I could even open my mouth, Bibi told him that Ali had brought me the book and taught me to read, and that Mohammad read to me whenever he came. She didn't tell him about Ali squeezing the pencil between my fingers. She bit the corner of her lower lip, glancing at me, and I knew I should not talk about it either.

Uncle Engineer told me to read from a page. "*bAbA A^B dad. bAbA naN dad.* Dad gives water. Dad gives bread," I read to him.

"*Afarin,*" he praised me. "It's always a wonder to me," he faced Bibi. "Agha Bashi was not much of a smart man. Well, no offense, Golrokh is not all that clever either, hardworking though. I wonder how her kids are so sharp and bright. Look at that Ali. With all his talents. What a pity. What a pity. All we've done for him, all that education. He didn't even finish his first *cycle* of high school." He rose to his feet and looked concerned. "This girl should go to school, Bibi," he said. "Let's see what we can do."

I couldn't believe it. Even this old man called her *Bibi*. My mother called her Bibi too. I even heard Mash Reza, the alley's shopkeeper, calling her Bibi. She must be very old to be everyone's grandmother. When I told her that, she laughed and said that Bibi means "gracious lady" and that I shouldn't be bothered by people calling her that. Instead, she said, I should be thinking about what Uncle Engineer just said. "He's an influential man, *babam.* Your father's relative. Who knows, you might be going to school soon."

"I don't want to go to school," I murmured, remembering what Mohammad had told me, that they'd punish you in school for not being good. Bibi said why, I should be delighted and throw my hat high in the air if something blissful like going to school happened to me. Then she waved her hand and said, "We don't have this kind of luck and fortune," and she left it at that.

A few days later, Uncle Engineer came by again with two women dressed in suits. I thought Bibi would slam the door in their faces as she always did when suited women came to the house. But this time, her face turned rosy and she offered the women cold lemonade. This time Bibi didn't send me to borrow chairs. All of them, including Uncle Engineer, sat on the small *Qashghaee* rug that Bibi rolled out on the porch. The women conversed softly with Bibi and admired the gardens. One of them had a small blue hat pinned to her hair.

The suited women asked me to read and write as Uncle Engineer had asked the other day. I read from a page and wrote the words they dictated to me. They seemed pleased: they kept smiling and saying *afarin, afarin*. They gave Bibi a letter, directing her to an address.

The next day, Bibi groomed me again, held my hand, and headed off with the letter in her fist. We walked through the alleys, along the golden cornfields and green sugar-beet fields. We passed the public bath, walking until we came to a huge brown iron double-door. The entire way, Bibi must have said to me a hundred times that I should be a good girl and do as the *ladies* instructed me. And each time I slowed my steps, she reached for my hand, asking why on earth I act so cat-like and that she wouldn't tolerate that kind of behavior. "That look on your face, it won't suit you, *babam*," she puffed and sighed. "It's not like you're going to get butchered. It's school we're talking about. Hey, hey, hey!" She slapped the back of her hand. "I wish I had someone this considerate when I was your age, sending me to school instead of the husband's house. So, shake it off!"

At the Mansoorieh Girls School office, Bibi and I sat next to each other on a leather chair. Uncle Engineer sat across from us, smiling. The women, all in suits, walked around their desks or talked to each other. A small blond woman came up to me, patting my head as if I was a puppy. Bibi rose to her feet before this woman who shook hands with Uncle Engineer and Bibi. She didn't kiss Bibi's cheeks like the other women meeting her in the alleys, and just introduced herself as Principal Sadati.

"How old is she?" she asked Bibi, pushing a strand of golden hair behind her ear.

"She's five and half," Bibi said.

"Well. As I told Mr. Engineer Fekri, it's a little too soon for her," she said, eyeing Uncle Engineer, "not being seven years old yet. But since she already knows how to read and write, we'll place her in the first grade. I can't make any promises." She looked sharply at me, throwing her hands in the air. "We have to see how she does in the first quarter."

Bibi thanked the blond woman and everyone else in the office. Reaching behind their desks, she even shook the women's hands, something I'd never seen her do before. She thanked Uncle Engineer too: "God bless you and your family." Principal Sadati gave Bibi a voucher to buy me a school uniform, books, and study materials, and reminded her to bring me back at 7:30 a.m. sharp on the first day of *Mehr* (September 21), the first day of school. Bibi's face blushed like pink peaches. I had never seen her so happy.

On the way home, Bibi told me to hurry up, so I could sit on the prayer rug and thank God, and pray for Uncle Engineer's health and blessing. "If it wasn't for his influence and title," Bibi said, "no one would've even bothered listening to me." I wondered why I couldn't thank God and pray right there near the beet fields. But Bibi said, "Though God is everywhere, this is no proper place to worship Him, with the public bath nearby and all kinds of funny smells around."

She said Mrs. Principal had to be *Sayyed*. "Sadati is one of those last names only *Sayyed* people could have," she explained. "In God's safeguard, who had ever seen a golden-haired *Sayyed* woman? I'm sure," she mumbled to herself, "those golden locks of hers come from an entire packet of color rinse."

# CHAPTER 19

The tarpaulin curtains are pushed to the side. Wireless radio in hand, Torabpoor converses with *Sister* Zahra from behind his desk. As usual, mothers and sisters hurry to the front gate to put down their names. They stand in line to beg Torabpoor one more time. Mina tells me that I should go again and plead with him for a visit with Mohammad.

Mahnaz is among the inmates waiting in line. She was transferred last week from the second tier. She has given birth to her son in prison, and her husband is among the eleven *oldies* still alive. She was arrested with a group of her comrades, according to the *Sepah*, living in a team-house. The house was bombed by the *Hezbollah*. Her comrades either got killed or arrested; among them was another pregnant woman, Azar, who had shouted at her captors, "Death to the fanatic regime!" as the *Sepah* guards shot her husband before her eyes. The *Sepah* had hanged her that very night, her three-month-old fetus still in her womb. The news exploded in the city with such impact that even the government-controlled newspapers wrote about the tragedy, questioning the authorities. The *Sepah* denied the crime and the chief of the Justice Department responded coldly that they would never execute pregnant women. To prove it, they have forced Mahnaz, then four months pregnant, to appear in a fake TV interview. The Justice Department, as well as the *Sepah*, deny that virgins are executed. The arrested girls are mostly under twenty-five, unmarried, and still virgins. According to Islamic laws, stoning or killing of a virgin is forbidden and against the principles and teaching of the religion. It is believed that the *Hakem* recites phony vows to wed the girls to the *Sepah pasdars* so they could legally rape the girls, now married, so as to defile their virginity before they are hanged. In this way, the government is convinced that they kill women legally and according to religion.

Mahnaz has recited the entire holy book of the Koran seven times so far and has read the entire Komeil prayers. She is the cellmate of Mrs. Hashimi who still pleads with God every waking hour, asking Him to forgive her only daughter. "Dear God, show me your compassion, show your mercy to my young innocent girl. She's all I have left." Mrs. Hashimi murmurs quietly so that the *Sisters* won't hear her. "Please God, all I want from you is for her to be sentenced to life in prison and not execution. Dear God, don't push me away disappointed from your door. You're all I have to plead to."

Bibi, too, must be pleading now like Mrs. Hashimi.

The last few times I stood in line, by the time every anxious mother, sister, and wife had pleaded with Torabpoor, and he had been interrupted by the telephone's constant ringing, the whispering into the receiver held closely to his fish-lip mouth, and the talking in a secret-code language to the *Sisters*, there was no time left for me to discuss my request. At this point, I shift my weight from foot to foot, holding my chador tightly under my chin, and pray to God that this time I will have a chance. I've been watching for days for him to enter the lobby and for the loudspeaker to announce that he is accepting appointments. I even leave my socks on at all times to avoid losing time so I can rush to him the moment he enters the lobby.

Torabpoor rests his hands on the table, pretending he's listening to Mahnaz, who is requesting a face-to-face visit with her son, now a toddler. He pauses, going through the stack of papers, facing *Sister* Tahereh. Mahnaz waits for his conversation to end. "One minute. That's all I'm asking. Just to hold him in my arms. I promise not to cry and not to say a word. Please, you have children. You know how it feels—."

"Enough!" Torabpoor interrupts her.

"Others are waiting," *Sister* Tehereh directs her back to the corridor.

Mahnaz turns her back. I can see bits of broken pride in her eyes. Tears bubble, but do not fall. Perhaps at this very moment she wishes that she were still on the second tier and that she had remained a non-repentant.

"I have come again to ask you please to allow me a visit with my brother," I say in my most carefully chosen words.

Torabpoor looks me up and down. Maybe he's still looking for some resemblance between the brother and sister. Looking for Mohammad's persistence, his frightening will, his wit. I doubt he could find much resemblance in an oval face framed in a black chador. Definitely my wheat-colored skin and dark brown eyes would not remind him of Mohammad's light complexion and large green eyes. The interrogators, too, were curious to see me, Mohammad's sister, and were surprised to see a small, thin, eighteen-year-old girl instead of, perhaps, a two-headed dragon or a wild tiger. I always see the same surprise in Torabpoor's narrow chicken eyes. He is lucky that he's relatively tall, able to hide that large gut of his, which stretches his tight uniform. A large-boned man with a big behind, he's got the chunkiest hands I have ever seen, chunky even for a man. His face is a large pox-marked round patty, his nose big, and his forehead broad under his receding hairline and close-shaven head.

"I have not seen *him*," I am careful not to use the word 'brother' too often, "for over two years now. I was hoping to see *him* and talk to *him* for a few moments." I swallow hard. "Is he at . . ." I stop myself before causing any damage. "I was supposed to answer a few questions and leave the same day. It's been six months, but I am still here and still not allowed any visit with my brother!"

"I am very disappointed in you," he says. "I thought you would make much wiser choices here, but you have proved me wrong."

"Would you please clarify what you mean?"

He looks up and stares at me for a good few moments. "I see. Now you want me to clarify things for you? Aren't *things* clear enough?"

"Please forgive my slowness. I don't think I'm following you," I say without looking at him.

"When was the last time you have talked to a *Sister*? I have never received any written report from you, and you have not showed any sign of cooperation. Have you? And you call yourself a repentant?"

I open my mouth to say something, but I don't know what to make of his comments. "I have done nothing against the prison's rules," I say finally.

"Have you been seen by the *Hakem*?" he asks.

"Yes. A while ago."

"If I were you, I would reconsider my demeanor. Trust me, you don't want to jeopardize your future."

I should walk away and never ever again stand in this line, pleading with this ignorant pitiless man who was nobody until a few years ago, but who now determines the life and death of young people in this city. "Please," I hear myself beg again. "If I could only see Mohammad for a few moments. Not a word. Just to see him." I don't know why, but I feel words come out of my mouth the way Bibi always pleads. Maybe the pleading would work and soften his heart.

He rises to his feet and walks around his desk. "We'll see," he says horridly, waving his hand.

I walk back to the corridor.

# CHAPTER 20

From where I am, in the corner of my cell, I can hear the guard's footsteps from the other side of the wall. Tonight is my turn to sleep on the cot. My back to the bars, I bring my face closer, breathing the icy chalk-covered cement, the cold, and the old pain. I close my eyes and let my ears take over. Maybe I can hear the Singing Lover again. The same inmate from Block 2 who used to sing at siesta breaks and at night. It's been days since I have heard him last. What could have become of him? Has he been freed? Maybe, now, he's singing cheerful southern folksongs to his beloved. What a burning honey voice he had, fluid and translucent. And how he poured out his sorrowful heart, its droplets trickling down somewhere in the depths of my soul. I wish it was Wednesday night and the *Komeil's* prayers were on, but it is only Saturday night and my eyes are already welled up and can hold on no longer. I cover my face with the blanket, feeling the warm droplets roll down to my earlobe. It is *Sister* Tehereh and *Sister* Marzieh's round tonight. Holding their flashlights, they pace the dimmed corridor in the opposite direction of each other. I bite into the blanket, suffocate my sobs. Three cellmates lie down on the floor. It is absolute silence, but I know that everyone is awake, pretending to be asleep. I face the bars again and this time let my memory takes over my hearing; it spreads its wings and lifts me up high and, and high, and higher.

Bibi was so overjoyed and impatient for the first day of *Mehr* that I couldn't tell if it was she or I who was starting school; after all, it was she who couldn't read or write, not I. We went to the Melli Cen-

tral Bank on Ahmadi Street next to Bazaar Vakil. Bibi took a stack
of tumans and a tiny red metal disc out of a small leather purse and
handed them to a man behind the glass window. The man counted
the money as fast with his fingers, as if he were the man in the magic
show at the Melli Garden. He took the metal disc, stamped the book
and handed it back to Bibi.

"What's that thing?" I asked.

"This is my seal. I have to have it with me when I come here, so
that I can sign." Before we left the bank, she pointed to a red mark-
ing and asked if I could read it to her. It was a long string of numbers,
so I read them. "7 5 6 2 0 riii alll s. Rials."

"Good. That's right. It makes 7,562 tumans. When I save ten
thousand tumans I could have Masht Nader come and build a large
bathroom and a kitchen," she said enthusiastically. At the entrance,
she let me use the revolving glass-door while she herself walked out
the huge double door. "God only knows if you ever get out of that
dancing door," she waved her hand at the revolving door. "Whatever don't they make these days. Once I got stuck in it; that was
enough for a lifetime."

Outside the door, a navy-blue-uniformed man took off his hat for
Bibi and wished her a good day. Bibi told him, "You don't have to take
your hat off for me, brother Jabbar. You know that." She handed him
her savings book. "My daughter," she pointed to me, "she already
read it." She scolded me, "Where's your manners, *babam*?"

"*Salam*," I said shyly to the man with the blue hat.

"*Salam* back to that moon-face of yours, child," he said in an
accent like Bibi's, and read the numbers: "7,562 tumans."

"Well. As I said, she read it to me. I just had to make sure. She's
starting school soon," she said, smiling. "We were just on our way to
buy her school uniform."

When we had walked a little way from the bank, Bibi said happily
that now that I could read, she would no longer need to ask any strangers to read her private business. Not that Mash Jabbar the Doorman
was a stranger. After all, he was from her old village. But she thought
there were still certain things that one should keep private.

We walked through the crowded streets, passed the Ahmadi
Square through zigzagging cars, and turned onto the Zand Avenue;

I spelled out the names to Bibi. She asked a few passersby for the address on the back of the voucher. We stopped at the front door of a corner store. On the wall-racks and from the ceiling hung all sizes of school uniforms. A heavyset man approached us and asked Bibi, "What grade?"

Bibi said, "Well, of course, first."

The man handed her a plastic wrapped package, which Bibi opened on the counter. There was a gray dress uniform, a white shirt, three pairs of white socks with lace around the ankles. He asked her if she wanted a plastic or a fabric collar. Bibi said, Plastic? Why plastic? The man did not seem to be in the mood to explain why, so Bibi said, "Fabric, of course."

The man turned around. "You'll notice the difference by the second month of school when you come back asking for plastic ones. The fabric, you have to wash it, starch iron it, and it's hard to keep clean," he said under his breath, going to the end of the store. Upon his return, he handed Bibi the white collar and a small red lunch box. Bibi waved her hand and said that the girl could use her brother's lunch box. I looked at her as we walked out of the store, hoping she did not mean Ali's tattered drawing briefcase.

# CHAPTER 21

On the first day of fall, Bibi woke me up and handed me the starched, ironed uniform. My mother had visited a few days back, and after her usual agitated bustle, managed to drag me to *Momon* Peymaneh, the neighborhood seamstress, so that she could alter my uniform which was two sizes too large with its skirt drooping way below my ankles. She scolded Bibi who was determined that I would eventually grow into it next year and the year after. Regardless, after much fussing and snapping, the skirt was tailored to my knee, and the shirt sleeves were also shortened by several centimeters.

Bibi undid my braids and pushed my hair back from my face with a white head-band. She handed me Ali's peeling brown briefcase packed with a week's worth of dried figs, puffed rice and wheat, and a bag of mixed roasted nuts that she had prepared over the summer. She took my hand and instructed me that I needed to keep my eyes and my ears open so I wouldn't lose my way to school since from the next day I would be on my own because she had to begin her winter-season jobs.

We left our house, reached the end of eight-meter Amir Kabir lane, and walked across to the edge of the abandoned gypsy field. We passed the corn field, the lettuce field, and the beet field, and went around a hard mud hill to the right of the public bath. There, at the foot of the hill, Bibi stopped and marked the black mulberry tree and told me never to climb over the hill for I might fall off into the deep ditch behind it. I should also walk along the shady pathway until I got to school. As we went down the path, past the one and only snack-shack, I could see the brown rustic double door of the

Mansorieh school wide open with the hubbub of girls in the school yard emerging. At the door, Bibi kissed my forehead and pushed me gently into the crowded yard as I refused to let go of her skirt . She promised me if I behaved and obeyed her now, she'd be waiting right there at noon to take me home. A few steps later, she turned around and ordered me not to buy anything from that shack because their fruit *lavashak* was old. Again, she forbade me to talk to or follow any strangers if I ever got lost on the way.

My stomach began to twist and turn at the sight of so many girls of all heights and sizes in the schoolyard, showing off their uniforms and shoes. I walked to a corner and leaned against a shady tree. A big woman approached, a line of girls behind her. She commanded me to follow her. "This is where you should line up in the morning before your class starts," said Khanoom Nazim, as some of the girls called her. The superintendent told us to line up according to our class and height. "First-graders here! Line up nicely!" she called out.

A bell rang and everyone faced the podium on the center stage in front of the glass double-door entrance. Through the crowd, I saw Principal Sadati approaching the podium holding a red megaphone. She said, "Good morning," and asked everyone to stay in line and sing the national anthem. The fat *Nazim* kept walking slowly, pointing her ruler to the white line in front of us, and yelling at those who pushed.

When the noises quieted down, a girl in her short-skirt uniform, almost as tall as Principal Sadati, stepped up on the stage and glided gracefully toward a flagpole. She raised the flag ever so slowly as a song blasted through the loudspeaker, vibrating the ground under my feet. The green, white, and red colors flew up. A yellow lion, holding a golden sword under a rising sun, sat on the white strap as if protecting the flag. Everyone faced the flag, singing loudly, "*Shah-anshah-e ma zendeh bada . . .* , may our King live forever."

My cheeks grew hot, as I watched this new spectacle. The one-big-loud-voice prayed that Shahbanoo Queen may live forever too. At the end, there were prayers for the teachers, for the parents, for their health, and prayers that the country remain eternally glorious. *Payandeh bad Iran*, the one-big-loud-voice shouted. After the morning salute, Principal Sadati gave instructions through her mega-phone. Her commanding voice echoed against the walls.

"As all of you already know, and for those of you who have just joined this splendid school, this is the school's routine from Saturday through Thursday. The line-up and morning salute start at a quarter to eight, and the first class session starts at eight sharp. There are two fifteen-minutes recesses. You may come to the school yard and play in the playground only during this time. School ends at noon. The second week rotates. The school starts with your first class session at one o'clock in the afternoon and ends at five. Remember not to get confused about the schedule of rotation. Every Saturday, hair, hands, and nails will be checked for cleanliness. Make sure on Friday, when you're off from school, to ask your mothers to clip your nails short. Your uniform must be clean at all times. Your skirt's pleats and your white collars must be ironed. Or else you'll be sent home to come back to the office with your mother."

We were then led to our classes line by line, starting with the first graders.

Our teacher's name was Miss Sadati too. She was the junior, she said. She smiled and told us No, she was not related to Principal Sadati, "Not that I mind that." We should call her *Khanoom Moa-lemm*, Miss Teacher. Unlike Principal Sadati, she was tall and thin and her long golden hair fell down her back to her waist. She kept tugging her shirt into her bell-bottom pants; a loose chain belt shone around her hips as she paced the room.

In the class, on the left side, the windows were half open to a yard filled with trees. There were rows of wooden benches with attached desks on each side of the classroom, making a one-meter center aisle look like a straight pathway to the blackboard on the facing wall.

We had barely sat on the benches when Miss Sadati instructed everyone to stand up as Khanoom Nazim entered the room, "*Bar pa*, all rise." Everyone stood up. "*Bar ja*," Khanoom Nazim said, waving her hands. "You may sit down!"

"It is imperative for everyone to make it a habit to stand up as soon as any official or elder enters our classroom. It's called respect," Miss Teacher said. "Your good manners here count toward your final discipline grade. And it's very important to learn that from the very beginning."

I peeked to see Khanoom Nazim. From where I sat, I could see her slim, narrow ankles and her small black flat shoes. The girl next to me chuckled and said that this was a fat Nazim. I looked up to see better. The girl was right. She was even fatter than Bibi. I wondered how her tiny feet could carry a fat body like that. She handed a stack of papers to the teacher. Even her hands were small and chubby. Both women whispered for awhile and the fat Nazim left the classroom. We got up and sat down one more time.

The teacher asked everyone to come and stand in the corners of the room, against the walls or in the doorway. "Let's see," she said, glancing at the papers in her hands. "There are thirty of you." She frowned at us for a few moments. Then she turned and looked at the desks. She put down the papers on her desk and asked us, one by one, to stand shoulder to shoulder next to each other. We were to be seated according to height, three girls at each bench. The taller ones sat at the end benches in the room.

"This is your permanent seat for the entire school year, unless you are told otherwise," Miss Teacher said.

I was to be seated on the front row bench in the left hand side of the class next to the window. I was happy because I could hear the birds sing and feel the cool morning air creeping inside. The yard was filled with the shade of mulberry and citrus fruit trees. Through the high branches, I could see the walnuts peeling off their green shells.

Our school books were stacked on the teacher's desk. She gave us each one copy and told us to keep it clean at all times. I took mine. My very first book. Its strawy, ivory papers smelled like the bunch of dry wheat Bibi kept on the top shelf in her prayer-room. The first time ever holding a new book. It smelled good. Crispy. Miss Teacher said if we wished, we could write our name right above the writing on the brown cover page where she read:

*Amoosesh & Parvaresh*
*The Ministry of Education*
*Iran, Province Fars, Shiraz*
*1st Grade Farsi Book*

On the first page, there was a picture of *Shahanshah Aryamehr.* On his head gleamed a bejeweled crown; a long velvet cape adorned his navy-blue military uniform. All kinds of colorful precious stones were sewed to his cape. A silk stripe of golden medals hung diagonally over his chest. On the second page, there was a picture of his queen, *Shahbanoo Farah Diba,* her face beautiful and sleek like a gazelle's. She stood tall and graceful in her long queen dress, her white gloves covering her long arms. On the third page was a picture of *Valiahd Reza Pahlavi,* the young prince, a boy perhaps Mohammad's age, sitting proud and dignified in his blue uniform on a splendid chair, his military cap resting on his lap.

When I turned to the next page, I spelled the beautiful bold lithograph: *In the name of forgiving and kind God.* The lessons and chapters followed thereafter.

At home, when I showed my book and the pictures to Bibi, she looked at them in awe and told me that it was said that the Shah was the shadow of God on earth. That he was the richest of all men and the father of all orphans. That the country will continue to prosper under his reign. Now that I went to school and prayed for his health, for a rich father of all orphans, I hoped that Bibi would become rich too, so she would no longer need to get up early and go to the sour-pickle factory, peeling off that mountain of eggplants. I tied a string around my finger to remind myself to pray extra for the King at the morning salute, so Bibi could stay home and rest her aching back until the cuts on her fingers healed.

That Friday, when Mohammad came to visit he brought me a rose flower wrapping paper. He wrapped my book's cover page in it and double-wrapped it in another plastic covering, so that the cover will remain clean and unfolded. In his neat handwriting, he wrote my name on the first page above the Shah's crowned head.

# CHAPTER 22

Finally, the electricity and water were working throughout our house, which was almost finished. Even all the ceilings were plastered and all the rooms were whitewashed, including the two that served as the guest room and the drawing room. Not only that, Bibi asked Mash Nader the Mason to design the ceilings' crown moldings with artful, carved chalk work. He tiled all four rooms and had his workers raise the roof as high as one meter, so in the summertime Bibi and I could sleep in the privacy of our own property, safe from stranger's eyes.

Even the front parlor, which separated the indoor living area from the courtyard, was covered with bright glazed tiles. In the center, thirteen narrow saffron-colored-mosaic stairs, the shape of a half-curved sleepy snake, looped up to the roof. At this time, on the cool dotted gray square tiles of the empty rooms, I pretended to draw a hopscotch ladder, or I jumped rope while Bibi dozed off, in her afternoon nap.

The courtyard was still a mixture of clay-mud and cement. The workers brought in a new small mosaic fishpond and mounted it in the center of the courtyard. Bibi let the top faucet run full blast and filled up the fishpond. She freed the goldfish into the sparkling blue water from the plastic bag she had brought from the market.

Most days, Bibi sprinkled the courtyard with a watering can, either early in the morning or in the late afternoon, so that the dust would settle. When Mash Nader suggested that Bibi reduce the size of the garden, eliminating half the trees, she shook her head in disbelief and said that there are tiny creatures of God resting in those trees and she had no heart to move them. "That's their habitat," she said.

Bibi would have been happier if the kitchen and the bathroom were already built. She still continued her weekly trip to the public bath, which took up her entire morning, only to come home huffing and puffing with cheeks as red as pomegranates and her forehead covered with beads of sweat. Sometimes she took me along; other times she gave me a bath with boiling water from the propane stove in one of the rooms. And each time, when she dumped out the hot water into the narrow gutter around the fishpond, she chanted, "*Besmellah, Besmellah,*" so that the jinn and evil-beings, who fear the name of God, disappear and never dare to harm us. She was always careful not to hurt them accidentally, by stepping on their invisible tails. The jinn, she said, were higher beings, immortal yet wicked. They were the cursed ones, expelled and banned from Heaven, worshipers of Satan who stole beautiful human children, and their entire intention was to lead us mortals to sin, and therefore to the fires of Hell. Though their bodies had a human shape, they had the look of four-legged beasts with hooves, tails, and small horns like a goat's. Opposing them were the good fairies, beautiful and pure. Their bodies were covered in transparent clothes made of lights sewn with silk and gold threads. Floating about like guardian angels, their purpose was to save and protect human beings from all evil, guiding us to everlasting life in Heaven.

Finally, when I came home from school one day, the pile of cement and chalk, the broken tiles, and the workers were all gone. The house was quiet; no more noise of squeaking wheel-barrels in the courtyard. Even our two-meter-wide entryway alley was paved with leftover tiles from the porch, the sparkly saffron color.

When my mother came, she ridiculed Bibi and asked why on earth the rooftop had to be tiled. "Couldn't you leave it plain black tar like everybody else's roof?" she mocked. "But no, you had to leave the courtyard untiled and dusty instead."

"God willing," Bibi said, almost to herself, "I'll have the mason build a bath and a kitchen by next summer before tiling the yard."

Sometimes, on the way home from school, Marmar and I crossed paths. She went to a different school and had been held back a couple of times; by then, she was in the second grade. Our plan was to

do our skip-rope before the sun went down, and to race all the way
to the end of the main street, paved only the last week, a smooth
black satin of asphalt that you could easily skid down in your slippery school shoes. Bibi would've gone mad if she had ever seen me
doing that. She said that she didn't have money to squander buying
me another pair of shoes. Keeping an eye on them, she taught me
how to walk straight, so the soles wouldn't turn lopsided. But after I
sobbed and begged and refused to go to school in my old shoes, she
finally gave in and bought me a new pair of black leather shoes like
the ones most girls in school wore.

Pushing the blue door of the house, I entered the courtyard only
to see Bibi kneeling in the parlor, pails of water and soiled rags all
around her. Her sleeves were rolled up and her white scarf was pushed
back on her head, just like the turban of Mullah Hossein, the Friday preacher, who came to the house once a week. In that mournful
voice of his, he read verses from a torn old book and made Bibi cry
for the martyr Imam Hossein, even though Bibi always fed him the
entire plate of bread-halva she'd meant to give away in memory of
the dead, and put a fistful of *moshgel-gosha* mixed nuts in the pocket
of his gray robe before he left.

Bibi was home from work early again, determined to finish washing off the front porch and the parlor floor. As she wished, Mash
Nader had designed the entire parlor's base—nearly half a meter
high—in the saffron mosaic that matched the stairs. She was scrubbing the base with a brisk brush and wiping off the surface with
a drenched rag. She scrubbed, rinsed it with water, scrubbed and
wiped it dry over and over until the tiny silver stars began to loom
through the mosaic and glitter under the fading sunrays.

As I came near her, she forbade me to walk barefoot on the floor.
I noticed her finger prints on the wall. "Your hands, Bibi. They're
bleeding," I shrieked.

"I know, *babam*," she said, dipping her hands in the pail of clear
water to wash off the blood. Then she wiped the red spot off the
wall's surface.

"I've got cuts all over; the whitewash burns. But it'll be all right.
Why don't you go outside and play, dear? By the time you get back,
I will be done, and I will fix your dinner."

I tiptoed to the bedroom, took off my uniform, hung it on the wooden rack, and ran to the courtyard. Marmar promised that as soon as her mother left the house, we'd go rope-skipping, especially this afternoon when the stream was running in the waterway down the sidewalk. This was the one day of the week when Hadji Javad would turn on his hilltop water pump so that the sparkling clean water would run down over his lettuce and beet fields at the base of the hill.

I snatched my rope, heading for the door.

Bibi sneezed. "Wait a minute!" she yelled.

I knew I had to wait, or else something bad would happen to me. Bibi believed a sudden sneeze from somone who was not ill was a sign from God to refrain from whatever act one was about to engage in. "God is telling you to wait and rethink the task you're about to do," she remarked. "It might not be to your benefit."

I waited a good minute, shifting from foot to foot impatiently, skipping rope. I was about to go outside but Bibi sneezed again.

"Not again, Bibi."

I turned and went to sit near her, even though she did not approve of it. She sneezed once more and then again. Bibi was ill. I should disregard her sneezes, I thought to myself, for they could not be the sign of God. I looked at her, her forehead was covered with tiny pearl beads. Streaks of sweat ran down her neck and her chest. She sneezed again. I got up to go. But somehow I couldn't. Bibi's eyes were watery as always, her nose was running, her hands damp. With the tail of her scarf, I wiped her forehead and her eyes. Her hands trembled as she scrubbed the mosaic surface.

"You're ill, Bibi. Why don't you let the workers finish it?"

"It's all right, dear. I am short of money. I didn't want to wait for my wages next month. Mash Nader has already done so much for me, I owe him a lot. I want to finish this parlor before I rent out the rooms next month. Who knows, maybe I'll get lucky and the soldiers coming from Isfahan or Jahrom will want to rent the rooms. We're not that far from *podegon* military base, you know."

It was nearly sunset now. The cold gust blew over the footsteps of winter, bringing the news of rain. I knelt next to Bibi, took a rag and dipped it in one of the pails. Bibi said I should move away and not get my hands dirty in the acidic water, which would burn my hands, and that Miss Principal would send for her if she saw my nails dirty and my fingertips cracked.

"Go on outside and play, dear!"

I no longer wanted to. Not when Bibi's fingers bled like that. I wiped off the surface and squeezed the water out of the rag into the second pail. "Is that how, Bibi? Is it the right way?"

"Yes, *babam*, yes. May I die for your delicate hands. May good fortune be upon your way all your life, *babam*." She wished me well under her breath, sneezing with each stroke of scrubbing.

Soon darkness fell and the Shirazi winds began to blow, bringing gray clouds over our rooftop. We finished the parlor; the entire mosaic surface sparkled with thousands of stars under the fluorescent lights in the ceiling. Bibi held my hand in her rough hands and glided it down along the surface. The cool mosaic, soft and smooth, soothed my hot burning palms and the tips of my fingers.

"Now I can rent out the rooms," Bibi sighed, hugging me.

I looked up into the dark sky. It was too late to go outside and skip rope.

# CHAPTER 23

The digital screen of my watch shows 11:00 a.m. To save ourselves from the heat and humidity released by the ever-moist hanging laundry, we take refuge in the cells on the left side where it feels a bit cooler. Pacing up and down the corridor is no longer tempting in this muggy humid recycled air, especially since under the chador we wear layers of soaked clothes. I have never been to the second or third tier. With the high ceilings, I can only imagine the unbearable heat the other inmates must have to put up with. Once in a while, a woman from the ordinary inmates shrieks at the top of her lungs, cursing and demanding that the *Sisters* let them hose down the entire tier with tap water. Ignored by the *Sisters*, they settle for splashing bowl after bowl of water in one another's faces. They steal each other's lovers and offer to ice down their private parts, cooing weirdly and talking in obscene phrases. Women gather around them, cheering and bursting into loud laughter; others break out in a frenzy, both of anger and envy. Again and again, the *Sisters* run up the stairs and struggle to separate tangled legs, sagging breasts pressed against breasts, bodies holding tight like two sides of a magnet, and. . . . Since beating is not done in the Block, the *Sisters* put up a show before us, presenting a good image of the followers of the saint Zaynab as if their hearts are filled with compassion and forgiveness for these miserable *damaged* women who have chosen to take the wrong fork in the road. Nevertheless, we can still hear them exchanging shouts and roaring at inmates who dare to challenge them. As usual, there would be soon another spectacle, both dismal and amusing, which could end with the arrival of the male guards and their batons.

The *normal* inmates are still lamenting the heat when the loud-speaker bursts out with a list of names being called to the lobby. The tarpaulin curtains are drawn and Torabpoor is in the main lobby. It must be the verdicts. My heart drops to the bottom of my stomach as I hear my name called. My cellmates jump to their feet, kissing my cheeks and saying goodbye. Everyone here believes that I have nothing to worry about and that I will be free. It's been over six months since the day I turned myself in. My heart races against my chest. I pray that my cellmates are right. I kiss them back and walk to the lobby. The voice in my head says I'll be set free, yet my heart warns against it.

All thirteen girls are already lined up behind the half-open tarpaulin. Mina makes room for me. I stand behind her. "Good luck!" she whispers. "Good luck to you too," I whisper back. For a month or so, Afsaneh, Mina, Farzaneh, and I have been sharing a cell. Friendship between the inmates is not allowed, but Mina and I have become as close as if we had known each other all our lives; we share a good laugh when the *Sisters* or the *Eyes* are not watching. Mina has been arrested on the pretext that she had read the Fadaee Party pamphlets and had distributed them among her classmates. She is my age and engaged to be married. The *Sepah* has contacted her fiancé's family and frightened them so often that her banker fiancé has called off the wedding.

Torabpoor verbally gives me my verdict: "Two years." Then he looks up and emphasizes that there is a possibility of general amnesty if I improve my behavior and decide not to act as I have been doing so far. "I want you to consider your mother's well-being," he says, as if I need his pathetic sympathy. "*Anything* is possible, forgiveness and freedom, or a sentence increase. The choice is yours," he adds as he motions for Afsaneh to come next.

Two years. Two years of prison. So, was that my trial? The day I was taken to that pot-bellied Hakem who wagged his pistol at me? Was that the Islamic Republic's court of justice? I didn't even get the chance to defend myself. I have been given two years for turning myself in, walking hand-in-hand with my own mother. I came in with the promise of release on that same afternoon, a promise that I would no longer have to live with fear and in hiding. Now, I have to live two years in this hovel; to live with the fear of being sent to the second tier, or of solitary confinement, of an increased sentence, or a revision to the death penalty. I hear the voice in my head pounding against my skull as I walk back to the corridor. My feet drag heavily as if I have just stepped out of a pool of molten tar. So this is the kind of mercy the Justice Department has been advertising on national TV! Mohammad, too, is back at the Sepah Detention, perhaps in solitary.

The girls gather around once more. "Two years will pass by quickly," they comfort me unconvincingly. Maybe they're right. Considering what I face in here every day, witnessing executions of so many innocent girls, the lashings, the revoked visitation rights, I should consider myself lucky for not being hanged or receiving a much longer sentence. As Bibi puts it, I should throw my hat high in the air and catch it with joy. Though *anything is possible* as Torabpoor said. Once you set your foot on the ground of this cursed place, only God and His angels would know if you'd ever be walking on free ground again. Both Mina and Afsaneh are also condemned to two years in prison. Nobody has been set free. The verdicts vary from one year to life in prison. Mahnaz is given a sentence of ten years. By that time, if she were to be set free, her boy will be in the fifth grade. Mahnaz's husband, Mohsen, has been sent back to the Sepah Detention.

# CHAPTER 24

My mother tries not to shed a tear as she switches the receiver from ear to ear. She's not good at pretending.

"I can't believe they gave you two years!" she murmers. Apparently, she's been given the news before me. I am thankful for that, because at least she had enough time to digest the bad news before seeing me behind the glass barrier.

"It's only two years, *Momon*," I sigh, trying not to look at her tearful eyes. I am not good at pretending either. "It'll go by fast."

"Will it?" she says, her eyes welling up. They shimmer. My, her eyes are striking. Two large almonds. "It's been over two years that Mohammad has been in here. Only God Himself knows that this two years of pain and suffering has been equal to whatever misery I have gone through in my entire forty-seven years of life."

"I know, *Momon*. I might receive amnesty. Maybe I'll be set free much sooner."

"Whatever God's wish," she says bitterly, wiping away a tear with her finger. She says that she has brought me more figs, cherries, and apricots sent from Deh.

I bow my head slightly. "How is *he*, *Momon*?" I ask, careful not to attract the *Sisters'* attentive, trained eyes and ears which are everywhere.

"I had a visit on Wednesday," she says in a stifled voice.

"How's he holding up?" I interrupt her impatiently.

Her lower lip quivers and her eyes well up again. Covering her face with her chador, she puts the receiver down on the counter before her and wipes her eyes with the chador which she finds more useful than

179

the drenched, crumpled Kleenex in her hand. It was a mistake to ask her that. The last thing I want is to make her cry, but she is my only channel to Mohammad.

"He's . . . just . . . skin and bones," she finally manages to say haltingly, covering her mouth with her fingers and swallowing her sobs "His face has become this much," she holds her fist against the glass. "What kind of world do we live in? I wish someone could explain to me."

I feel tears boil under my eyelids. I move further to the right and try to turn my torso as far back as possible to avoid the watchful *Eyes* behind. "Does he know, *Momon?* About . . . me?"

She sighs, nods her head, and shows two of her fingers. This way she tells me how she had used sign language to tell my brother about my verdict. "He couldn't believe it. He felt horrible, dear. You should've seen his face when I told him."

"It's not his fault, *Momon.*"

"He sends you his warm greetings and said I should tell you he only meant the best for you. I guess he fell for their promises too. He said I should tell you not to do anything hasty. Stay strong and don't lose faith and don't do anything against the authorities' wishes here. What can I say? I blame myself for it. But it's spilled milk, dear, think of your release now! Be very cautious not to worsen your situation in prison just as it happened to your brother. . . ."

My mother's voice is cut off through the receiver. The fifteen-minute visit is over. "Time's up," yells *Sister* Zahra, not a bit concerned if her voice is being heard by the *Brothers*. My mother puts her palm against the glass barrier. "Be very careful!" her mouth moves soundlessly.

# CHAPTER 25

Tons and tons of white boxes were stacked on Khanoom Moalem's desk. A girl in school uniform, holding a cookie to her mouth, smiled at me in the drawing under the arch label *The Gratis Nutrition*.

Two women in navy blue suits entered the classroom.

*"Bar Pa!"* commanded Miss Tabatabaee, our second-grade teacher.

Everyone rose and sat down again at the nod of the Blue Suits.

"These ladies are from the Ministry of Education," Miss Tabatabaee explained. "They are here to present us with their generous offer, promoting free nutrition in the elementary schools."

"Yes. That is correct," one of the women confirmed. Holding one of the boxes in her hand, she went on. "We have an obligation to visit each school and observe children's nutrition all over Iran. Our goal is to make sure that you children, the hope and the capital asset of the country's future," she smiled and looked around the classroom, "are nourished properly. As the saying goes, a healthy mind begins with a healthy body." She nodded her head both to the other lady and Miss Tabatabaee.

The women distributed the boxes, giving each child one box containing twenty rectangular cookies to take home.

From then on, every Saturday morning, the Free Nutrition trucks arrived at our school with the food ration for the entire six school days.

"You should be thanking God for such a fair King," Principal Sadati reminded us again at the morning salute. "Where else in the world is a schoolchild being served this sort of healthy nutrition, let alone free? There are starving children dying in India, in Africa, yet the best of the best is here at your hand."

Shielding her face with a handbook, the superintendent scanned the lines of gray uniforms in front of her. "Would you girls quiet down a bit! What is it? Do you have the tickle ants?"

Looking at each other and at the superintendent's ruler, we fought hard not to laugh.

"Do not push each other!" The scratchy voice of Principal Sadati blasted through the loudspeaker. "You'll get to your classes momentarily. Look at those juicy oranges. Do you know where they come from? Lebanon. The bananas come from Mexico. Not even your fathers could dream of a time like this! You know how far away Mexico is from here? In one day, we feed you dates from Ahvaz, best cheese from Switzerland, and Lavash bread from Tehran."

This time, she asked us to pray for the King even louder, now that our bellies were full. Every day, a different snack or fruit was distributed. In the morning, right after the first recess, we were given two cookies and a bottle of cold pasteurized milk. Miss Tabatabaee, pacing in the classroom, her hands clasped behind her back, made sure everyone ate the cookies and drank the entire bottle of milk. Some of the girls refused to eat or drink, saying that cold milk made them nauseated and gave them a stomachache. Others, on the other hand, asked for a second round. The teacher said that she'd heard that some of the pupils—"Who I'd rather not name,"—were taking their share home, for their parents to eat or even to sell to the snack-shacks.

"What an awful way to make money out of the mouth of your child," said Principal Sadati to Miss Tabatabaee, who nodded in dismay.

I told myself I had better eat my entire share of food and not take any home for Bibi. Not that she would sell anything. It was just that she didn't have any of her teeth any more and she really cared for bananas; they were so soft, she said, they melted right in her mouth like sugar cubes. She would have bought them if the nearby greengrocer or vendors coming to our alleys sold them, but she had to go all the way uptown to get them from the special green-markets. I loved them too, so I kept staring hard at my nails to fight my craving, a trick Froozan showed me. She told me I could do anything if I just stared. I stared a lot. Then I gave in. I took a bite or two, and sometimes, by the time I got home, it was all mashed in my fist.

"Why don't you eat it yourself, *babam*, and save me the guilt and the big-belly label, all together," Bibi would remark, amused.

There were parents who did not like the idea of free nutrition. Rumors had it that the program was designed only for grade schools in the working-class and the lower-income areas. They said that they did not send their children to school to be labeled "charity cases." Soosan's family, for instance, who'd just moved to our lane, was among these parents. Besides the brand-new sedan Soosan's brothers drove, there were always Japanese trucks and a Buick parked in front of their house. Her brother, Mehran, was just out of high school, but he was driving a Paykan Javanan. Sometimes, he came to pick up his sister from school, and Soosan asked me to drive with them. Our house was not that far away, but Mehran would take the longer way home, and let us play right before the all-girls Pirnia High school. Soosan hardly ever took home any of the free cookies so as not to shame her mother.

On our street, the wealthy and not-so-wealthy lived wall to wall next to each other. New neighbors were arriving one by one, each building a more modern house than the last one, the kind with an indoor kitchen and bathroom, instead of out in the courtyard like ours. Bibi's daughter never got over this, tormenting her each time she came to visit, saying that Bibi still lived as if it were in the *Caravan-Age*; the time when people used to have separate kitchens from the main indoor living quarters, and pissed in the back of their courtyard. Our house was among the largest in the lane. If only the owner of the abandoned lot adjacent to our house would consider building on it, Bibi would have been real pleased. Lately, with less and less land around us, this lot had become a soccer field for the neighbors' bully boys. They shouted and laughed so loudly at the midday rest time that Bibi couldn't take her afternoon nap in quiet. Not that she really minded their frenzied cheerfulness each time they planted a goal or won against the other team: "laughter brings health," Bibi would always say. But a quiet, civilized next-door neighbor was what she really wished for.

The Free Nutrition ladies were not the only ones who came to visit our school. Once a fat man came who handed everyone a small blue leather-covered booklet as he went bench to bench. Miss Tabatabaee followed him with her black-ink *BIC* in her hand, writing each person's name on the first page of the savings book. "Fifty *tumans* is already after your name," the unsmiling fleshy face said. The man's big body towered over our heads; our necks stretched up to meet his black eyes. The skin of his neck was beet red and he smelled like good, expensive Kermanshah butter.

"Have your parents take it to the nearest local Saderat Bank and register your name. You have to learn, from now on, how to save money." He breathed hard and dabbed his shiny forehead with a white handkerchief, but didn't bother to put it back in his jacket pocket. "If you add fifty tumans each month to this book, by age eighteen, when you graduate from high school, you'll be a *rich* young lady ready for higher education at the country's best universities," he puffed, extending his chubby arm over the benches to reach those sitting far behind. "Remember our generous Shahanshah. . . ."

Quickly, we rose to our feet and chanted: "*Javid Shah*. May the King live forever."

"Yes. Yes. Well learned. You may be seated."

Everyone sat down again.

"As I was saying, the ever-crowned Father of our country wishes to have proud children all over Iran. Do your best! Learn well and grow up to be a proud Iranian serving your country. Don't ever forget that *we* are the true descendent of Aryans, always strong and victorious."

When I took the savings book to Bibi, she was beside herself with joy that I was fifty tumans rich that day. She, too, said that I should be thankful to live in the time of such a Shah who cared about the children in this country. "The kings before him just bankrupted the country and built castles for themselves with the money they stole from the national reserve. Just look what the Ghajar Dynasty did to this country."

I knew Bibi would become irritated at any moment. Every time someone talked about the Ghajar Dynasty, she got all edgy and cheerless.

"All they cared about was pleasure and hedonism," she sighed. "If it wasn't for their lack of power and jurisdiction, the English would never have dared to set foot on this land." Here she was going at it again, at the English, whom some day I'd like to see with my own eyes, to see why she resented them so much. I should've expected it when she began again, "At your age, I saw war. Famine and disease swallowed young and old. When I was your age, I had to herd the sheep for my aunts so that they'd feed me a morsel of food."

I knew the rest. She didn't need to tell me any more; that when she was my age, she was sent to the husband's house. "Hey, hey, you unfaithful world! What would've happened if I'd been born half a century later?"

Moments later, she said that she could never afford to put away fifty tumans for me. "I barely make five hundred tumans a month. I wish I could. This is a good notion, a real bargain for someone who can afford it."

My pocket money was one tuman a week. If I'd save it in my safe-jug, Bibi told me, she might be able to come up with the rest and make it ten tumans a month at the most. But I had to promise her not to touch any of that money until the day I turned eighteen.

# CHAPTER 26

My second year of school might as well have been called the year of vaccinations. The Corps of Health & Hygiene came to our school, checking our hands, heads, hair, and our eyes. Miss Tabatabaee gave us many lessons about the three Corps, "You must learn these lessons very well!" she repeated over and over. "As part of our competent Shah's White Revolution plan for Iran's rapid modernization, the Corps of Literacy, the Corps of Health & Hygiene, and the Corps of Development & Cultivation are established with the purpose of improving general conditions in the cities, as well as in the remote towns and villages." We were even tested and graded on these lessons in history and Farsi subjects.

Almost every day there was a new vaccine. The ladies from the Corps of Health gave each one of us a health-book to write down all the necessary information. Class by class, line by line, we were led to the nurse's office where women in white overcoats, a sharp needle in their hands and a devilish look in their eyes, gave vaccinations. Sleeves rolled up, left arms held out, we pushed, for the first time ever, not for the privilege of being first in line, but to be last.

In the nurse's office they asked me about my father and my mother and the entire household; about their ages and their income; if I had any brothers and sisters; what were my father's and my mother's occupations; were there any diseases in the family, or if someone had died from a disease. There were so many questions, my head began to spin. I had no clue what the nurse was talking about. I didn't even know my father's name, let alone how old he was and if he had any diseases. I told them my father died on the prayer rug right after he returned from the public bath. I have brothers, but I don't know how many and how old they are. The nurse gave me a form to take home and have my *parents* fill out the questionnaire, sign, and return it to school.

I told her I have my Bibi at home, but she can't read. The Lady Nurse shook her head, let out a pitiful sigh and stared at me. "That's a disaster. Just a catastrophe!" She said to another nurse who was fiddling with a syringe, "We're lucky if we get ten forms returned to us correctly, and here we're trying to modernize this country. Breaking an elephant's tusk with your bare hand is easier than doing this job. For whom? For these?" She pointed to me with her red polished nails. "You mean you live with your *grandmother*. Right? What's *Biiii-biiii?*" she stretched the i's mockingly, "we don't live in the stone-age any more. Say *Momon bozorg*, grandmother. Speak properly, like a modern girl!"

The entire way home, I thought about what the red-nailed woman had said to me. The sharpness of her tone still burned the back of my neck; it made me want to scratch the red bump where her chicken-pox vaccine needle had stung my skin. Fighting tears, I went to Bibi, hoping to find the answers to all those questions. Already I could imagine her gaze floating to a faraway place, the gaze, which always returned whenever I asked her a family-related question.

I reminded myself not to cry or tell her anything that the nurse had said to me. Last time was enough. She had made such a fuss that the entire school knew her. Miss Tabatabaee had pinned my penmanship test to my back, and asked the class monitor to take me class by class to make an example of my zigzag scribbling for those who still write like a frog hops. I didn't go home that day. I went directly to Bibi's work and burst into tears right there in front of the hill of eggplants before the eyes of a bunch of toothless women. The next day Bibi came with me to school. She barged right into the office, asking for that ungodly woman who had done such a thing to an orphan child. I kept pulling at the hem of her chador, hiding behind her from the stare of Miss Tabatabaee. Principal Sadati promised Bibi that she would talk to my teacher personally, and made me promise to work on my penmanship, a very important subject, not to be ignored.

# CHAPTER 27

Winter came uninvited and made itself right at home. I didn't mind the cold as much as Bibi did; she was in such a fuss about how to keep her room warm without burning the propane heater for too long, for she believed its filter gave her a headache no matter how often she trimmed it evenly. The courtyard was more than filled with scattered, lifeless leaves; I didn't mind that either. What I did mind were the newly arrived *guests*. That day Ali was wearing his beige slacks and his sky-blue wool turtleneck sweater instead of his army uniform. He walked about with his camera dangling around his neck, taking pictures of Bibi's daughter, Golrokh the Flower-Face, and her sons, sitting at the edge of the fishpond. I watched them quietly and marveled at how they all looked alike, the same large honey-brown eyes and black eyebrows, the same cheeks, nose and mouth, even the same melodic, chic accent. How could a boy's face resemble his mother's? I wondered. It was the first time I had seen them all together. *That boy sitting on the stool must be Rahim, and that one must be Hossein, looking lost, standing right there next to Golrokh. And that one must be Amir, climbing up to his mother's lap.* The boys wore matching outfits, argyle V-neck wool sweaters over their white collar-shirts and cream-colored trousers with creases as sharp as a watermelon knife. Only Mohammad was at ease and familiar with the house, coming here so often, he couldn't stop running in and out of the arbors. His face was flushed; I didn't know if it was because of the cold air or that he was delighted to be back at the house once again.

I watched Rahim as he sat on another small wooden stool, away from the rest of them, his brown eyes, so large in his gloomy face.

The Flower-Face wore that lovely outfit of hers again; I had seen her wear it once before: the knee-length pleated skirt with a print of large red roses and matching long-sleeve shirt. Her short hair, straight as a string, was parted in the middle and gathered at each side of her ears, tied with a black elastic at the ends. I have never seen her smile or wear any makeup as my teachers did, but that day her face was rosy and full of beautiful smiles. She shied away from Ali's camera each time he asked her to look in his direction. Turning toward him ever so calmly, she brought the tips of her knees together like an elegant lady, and reached for her boys about her.

A few steps from them, by the fishpond's gutter, Bibi washed her clothes in a tin basin. Her scarf was knotted behind her neck, her sleeves rolled up. Ali zoomed his camera, clicking and pointing at anyone in his sight. As for me, I was invisible. Minutes passed before Ali zoomed his camera in my direction, asking me to come and sit.

"She has to get cleaned up and change her clothes if she wants to be in the pictures," the Flower-Face told him.

I frowned at her, and turned away. Bibi called after me, but I shrugged and walked toward the parlor. When I stood there watching them for so long, no one asked me to be included. I no longer wished to be in their pictures. I just wanted to sit on the stairs and ignore her. Soon, the sun will set, I thought, and she will leave with her boys back to wherever she came from, like the other times when she came, always worried about catching a taxi before darkness fell.

But the guests never left that night or the nights after; instead, they camped in the parlor. "When do the guests leave, Bibi?" I asked her when days went by but they were still at our house.

"They're not guests, dear," Bibi said. "They're family, your mother and your brothers. They're here to stay, my *babam*."

A week or two passed. I was in the vegetable garden plucking out the weeds around the eggplants and the red chili-peppers, when Golrokh appeared behind me; she had a shovel in her hand and began to tend the garden. She sank the sharp metal deep into the vegetables. With each dig the tiny cucumbers, the yellow squash and pumpkin flowers, the peppermint and basil leaves, and the half-green-half-red tomatoes sprang out of the soil. With their white stringy roots still attached to them, they were strewn all over the ground.

I rushed at her and reached for the shovel's handle. "You're ruining my vegetables," I almost screamed, holding on to her hands.

With her palm she pushed me away. "Get away, you little rascal. Look what she made out of you! Look at your hands! Look at the way you look!"

Bibi was not home and Golrokh's tall shadow, like a wounded bear, bounced over my head. "Leave the courtyard!" she ordered. "Go do your homework. Never mind mingling with grownup business!"

My gasp turned into a sob as I gathered the pumpkin flowers and the bruised cucumbers. I was afraid she would hit me if I said another word, yet I heard my voice tremble, "Bibi will get mad. You'll see. She will ask you to leave *our* house."

Clenching her teeth, she bent over and pinched my calf. The pain vibrated across my leg. I reached for the burning spot and rubbed it. I stared into her eyes. They looked even larger now, somehow rounder, no longer pretty.

"The size of your tongue is one meter, isn't it? I will cut it out for you so you won't talk like that to your own mother."

Still on my bottom, I crawled backward, but I kept staring at her. Her voice echoed louder in the yard, making my lips and knees quiver. I drew my knees to my chest.

"What are these? A bunch of good-for-nothing weeds. She brought her own village to this house." Golrokh pointed to the garden.

*Tagh, tagh, tagh.* . . . Someone knocked. Masht Akbar, the gardener, peeked inside the courtyard. "*Ya Allah! Ya Allah!*" he said out loud from the door. Golrokh ignored his customary gesture of letting a female know that a non-family man was about to enter the house, and without bothering to cover her hair she yelled, "Come in already! It's not like the Prince of India's arriving. Who would consider you even if you were the last man on the earth? Just come in and get this mess over with."

"There's no need to get all spiced up, *khanoom*." The gardener puffed and shook his head as he set down his canvas sack. He reached inside and a pair of long gardening scissors and a sharp-toothed saw appeared like magic.

I wiped my face with the back of my hands and didn't even trouble to greet him with a *salam*. Together, they yanked out the vegetables. She must have arranged with him to come in when Bibi was not home. In horror, I watched the vegetable garden disappear before my eyes. Baffled. Lost. The two of them began to shear the creeping vines. From every corner of the sky the branches and leaves fell down. Masht Akbar sawed the wooden arbors and jerked them out. The gardens turned into a bare ugly meadow. A tornado seized the courtyard. The sparrows flew overhead, chirping noisily. They settled on the electric wires above the rooftops, as if they too had sensed the unexpected early winter. Golrokh told Masht Akbar that she couldn't stand dust or the dry leaves scattered all over the courtyard.

In the midst of the confusion, Bibi came home. The moment she entered the doorway and saw the mess, she knelt in front of the heaps of broken branches and green leaves and cried like a little girl who has lost her candy stick.

"I told her you'll be mad." I ran to her and hugged her. "I tried to stop her, but she didn't listen, Bibi. You have to tell her to leave."

Bibi, flustered, just sat there. She reached for the pile of branches, pulled out twigs of tomatoes which were still green and smelled like summer.

"Who gave you the permission to do such a thing to my gardens?" She raised her voice as her daughter went on reaching for high branches, cutting and pulling, ignoring her mother. Masht Akbar stopped filling his sack with twigs.

"I thought you knew about this, Bibi," he said with astonishment, casting a piercing look at Golrokh, shaking his head. "You should've told me this was your doing. Poor woman, she worships this garden."

Who is this woman in my grandmother's house who dares to do whatever she wants as if she owns this house? Why won't Bibi ask her to leave? Why doesn't she chase her out of the house instead of sitting there and grieving?

"You should've waited till I was home. You ambushed the entire gardens. These poor, tongueless creatures." Bibi began to sob.

I helped her to her knees. I knew she was exhausted from work. In her room, she cried for her trees and I for my cucumbers.

At night, Golrokh called my name, demanding that I go to her. I refused and hid behind Bibi. She called for me a few more times. Again, I didn't respond. She marched into our room, grabbed my arm, and pulled me toward the door. "No! Let go of me!" I shrieked and held on to the doorframe, pushing against the wall with all my strength. "She's old enough to sleep by herself." Golrokh's voice echoed off the walls. She dragged me to her room.

In Golrokh's room, the boys sat on their bedrolls. They must have been awakened by my shouting for they looked at me with fearful eyes. Hossein stared at everyone quietly. Amir clung to his mother's legs. Rahim's body was curled into a big ball. I lay down on a bedroll next to Golrokh, pulling the sheet over my head, so she would not hear my sobbing. If only I could fall asleep. It was so quiet in this room, I could hear my brothers' breathing. I could hear them tossing and turning. There was no sound of late night playing from Bibi's radio. I wanted to be with Bibi, the way she always held me, caressing my hair, untangling my braids. I wanted to hear her voice telling me stories before I fell asleep. Stories from the Koran, about Josef the Beautiful, who was so handsome that the Empress Zoleikha lost her senses the moment her menservants brought him to her palace; how all the elite women of Egypt fell in love with his beautiful face the instant he entered the Grand Hall so that they cut their fingers with the knife instead of the apple in their hands. She told me all the love stories of the world, the story of Shirin and Farhad the Mountain-Breaker who carved a bridge through the Beesetoon Mountain with his bare hands. The more he suffered, the more he carved the stone, wishing for a glimpse of his beloved Shirin's face. I moped under the blanket.

"Stop the whining!" Ali barked.

"I want Bibi," I moaned.

Golrokh elbowed me, telling me to be quiet. I cried louder, "I want to go to Bibi." I sat up and hugged my knees.

"Lower your voice!" Ali warned again.

Mohammad crawled to me on his knees. He held my hand and offered to move my bedroll next to his, pleading with me to calm down. "I'll tell you a story, if you stop crying," he whispered in my ear. But I wanted Bibi, who was so far away from me. This was a strange place where I did not want to be. "Take me to Bibi then," I sulked.

"Mother, let her go to Bibi," he begged. "She's very frightened."

"Go back to sleep!" Ali shouted. "She has to learn how to obey her elders."

Where did these people come from? This woman who claims she's my mother. She's mean. Now that I suddenly have a mother, why can't I have a nice one? Like Soosan's mother, who braids her hair every morning before she goes to school, and sews her pleated skirts? If only Golrokh would leave Bibi and me to ourselves, just as we used to be.

The lights went off. The silver stream disappeared. Around me, the air smelled like naphthalene and cedar. I wished I was in Bibi's arms. She would have been telling me now the Imam Ali's stories, or the camel-man's tales. The man who lost his camel and searched for it in the high seven sand dunes, playing his flute all night because he couldn't fall sleep. He wandered about, walking through the desert, calling out to Imam Ali to help him overcome the cold night. Just the way Bibi prayed right at this hour, pleading for help from all the saints and the prophet Mohammad.

It must be very late, the time for the late-night programs, but Bibi's radio was quiet. My eyelids felt heavy. The darkness swallowed me.

A few days later, a big truck unloaded the mahogany walnut commodes, the colorful satin and velvet bedrolls and blankets, and Golrokh's other belongings.

Though she did not talk to me and I ignored her, Golrokh's eyes warned me that she was there to stay each time she looked at me. She was there to stay and I had to get used to her and the changes she demanded. I kept hoping that one day when I came home from school, they would all be gone, except Mohammad, who played with me and taught me karate, even though Bibi scolded him not to teach me to be like a boy. "Enough bully boys in this house. Let her be the girl she ought to be," she would say. If I ever broke my bones, she told him, she wouldn't have the money to take me to the hospital. In her room, she whispered that I should not kick in the air, and worried herself about some flower I might lose even though I had none.

"If you ever lose your flower, who's going to marry you when you grow up?"

Once they moved in permanently, Rahim and Mohammad began school at Ahmadi high school, both of them in the seventh grade. Hossein started third grade at the Rahmat's Boys school, adjacent to mine, and five-year-old Amir stayed home with Golrokh.

When the newcomers finally settled, once again the deafening noises of the construction workers began to fill the house. The brick-layers left, the plumbers showed up; the plumbers left, the electricians arrived, then the tile workers, the painters, the cabinet people, until the house was introduced to all professions of the world, like a new bride whose face was being made up especially for the bride-groom.

On the left-hand side of the courtyard, what had been the orange garden was filled with cement, flattened as the yard's surface. Now the foundation of a new kitchen, a bathroom, and an additional room was taking shape. Golrokh did not approve of the public bath and was determined to build a bathroom even before the kitchen.

Golrokh was the cleanest, the neatest, and the most organized person I have ever seen. She didn't get along with anyone who did not share or appreciate her distinctive trait. The chicken coop and the fresh-laid eggs were long gone; the chickens were cooked, roasted and eaten on platters of her steamed, buttery rice. Instead of the sound of the rooster in the morning, now I would wake up to Golrokh's banging tin pans and pots, and the whooshing noise of an *Abadan-e* broom—made from dried palm leaves—she brought with her from her Peninsula. She woke up early, right before sunrise, yet never did any morning prayers. Instead of the ablution ritual, she held the end of a long green hose, watered all the plants, the rose bushes she adored so much, and scoured the entire saffron-tiled courtyard where once the vegetable garden was. The tiles shone in the early sunrays like sparkling dots you just wanted to chase. Not to mention the fishpond which always sparkled crystal blue like a mir-ror for the sky. Then she went to the stores, bought the fresh-baked bread, the same morning-made *halim*—sweet porridge—and a jug full of boiled milk. She prepared a big breakfast *sofreh* in which one would always find red cherry or quince marmalade that she made herself, along with butter, thick cream, cheese, scrambled eggs and fruits of the season.

Golrokh had the painters paint all the bedrooms in soft pastel colors. With half of the gardens gone, and trees no longer moving wildly every which way, the courtyard seemed smaller, less intriguing, but charming. At night, the fluorescent lights reflected a powdery silver over the green waxy leaves. Divided into four rectangular small gardens, trees embraced the courtyard from all around. Against the wall and in the back, now, there were only rose bushes, night jasmine, white *nastaran*, and squirming *laleh abassies*. Next to them rose a brand new small vegetable garden. The mother *askari* grape-wines grew back again, creeping over a much reduced arbor, leaning against the wall towards the newly built room. I was glad that the persimmon tree, a few of the tangerine and orange trees, and the black grape vines were still there, shading the doorway all the way up to the front porch. The hot water, too, ran throughout the house. Most mornings, she carried big plastic containers of propane oil, filled the big tank and turned on the heater so the boys could shower with hot water. There were times that I would see her holding ten-liter containers in each hand, standing in the line in front of Neamat Nafti's oil-shack, the propane seller. She carried them herself to the house and kept them in the storage room.

Our house was transformed into as stylish a house as the neighbors'. Everywhere you looked, it was redone, except Bibi's room, untouched and unchanged. "The house is not enough to be tormented by you? Leave my room alone! This is how I like it," she'd argue with her daughter every time Golrokh came near her belongings. On the other hand, the corners of her room seemed to be disappearing bit by bit with the collection of newly made bedrolls, which Golrokh carefully stacked against the wall, for my brothers or any unexpected guests. There were days when I came home from school, impatient, because the smell of food coming from Golrokh's kitchen wafted down our lane. The smell of *ghormeh-sabsi*, chicken or lamb stew, and this newest smell, the smell of roasted fish she cooked so deliciously that even the neighbors talked about it. "She brought with her the sea, the smell of the harbor of Abadan," Bibi would say through a mouthful of grilled fish and cooked rice. "What beautiful fish, what cooking. Twenty years of living by the Gulf did her at least this much good."

Sometimes Golrokh sang a sad tune, a song she said the fishermen sang on their boats as they pitched their fishing nets into the deep emerald water, bringing to the shore their daily catch. At these moments, she was good to me. Her face became soft and her brown eyes smiled again. She told me to sit next to her and gave me a chunk of hot roasted white fish wrapped in the Lavash bread as she gathered my hair in a ponytail. Quietly, she murmured about how she missed Abadan and its harbor, how she used to go to the fish market to buy the just-caught fish of the day with skin fresh and smooth like unworn silk. "Too bad the fish in Shiraz are not as good and damn too expensive," she complained. "They keep them in ice, you know? They bring them from Bander-e Bushehr."

It was at times like these, when I listened to her soft voice that I wished she would remain like that eternally, even if she did not care to hug me. I would have held still forever so she could braid my hair if she would just tell me more stories like that, because a tiny voice in me wanted to burst out, calling her *Momon*.

# CHAPTER 28

Though it was the last month of winter, the *Esfand's* afternoon air was gentle and not too cold. Yavar the Cross-Eyed still pushed his ice cream cart, parked it under the big sycamore tree, waiting for the school bell to ring. *Mohammad should be here by now.* He said I was to wait for him outside at the last school bell. I ran the entire hallway and schoolyard until my breath grew ragged. At the entrance, I stretched my neck to the right, then to the left, looking for him. He impatiently looked to his new watch "I've been waiting more than fifteen minutes."

"I was looking for my pen. I think I lost it," I lied.

Well. Not exactly a lie. I did lose my pen, a few days ago. Ali brought it for me from Tehran. It was a special pen, it wrote in five colors. I had a feeling that Azar, the lice-head-girl, took it, but she pretended she had never seen such a thing. What really happened was that this morning Bibi made a big fuss over the glob of cherry marmalade I accidentally spilled on her Qashghaee rug, saying that an entire army of ants would soon swamp her room. I rushed out of the door, forgetting to take my notebooks to school. Miss Tabatabaee was not able to check my homework and the penmanship I had worked so hard on. So she forbade me to leave at dismissal and made me clean the blackboard with a wet sponge. I didn't tell Mohammad any of this. He, himself, was always good at whatever he did; he couldn't understand when I did something sloppy. He had such neat cursive writing, so pretty and within the lines, that it looked like a page of a book. He did most of the artistic scripts in various programs at his school and couldn't believe why, despite all the exercises

197

he'd given me, my penmanship still looked like a wiggling tail of a scorpion on the page. He finally gave up and went back to reading his own book, completely ignoring my bad practice. Most nights I went to bed and prayed that when I woke up in the morning my penmanship would be as pretty as his, so everyone would be pleased: my teacher, Mohammad, and me. And as if he was not precise enough, he had to get this digital watch to tell even the seconds. He played chess against the boys from another high school, came in first, and won the grand prize: this very watch.

He had more luck teaching me ping-pong and chess. He'd taught me chess with so many different moves that he expected me to do much better than our brothers. Usually, he became agitated if I took too long and couldn't decide on the right move, or if I stared at the figures. "In the name of the Prophet, concentrate," he'd chide me. "That's a bad move. You don't have to be Einstein to see that. It's as easy as drinking a glass of water. There, that's the move you should do," he'd say, moving my queen. "Never ever lose your queen! Anything, but the queen," he lectured. On the other hand, when I made a right move, he'd get excited. "Ahhaaa! Now you're tuning in. That's it. Good move! Pay attention. You have to attack his king from all around. You surround him with your queen, the bishop, the rook, and the knight. There. Checkmate! You defeated your rival." This is how he taught me his secret: winning in only five moves.

"Hurry up then, before the library closes," he said.

I couldn't wait to go inside the famous City Library where he was a member of the Youth Chess Club. Most of the time, he brought me books; this time, he promised that he'd show me all the books in the world and that I could have my own library card.

Together, we walked a few blocks to the main street and took a taxi to Mossadegh Square. Across the street, the Prince Valiahd City Library sat in the middle of a park surrounded by short trimmed green hedges and colorful gardens. The *atlasi* flowers perfumed the air and the grass looked a damp luscious green. A cool, shady mosaic-tiled pathway led us to a full-size, double-door glass entrance and to a lofty rom where people sat on wooden benches or in leather chairs. We walked up to the front desk. A woman with saucer-sized-orange-framed glasses sat behind the desk, going through open books and a

stack of magazines before her. The beautiful face of a woman, holding her index finger to her lips, stared at me from a picture on the
wall. *Silence* was written underneath the picture.

"*Salam*," Mohammad greeted the woman in a quiet voice. "This
is my sister," he nodded at me. "I'd like to sign her up at the library
so she can check out books herself."

The librarian brought her glasses to the tip of her nose. I stood on
my toes and peeked from behind the polished wooden counter so I
could see her better.

"Certainly," she said, facing Mohammad. "You should be proud
of having such a smart brother, young lady," she said, smiling.

I squeezed Mohammad's hand.

"What grade is she?" the woman asked.

"Second. But she can read very well."

She asked my name and address, and requested a picture. Mohammad answered all her questions and handed her a picture which I
did not like. It was my last year's school picture with that thick ugly
white plastic collar, taken before the school year ended. But that was
the only picture I had that was good for a library card.

"All right then, I'll show you the children's section," said the
librarian, smiling and handing me my new card.

I followed her.

Mohammad told me that I should stay in that section, busy myself
with any books I liked. He'd meet me back there in exactly an hour.
Then he headed for another section across the hallway where a sign
said "Discovery & Science."

From the joy of being surrounded by so many storybooks with
colorful illustrations, I was nearly bursting out of my skin. I held the
card with my picture on it to my chest and sat down right there on
the purple-carpeted floor, staring at the rows of tall wooden shelves
filled with books. All those books!

When Mohammad came back, a stack of books in his arms, he
examined the pile of books I had heaped before me. "*Waay*," he said,
"this is a good one, I read it a long time ago . . . you should take this
one . . . look here, this is the best . . . now, that's a lot of adventure
in there." On the floor, almost an entire shelf was out before me,
because I couldn't make up my mind which five ones to pick. "I'll

bring you every week so you can pick as many books as you like. We just have to save our money for the taxi-fare."

On the way out, he bought us a *Paak* chocolate-covered, vanilla ice cream bar from a vendor. We sat on the tiled steps in front of the entrance, eating the delicious treat. I put my books down on the step so the ice cream wouldn't stain the covers.

"You're my best brother," I said to Mohammad.

"I know that, *koochooloo*."

And I knew then that I did not need to be afraid of anything as long as I had my big brother by my side.

# CHAPTER 29

We had a new tenant, a tall bony Sergeant Hamid from the remote town of Sarvestan, who acted as if he was from the Capitol City and put on a Tehran-e accent, trying to be chic and city-like. He dabbed on so much aftershave that even when Golrokh washed his army shirts with Tide detergent and hung them on the laundry line, the courtyard was still saturated with this brawny spicy scent. He rented the small room next to Bibi's, which Golrokh kept impeccably clean. She washed the windows so often that when the sun beamed down through the branches of the persimmon and orange trees, a rainbow of colors rose from the small Kerman rug, reflected over the wall, danced on the ceiling and fell back to the cot next to the window. She polished his army boots, changed his bed sheets, swept the floor, and dusted all the shelves, because Sergeant Hamid, like herself, had no tolerance for untidiness and dirty places. Bibi said that Golrokh has found her dust-free soul mate.

It was a lazy, late afternoon. Golrokh and Sergeant Hamid entered the courtyard, carrying several square boxes. Cautiously, they carried the mysterious boxes to the guestroom and placed them on a table. Hamid cut the borders gently with a sharp kitchen knife that Golrokh handed him. A big chestnut-colored wooden cabinet with sliding doors appeared like magic. He attached four long legs to the bottom and positioned it in the corner of the room. Then he slid the door open and knocked on a grayish-greenish glass screen with the tips of his fingers.

"It's the peep-show." Rahim and Mohammad clapped their hands. "Just like the one we saw at Uncle Engineer's house."

"I'll be damned!" Bibi said, looking suspiciously at the gray glass screen. "Is this the magic box? *Allah-o-Akbar.*" She smacked the back of her hand.

"It's called television," Sergeant Hamid corrected Bibi mockingly. "If you pay attention, you'll see people talking."

We sat cross-legged in front of the magic box and waited impatiently while he fastened a long wire to the back of the box, dipping the other end into a bowl of water. From one of the boxes he took out a long rod and attached it to a rectangular rake-shaped tool he called the antenna. He went up to the rooftop and mounted the antenna on the roof blockade. He dropped another long wire down to the window and asked Rahim to watch the screen for a signal.

Back in the room, he fooled around with knobs and pushed a button. Millions of gray and white dots marched across the screen. Again, he ran up to the rooftop and rotated the antenna. *Fishhh . . . shhh . . . tttttttt . . .* filled the room; a black-and-white twin-lion symbol came on.

"The program hasn't started yet." The Sergeant looked at his watch. "In a few minutes."

"Ladies and Gentlemen!" A husky voice sounded in the air, followed by a clean, handsome man dressed in a black suit and tie. "Good evening. This is Iran, the national broadcast of Jam-e-Jam. With warm *salams* we present to you tonight's programs."

"That's it. I got it," Sergeant Hamid said excitedly. "Now, everyone be quiet. Just watch!"

After the announcement, the national anthem began. Sergeant Hamid made us stand up and salute the screen.

It was magic. Just like Uncle Kalimi's peep-show-box he brought to the alley and for two *rials* let us peek into a hole and watch the pictures of different places in the world. Bibi brought her scarf closer to her face to cover her hair from the eye of the strange man on the screen. "Where on earth is it safe any more? You can't even be uncovered in the privacy of your own home," she said.

"Silly woman," Sergeant Hamid ridiculed her. "He won't see you. This has been filmed in a studio."

But to be on the safe side, Bibi went to the screen and touched it carefully. "Is it *cimmema*? Like the one Ali used to have in Abadan?

This is glass, though. What's happened to the white curtain? *Allah-o-Akbar.* What wonders! It's the end of the world. What else would the two-legged man not invent?"

From that day on, my brothers and I sat impatiently in front of our new black-and-white Belair TV screen minutes before five o'clock in the afternoon when the programs would start. And we became glued to the screen until the last program ended on the only channel at ten p.m.

Every afternoon, at first, Mr. Oskooie delivered half an hour of national and local news. Then the children's programs began, cartoons and puppet shows, followed by silent movies with Charlie Chaplin and Harold Lloyd. At the end were the night series like *The Wild Wild West, The Farm of Chaparral* and other movies about horses and half-naked, reckless, red-skin Indians who were killing and scalping the handsome, blond, blue-eyed Americans everyone adored so much.

Soon, the news reached our near and distant neighbors. One by one, adults and children came to our house to witness the magic box with their very own eyes. Some of them even brought blankets and a pot of cooked dinner and made a picnic right in our courtyard. Mother passed around tray after tray of cups of hot tea and offered everyone lime punch as if it were the mourning month of *Muharram* when at night everyone gathered at the local mosque and listened to Mullah Asghar preach about Imam Hossein's battle in the desert of Karbala. Bibi said, "In God's safeguard, you couldn't gather this many people in any commemoration even if they were given free lunch and dinner." She feared that Mullah Asghar might lose his crowd to our American Belair TV and our house would be a damned place where no angels ever would come again.

Night after night, Mother added another plastic straw-mat so everyone who came to the house would have a place to sit. Children were everywhere; the older ones usually sat at the edge of the fishpond or on the edge of the short wall surrounding the courtyard. Their feet dangling high above, they sniggered and repeated word for word what the actors said or predicted the next scene, "And now, he'll punch the bad guy. You'll see. He'll kick his butt."

"Shhhh!" yelled one mother.

"Watch your language!" said another.

More people kept coming until they began to get on Sergeant Hamid's nerves. He told Mother not to open the door to anyone, "This is not a private residence any more! It's worse than an African village." He complained that he had no privacy and could no longer enjoy the TV when everyone talked. Mother tried to somehow get the message across to the uninvited guests by cutting down on the lime punch. When they ignored her hints, she diluted the tea with too much hot water. Then she cut the offerings all at once, closed the house door before five o'clock, and told everyone that the TV was broken.

Thanks to our brand-new Belair TV, I had many friends to play with. Suddenly, all the alley kids were actors. Someone was the bad guy. Another one was the good guy. No more playing skip-rope and five-pebble games for me. Who wanted to do that when we could play sheriff and arrest the robbers who attacked trains and coaches? At midday rest time, no one napped any more. Instead, my brothers and I reddened our faces with Mercurochrome, chased our rooster, and plucked its longest, colorful feathers to accentuate our Indian features. Just like the mean redskin Indians, we ran wild in the alleys, chasing the beautiful blond Americans, the good guys, shouting: "Heehaw, heehaw."

We mimicked the movie stars' accents, the way they walked or posed. Everyone had a favorite star. Ali liked John Wayne, and Rahim pretended he was Kirk Douglas because he had the same chin-dimple. Mohammad favored Robert Redford. And I just couldn't get enough of Immanuel of Chaparral. I loved the sound of his name. *Immmmanuel*. And I liked the way Elizabeth called him, "Oh my darling Immanuel."

Before the next winter, another channel was added and an additional two-hours of programs during the midday rest time. The neighbor kids kept asking me about the new series that had just started: *Peyton Place*, *The Waltons*, *The Little House on The Prairie*. I got tired of Immanuel and traded him for John Boy who looked like Mohammad and wanted to become a writer. Even Bibi watched this show with me. I told her when I grew up, I wanted to have a family like Laura Ingles' family. Rahim and Mohammad were hooked on the *Adventures of Huckleberry Finn* and *Tom Sawyer*. Rahim promised me that when he grew up, he'd take me to America so we could water-raft on the Mississippi River just like Huckleberry Finn. Bibi protested that he should bite his tongue and not fill my head with such dreams. "You won't take her to any *Michipichi* place, not while I'm alive."

We laughed so hard our eyes watered. "Not *Michipichi*. Mississippi." Rahim tried to teach Bibi how to pronounce the name of the American river. He brought his atlas and showed her where America was, and where the Mississippi River ran, and pointed to a mass of blue on the bottom. "That's the Pacific Ocean." My brothers and I lay on our stomachs before our TV screen and dreamt of beautiful America. "Some day I will take you to America," Rahim promised again.

"And we will swim in the Pacific Ocean," I sighed.

# CHAPTER 30

A long time ago, even before I started the first grade, Bibi made me a chador and taught me how to wear it and how to stand at a right angle, facing in the direction of the holy House of God in Mecca and recite *namaz*, the five-times-daily essential prayers. I had not worn the chador for some time because it was now up to my knees. I was not quite nine years old yet, the required age for a Muslim girl to wear a headscarf. But Bibi was determined that I was ready for the ritual purification of body and soul. In order to do just that, she said I needed a new chador that I would wear at the *Rouseh* sermons in the neighbor's houses, where women arranged a gathering, reciting verses of the Koran and prayer books. Though the sermons were held at all times, especially on Thursday evenings, they were mainly popular during the two mourning months of Moharam and Safar. The women would hire a female elegy preacher to come and make them cry in commemoration of the third Imam, Hossein, who was martyred over fourteen hundred years ago.

From one of the fabric chambers at Bazaar Vakil, Bibi bought me a full piece of white fabric with a pattern of tiny purple flowers. In a silver tray, she laid the folded fabric, a china saucer filled with almond sugarplums, a bowl of water with floating green leaves, a small holy Koran, and a brand new, never-folded note of five tumans. Together we went to *Momon* Paymaneh the Seamstress.

"May your hands be saved from any pain," Bibi greeted the seamstress. "I have brought my child for her first prayer chador."

The seamstress asked me to stand on a stool in front of her. She threw the fabric over my head and measured the two bottom sides so the chador would have an even hem. The moment the seamstress set the sharp scissors to the fabric, asking Bibi's permission to cut, Bibi let out a muffled cry. "My bunch of flowers, my daughter, is growing up."

"*Mobarak, mobarak,*" congratulated the seamstress.

Bibi filled her fist with white sugarplums and threw them over my head. "This is a blessed day, *babam,*" she said, holding my face in her hands, placing kisses on my forehead. "From this day, you're invited like a grownup to face the holy House of God and talk to Him, the only creator of the universe."

I had accompanied Bibi to the *Rouseh* sermons many times before that day. If the sermons were held in the farther alleys, she'd ask me to walk with her so I could warn her of those not-so-visible rocks in her way or the mud-holes which sprang out like wild mushrooms here and there even after a light rain. Once, crossing the street, she got hit by a careless bicyclist. She didn't leave the house for ten days, petrified that she was going blind and would be housebound like a wretched cripple. Since she no longer worked, she believed more and more that she ought to spend her time praying and listening to Karbalaee Fatemeh, the Lady Preacher, who got invited left and right to the houses of affluent women in the neighborhood. Mother was in awe how someone could earn a living making women wail, whereas someone like herself had to dog-run from dawn to dusk to make one tenth of what that woman made. The Lady Preacher drank golden-trimmed delicate glass after glass of sweetened cardamom-laced hot tea offered to her by the ready-to-wed girls who carried gracefully the trays of glasses, presenting themselves to the mothers and sisters of any eligible suitor looking for a future bride.

In *Rouseh*, women chatted about their husbands, housework, the never-ending nagging of the mother-in-law; they asked each other for the recipes of that special dessert at last Friday's festivity; they bragged about the price of their gold bangles or the jewelry just pur-chased at the Gold Bazaar. They wanted to know which face-maker tended to Parivash Khanoom, the neighborhood's midwife, that her face was so hairless and her eyebrows so perfectly arched.

We smaller girls were not allowed to carry the trays of glasses brimming with hot tea or cold lemonade to the women. Our job was to organize the visitors' shoes in the courtyard or in front of the host-ess's parlor since no shoes are allowed inside the living area of one's house.

That year, the mourning months of Moharam and Safar began even before summer ended. At least one house in each alley hung a black or green flag to invite visitors to come and purify their souls by listening to the preaching. *Rouseh* was arranged only in the houses, the women's territory. Men were to leave the house before the com-memoration began. They usually attended the mosque's gatherings or went to the *tekyehs*, the temporary tents and stands decorated with colorful tapestries, religious motifs, and fanciful drawings of the saints and their battles.

The difference between the sermons was that *Rouseh* was held dur-ing the day, whle *tekyeh* took place at night when men were off work and mourned in their black shirts to show their respect for the mar-tyred Imam. They, too, hired a Friday Preacher or a man who pos-sessed a deep, sorrowful voice to recite the commemoration through a loudspeaker. Women and children were allowed to attend *tekyeh* only in a separate section where they could listen to the sermons and watch the men mourn.

In the months of mourning, wherever you set foot, on the streets, at the houses, in front of the stores, and in the mosques, people gave away free lemonade, sweetened Egyptian willow extract water, and sweet yellow pudding, in the hope that the saints would grant their *nazr*, an urgent wish. Music and celebrations were frowned upon, and weddings had to be postponed until after the months of mourning.

Handing me my brand-new chador, Bibi required me to go along to *Rouseh*. There, she asked me to sit right next to the Lady Preacher and recite my *namaz* prayers before her, so she could correct my ritu-als. In the third grade, Arabic was added to our mandatory curricu-lum, only one hour a week, even shorter than the two-hour sports class. Bibi wanted me to read out loud the verses of the holy Koran in front of the alley's women now that I also knew how to read in Ara-bic, even though I could barely write a sentence. That very day of our visit, the Lady Preacher suggested that Bibi have me start wear-ing a scarf to school.

I knew this wouldn't happen. No scarf or chador was allowed in school, not even if you were a fifth-grader, or even if it was the holy month of fasting, Ramadan, or the mourning days on which the Imams and saints rose up to heaven. Anyway, the school was closed on these special days. Once, in the school yard, Principal Sadati took the *magnaeh*, a long tent-like head-covering, off a girl's head. "If you want to be religious, go to a mosque or stay at home or do it somewhere else," she yelled at the trembling girl. "*This* is a school. You're here to learn and become a modern, educated young lady. You *must* follow the school's rules!"

Some girls, whose parents wouldn't allow them to go to school without a head covering, removed their scarves before they reached the school property. When I told that to Bibi, she did not seem surprised. She told me stories about the Shah's father, the Great Reza Shah, who did the same thing. "When he, supposedly, freed the women from chador, *Kashf-e-Hedjab* he called it," Bibi mocked, "I myself couldn't leave the house for many months. I was not even twenty years old then and was pretty much new to the city from my village. I feared that the Reza Shah's soldiers would tear off my headscarf, and I would lose face in my neighborhood." Bibi lowered her voice. "It was right after the big war. I remember it as if it were yesterday. When the English brought him into power, Reza, the plain bully soldier, all of a sudden became first Reza Khan and then Reza Shah. He changed his name to the ancient Persian script, *Pahlavi*, and ordered all the women in the entire country not to wear their black chadors and their hedjabs in public. He said women ought to cut their hair short, put on a small hat, and wear a skirt-suit like the *farangi* women. He even forced the men to give up their long robes and turbans, which were the custom those days, and to wear only suits and hats. God knows how many yards of fabric they brought into the country from England. Not to mention their tailors. What seamstress knew those days how to make a *farangi* suit? Well. The English didn't only make money off this country's oil, they even filled their pockets with the money they made over the new suits, with the stolen cotton from India or God knows where. So, if anyone didn't obey the new rules, Reza Shah's soldiers would cut their garments with scissors and rip them open right on the spot."

Not that it was any of her business, Bibi muttered, she hated the black chador. After all, in her village, no one covered themselves. "We were all related, cousin of that cousin and so and so. But in the city if you were a young widow, people would talk behind your back and ruin a good woman's reputation for no reason. With all that," she looked thoughtful, "the man is gone, may he be in heaven like the rest of the slaves of God, but who in his right mind would want to do such a thing to the women in a Muslim country by force, I'd like to know? Religious men were hiding their wives and daughters in their closets. The *Ulama*, the clergy, preached over their pulpits and called Reza Shah's order an act of *kofr*, blasphemy and a satanic sin. They raised objections against him, took sanctuary in the mosques for many months, and summoned all good Muslims to take to the streets before the world came to an end and the county was drowned in a sea of sins. Now, look around! Eventually all young city women went to the mandatory schools. They began wearing uniforms and working shoulder to shoulder with men. Only God knows people's true intentions. Some said that the man thought, God forbid me for saying that," Bibi looked up into the sky and bit between her index finger and her thumb, "he thought that religion kept people in ignorance. Some said that he had become an infidel and lost his faith."

In school, we learned that the Great Reza Shah was a brave patriot and loved his country above everything. We celebrated his birthday, and the entire school left the classrooms to gather in the big auditorium, and watch a film about his life. Our teachers told us that he was a courageous man who wanted only good for his people. He wanted a modern Iran, a free and proud country. In our history book, we read that he freed our people from the Arab's ignorance and the superstitious beliefs they had imposed upon us for centuries, and that he gave us back our true Aryan and Iranian heritage. Showing us a repeat movie, our teachers also taught us that the Reza Shah had introduced our country to new inventions like electricity, locomotives, railroads, running water, and all the modern things, and that he had established schools and hospitals and had educated women throughout the entire country.

I told Bibi all that I had learned in school. She nodded her head and said, "So, I guess he's done a good thing. After all, in a way, he did stand up to the English and the Russians." Lowering her voice, she said, "I don't know if they teach you this too in school, but the English, I tell you this much, after all that topsy-turvy, they banished him, just like that," Bibi snapped her fingers, "to go and live in some faraway country I don't know its name."

# CHAPTER 31

In our house, one could always know the seasons by Mother's jams and preserves, like now that it was fall, the season of quince. And the fruit peddlers knew that when they knocked at our door, they need not look farther in the alleys to find a better customer for most of their fruit than Mother, better than selling a few kilos here and there to the other neighborhood women.

She had a fascination with modern home appliances. As soon as we saw something advertised on TV, the next thing we knew, that item would appear magically in our house. Without Bibi's consent, she'd sold all the copper pots that Bibi had bought several years ago.

I remember the day Bibi bought the pots. We went to the holy Shrine of Shah-e-Cheragh. At the entrance, Bibi bought a stack of white wax-candles from the courtyard's vendors; she even gave me one to light. Bibi knelt in front of that splendid candelabra, splashed some rose-water onto my face and hers too, and pleaded with the dead Imam, "Salam, my Saint, King of Light, dear brother of Shahid Imam Reza. Bless your pure soul for giving me the strength to finish the house before I was too old to see the fruit of my hard work!" She cried with joy. "You have granted my wish. It is time for me to deliver my promise and pay my debt of *nazr*."

Then she took me to the Gold Bazaar at the crossroads of Ahmadi Street. She sold whatever gold earrings and bangles she had to one of the merchants. From there we went straight to the Bazaar Vakil. In the copper chamber, over the deafening sound of sweaty workers hammering large pans and pots, she bargained with a man in a white undershirt and bought several large pots. She bought them to lend them to the neighbors whenever they had a nazr of *Sofreh*, like Marmar's mother, who borrowed the largest pot for their New Year's *Samanoo*, the sweet wheat-extract pudding.

The pots were so huge that if three more girls and I hid in them no one could've guessed that we were in there. And since they were copper and very heavy, Masht Akbar the Gardener had to bring his wheelbarrow; with the help of two other men, to carry the pots to this house. People usually returned them with a bag of sweet hard honey candies to show their gratitude and blessing. Bibi never accepted any money from the people; it was her *nazr*.

Mother sold the pots one by one to Uncle Kalimi when Bibi wasn't home. With the money she got for them, she bought new light-weight pans and pots she saw advertised on TV. Bibi cried when she found out . . . "You have no respect for the saints. No faith," she told Mother, who just shrugged. "They take up too much room, they're old-fashioned and too heavy. People use them only a few times a year, and amyway, I bought some of them myself."

Mother worked, but I didn't know what exactly she did or where. She was the only woman in our neighborhood who worked, except for *Momon* Paymaneh the Seamstress and Tahereh Khanoom who helped her husband in his grocery store. Even at school, I didn't know any girls whose mothers worked. She would leave the house early in the morning, even before I left for school. Most days she didn't return until late in the afternoon, carrying bags full of groceries she'd bought from the market. Then, she'd lie down on her back in the front drawing room, closing her eyes for a while before she'd go to the kitchen to prepare our dinner and lunch for the next day. I'd watch her at these moments. Her face had lost the color it had in the morning, and her hands looked wrinkled and swollen. "Where does she go, Bibi?" I asked her once. "Oh, dear. She goes to work," Bibi sighed without any more explanation, brushing off my curiosity.

Now, Bibi was talking to Mother. Her voice was too low; I couldn't hear what she was saying. The door to Mohammad's room was ajar. *Maybe I should go to his room and look at his English books.* He had gone to Tehran to attend the National Youth Chess Tournament. He had become first in the entire province and now he was competing nationally in the final tournament in the presence of the Valiahd,

Prince Reza. I couldn't wait for him to come back and tell me all
about his trip. How exciting, to play in the presence of Prince Reza!
If he won, he might even go to the Shah's Palace. And he'd promised
to buy me a set of ping-pong rackets just for myself as soon as he
came home.

Mother paced around the fishpond. Suddenly, her voice rose. She
walked up to Bibi. "You don't ever understand, do you? You're not
listening to me!" Bibi shook her head. *What are they talking about?*
*Why is Bibi rubbing her chin?* She did this gesture only when she
was agitated. Mother's face stiffened again, losing its softness. Bibi
noticed me, but didn't stop talking. "Why don't you go and work in
the sour-pickle factory?" she asked in a much lower voice. "It's close
to home and you don't need to drive all the way to the other side of
the town to earn a morsel of food."

"You want me to go and chop eggplants for thirty tumans a day,
just because it's close by?" Mother shook her head. "That's petty
money, with all these children I have to feed and clothe." She pointed
to me. "There are expenses sticking out at me from every corner of
this house. I have orphans. They're school kids, you know. I'd rather
work hard to earn more money than send my children to school barefoot or in rags."

Bibi got to her feet, but Mother kept on. "It's no shame to work
and make a living using your own arms. They give good money.
They like my cooking; they pay me one hundred tumans a day." Her
voice rose again. "You know what that means? I can do lots of things
with it. Not even a woman whose man has a one-kilo-ball hanging in
his underpants can dream of this kind of money. I don't have a man,
that's true. But I'm not going to wait for one to come and knock on
this door to better my life," she shouted at Bibi.

"It's not a shame, dear." Bibi said. "I just meant it in a good way.
The walls have eyes, and the eyes can see." Bibi glanced at me. "I
just said that people may badmouth you behind your back. You're
young. You could still get married. I wasted my entire life in this factory and that factory. Why should you? If they hear . . . you work. . .
you might not have a suitor."

"Ah! Shut up! Suitors my ass! What do you think I have been
doing all these years, huh?" Mother sniffled. "Since that day you

sent me, supposedly, to my husband's house. That day, I became a housekeeper. Remember? I was nine years old. Just take a good look at that girl! See her body, how small she is? Imagine me sending your darling granddaughter to the husband's house instead of school."

I wanted to run back to the gues troom. I wished I were at school. I wished Mohammad were here. I knew the house couldn't stay quiet long. Somebody had to yell. Someone, always, had to cry. This time it was Mother.

"Why do you keep sprinkling salt on my wounds?" Bibi moaned. "It was another time. I was ignorant myself. A lone woman with no support."

"Well. I'm just reminding you, and I will remind you for the rest of your life that I was that small when I became a laborer, only I wasn't being paid."

Mother cried hard. The first time I ever saw her cry. And how bitterly she cried. I felt a lump in my throat. My eyes burned. I wished I could go to her, but I couldn't move. Bibi was silent.

"When I was in Abadan," Mother sobbed, her words chopped, "they called me so-and-so daughter-in-law. The poor, pitiable daughter-in-law. Goly, do this; Goly, do that. I was running an entire clan. None of what I'm doing now is new to me. So what do I care what people might think of a working widow? Shame on them! Let's have the neighbors talk behind my back. Let's have them say that I'm a laborer. It's better than starving these kids. They deserve to have all the good things, like the ones with a father. I don't want them to grow up with anything less than the kids at school. After all, a mother should have dignity."

# CHAPTER 32

By the sound of the uproar of the women outside in the alley, I could definitely tell that this was Propane Day. Even though the propane-cylinder driver was a little more sympathetic than the Pepsi Cola driver, yet he too would arrive, stopping right in the middle of the street, honking for the women to come and exchange their empty propane cylinders. This one, at least, was obliging and did something more; he showed the women, who came huffing and puffing, how to hold the grip and drag the cylinders on the soft side of the asphalt, a much harder task than pushing a crate of Pepsi Cola with the tip of one's shoe. I never dared to touch any of the cylinders, empty or filled. Luckily, Mother was home; unlike me, she was very strong.

She was dragging the twenty-kilo cylinder into the courtyard when Mohammad walked in behind her. He put down the books in his hand, "Let me help you, Mother," he said, reaching for the cylinder. "This is absurd!" he added, shaking his head. "Hard to believe that our country is the number one nation in the production of natural gas in the entire world, but there are no gas pipes in any houses for heating!"

Ali, who was standing near the fishpond, darted toward Mohammad and slapped him on the back of his head. "This kind of giant-farting talk is none of your business," he scolded. "Do you want to blow up your head for saying things like that? Don't you know this sort of talk is against the Shah?"

Mohammad, taken off guard, looked flabbergasted. Without saying a word, he went to his adapted corner-room and closed the door.

"You don't extend a helping hand yourself, yet you have to strike the poor boy who just came home, hungry and thirsty, after a long day of work," protested Mother. "He speaks the truth. Where? Where do you see natural gas burning in any houses around here? Places in Uptown yes, but not in our quarter."

"You talk nonsense too?" Ali stepped forward. "Instead of scaring him off from this kind of talk, you're encouraging him? Do you want him to lose his head? He's not fifteen yet, but, already has a money-making job, more than any boy his age. Do you want his future to be ruined?" He shook his head and went back to the parlor.

I went to Mohammad's room. He was lying on his back, his eyes closed. "Why is what you said against the Shah?" I asked quietly.

"I'm tired. I don't want to talk about it now," he said as he stood up.

"Mother wants you to come and have dinner. Would you rather have your dinner here? I'll bring it to you."

"It's all right. I'll be coming out in a minute."

Mohammad was the only one who dared talk back to Ali.

Every time Ali came home from his week-long absence or just a day trip, the house suddenly turned into a mute beehive. Everyone got to work on something, read a book, rechecked homework, completed unfinished artwork. Ever since he had started working on the passenger bus, Ali had been acting more and more peculiar. Returning home with his coat hanging over his shoulders and his sleeves dangling around his arms, he behaved as if he was a *Johel*, a tough guy. He wore a black hat, folded the back of his shoes inward, and clutched a red *Yazdi* handkerchief in his hand. One thing was sure, Bibi said, he did not have even a bit of Ebrahim's meekness, a brother only a year younger than he.

Good thing Ebrahim was home; in case things were to get ugly he could guard Mohammad, since he was the one who usually came between the boys, calming them down whenever they got into one of their bloody fistfights. Only eighteen years of age, he already managed Masht Kazim's welding workshop. At midday rest time, Mother usually prepared a bowl of cut, raw potatoes soaked in chilled water so that he could rub his eyes with them to soothe the burning from the welding sparks. No wonder Bibi called him a hard-working, tongueless lamb. When his eyes were not bothering him, he'd poke his head into *Sports* magazine crammed with soccer-match pictures. Since he was a member of the Persepolis City team, most evenings he rushed to soccer practice. Mother warned him that he'd shrink even shorter if he kept squandering all his energy playing soccer instead of resting his aching back. But everyone knew that his practice, especially his Friday soccer match, was virtually a holy day to him.

In the parlor, Mother was busy preparing the dinner *sofreh*. Leaning against a few cushions, Ali already had his head in the fold of the newspaper in his hands, reading an article to himself. Noticing Mohammad entering the parlor, he looked up and said in a voice much softer than before, "He's a good Shah, a clever one. He does a lot for the country. Progress is everywhere. He's not like his father who came and overnight took the scarves from the women's head. This Shah does things differently. He goes to visit the Shrine of Imam Reza in Mashhad. He visits the House of God——."

"Bunch of formalities," Mohammad interrupted him, "all foolish acting. Besides, everyone should benefit from progress, not only a certain class, not just the rich in the wealthy neighborhoods. What he's building is a mirage. Things look good on the surface, but let's dig a bit deeper, let's scratch the surface, let's stop the stage acting and step out of the shadows."

"That's exactly the point," Ali said. "That's why he's a smart shah. He's supposed to act. To make everyone believe that he's a faithful man who respects the tradition, and wink at the super powers that he's pro-West and reform."

"But that's not how it supposed to be," Mohammad cut him short again. "His job is not to please the West or any foreign super power, but to serve the citizens of his own country. A king, and a just king at that, if there is such thing as a just king, should only feel obligated to his own people."

"It's easy for you to say," Ali said. "It's thanks to those super powers that he's still in power. They're the ones behind him; he has to, must do, what he's doing. . . ."

"It's always been like that," Mother intervened nervously, worried that her two sons would snap at each other again, "but there's always someone who'll disagree with what the boss of a country does, king or no king." She said to Mohammad, "What would you want to eat for dinner, dear? I made *Ghorme Sabzi*, the herb stew. It's not for us to criticize the ones on top. The *Ulama*, for example, no one can really speculate if they're for the king or against him." She asked Bibi, "Do you remember when Mossadegh was the Prime Minister? What the Mullahs did to him?"

"Don't I remember?" Bibi said. "It doesn't seem like it was twenty something years ago. The first time I ever set foot in Abadan. It was 1953. Ali could barely walk. He was a very heavy boy, I'll tell you. It was all because of the British. One morning people took to the street and cheered Mossadegh, they shouted Long live Mossadegh! That same afternoon, a bunch of thugs led by Karim the Brainless ran down the streets, shouting Death to Mossadegh! The Shah left Iran. But the blue-eyed *farangi* brought him back again. Next thing we knew, we heard him giving speeches on the radio, saying that he only went for a short *farang* vacation."

"You mean our shah, Bibi. Mohammad Reza Shah?" I asked, thinking she'd mistaken him for his father, Reza Shah.

"No, dear, our shah."

"Because Prime Minister Mossadegh demanded nationalizing the oil industry," Mohammad said. "He wanted a people-governed, democratic Iran, independent from any foreign powers, he did not want another monarch."

"Your mouth still smells of your mother's milk," Ali said angrily this time. "Why do you have to talk like that? The country needs a king. It has always been like that. Read our history. This is a land of monarchs."

"Don't browbeat the boy," Bibi scolded Ali. "And let us talk. I have worn a few more shirts in my life than you." She sighed. "Speaking of Mossadegh, well, he was not very fond of the shah or his father, Reza Khan; the English made him a shah, not the people," said Bibi. "You are all too young to remember any of it; none of you was even born yet, for that matter. Let me tell you something. I know I'm not an educated woman, but I lived in that time. Under Reza Khan, Mossadegh was an important senator in the *Majlis* parliament; and when Reza Khan wanted to be crowned, Mossadegh was reluctant to support him, let alone give him his vote in becoming the Shah of Iran.

And of course, Reza Khan never forgot that; when he became the Shah, he forced Mossadegh to live in exile for some years. I don't remember how many painful years. Now, our Shah, like father like son, he never liked Mossadegh and was afraid of him. I remember how we would hear those days that he sat right there on the floor of the *Majlis* the entire day, demanding the Shah change his policy with the English. Instead, he ended up being confined to his house. Ah, how he fasted for days; how he said that people were better off to pour the country's oil into the sea rather than give it dirt cheap to the British. It was such a hurly-burly time. The *Ulama*, too, were angry with the Shah. At least for a while."

"We lived in Braym then," Mother added, "in the Engineers' housing section. Uncle Engineer would come home every night with different news. I was very young then, didn't know anything about this world, but those were days that everybody in the house wouldn't stop talking politics, because all the relatives worked in the oil refinery, and of course the entire quarter where we lived."

"God knows, all our problems are because of that damn oil refinery," Bibi said bitterly. "I remember everyone, all the neighbors telling me your daughter lives in Abadan, the city of oil. They'd say to me, you never know, maybe Golrokh is sitting on one of those lucky wells and is a rich woman now. It was those times that I kept writing letter after letter to Abadan to go visit your *Momon*. I was crying for her and the women were telling me why worry, you sent your daughter somewhere where people sweep money in the streets instead of dead leaves. And when I went to Abadan, instead of dead leaves I just saw English and their servant Indians, some of them in turbans, some of them in shorts like schoolboys. What money? What black gold was my daughter sitting on? Sometimes you didn't dare walk in the street because of all that hurly-burly. And when I'd return from my visit to Abadan, the neighbors would all come, wanting to know if it was true that you could dig a shovel in dirt and oil would gush out."

"Ya, the country sits on a sea of oil," said Mohammad, "but thanks to the English and foreign powers, Iranians themselves had no control over their own assets, neither do they have any now."

"Part of the problem was the very Mullahs' meddling," Ali said. "They played Mossadegh against the Shah and vise versa. They allowed foreigners to have control here. An intelligent person ought to ask what a Mullah really knows about politics? Ever since we remember, they preached at the mosques or read prayers or recited the Koran for the dead in the graveyard. It's not like they went to the university and became economists and historians so they would know about politics. They went to religion school and ministry in Qom, in the name of the Prophet."

"If it was so, it was because the Shah made them powerless, stifled them," Mohammad retorted. "Not only them, he made every conscientious, religious person into a prayer machine, not an active, outspoken citizen who could have a say about the wrongdoing of the government. The problem with you is that you have no idea how people are being prosecuted as you and I are speaking right now. Since Mossadegh was pushed out, the Shah has been repressing and banishing dissidents, letting a few agreeable Mullahs run the show. And this is exactly the kind of disrespect that the true clergy as a whole has been putting up with for decades. It's nothing new, but things have got to change. As Dr. Shariati says, we need a progressive interpretation of religion today. Things are going to change. You'll see!" He left the room abruptly, without touching his food.

"Dr. Who? What's he talking about. He's gone *siasi*," Ali said, smacking his thigh. "Don't you have enough in life to complain about, without causing yourself more headaches with this kind of nonsense?"

# CHAPTER 33

Bibi could not stop kissing the picture, insisting that Mohammad ought to frame it and hang it on the wall. She handed me the manila envelope and several large prints of black-and-white pictures, pointing proudly to the one in which her grandson was receiving his accomplishment certificate from the director's hand. Mohammad took the picture, stared at it and tossed it on the floor.

"Don't you want to frame it?" I asked.

"Can't you see?" He picked it up and handed it to me.

All I could see was my brother receiving his certificate before a well-dressed group of older men.

"Look again," he said. I saw men in expensive suits sitting in the front row. Behind them, sat young workers in their overcoats, applauding. "I don't see what's wrong with the pictures," I said.

"Can you see that boy in the second row?"

Ah, that boy! I did see him. The boy sat in the second row, staring with large lamb eyes.

"He comes from a small village in the vicinity of Ghalat. You know how old he is? Twelve. He uses his dead older brother's birth certificate, pretends he's fifteen so he can work at Siemens to feed his entire family of eight back in his village. It's just too much poverty, too many hungry people, and the Labor Committee . . . all just a big show."

"Well, you started working yourself when you weren't even fourteen, didn't you?"

"That was different. Mine was a paid internship, on the way to becoming a technician. I design the telephone moldings—a clean job—and I'm not working to feed my family. But this boy, his job is to clean the grease off the machines and keep the workshop neat. He barely knows how to read or write. I'm trying to talk him into going to night school or let me teach him how to read. We'll see. I can't believe that with all this poverty, the Shah squanders the country's money for a celebration party to impress foreigners while his people suffer like this."

"Our teacher says that we celebrate the anniversary of the 2500 years of our kingdoms, our true Aryan heritage," I said, astonished at Mohammad's attitude.

"Monarchy, empire, honoring the dead king's traditions," Mohammad snapped. "Aryans, superior race, like we're a herd of cattle or horses. This race is better than that race. We're better than Arabs. We should stick with Europeans instead. Americans are superior to us. This is all *gharbzadegi*, eulogizing the West, the Westerners, and their hierarchal, corrupt ideas that we try to mimic so blindly. What our history books leave out is how these kings killed and banished brave people who opposed them, and ruined the country decade after decade, giving away its natural resources to foreign powers. What the Shah is forgetting is that you can't celebrate the past at the expense of today's poor people. The thing is that he squanders the wealth of this country to glorify himself in the eyes of the western world, to pretend that in this country everyone lives first-class. Glorifying a lie."

The tip of my fingers felt like ice. I remembered that Ali warned Mother that Mohammad would lose his head if he kept talking like that. I had never heard Mohammad talk so angrily, so boldly and openly, let alone about the Shah. The one thing Mohammad was not good at was getting angry, so it was hard to believe. Because he worked during the day, he'd been attending night school at Ahmadi High School in order to get his diploma. In his room, he had taken down all the posters of Bruce Lee; instead, he had pinned a black-and-white picture of Malcolm X on one wall and one of Mohammad Ali the boxer on the facing wall, and he kept forbidden pictures of Che Guevara and other foreigners under his bed. He wasn't interested in Jesus Christ any more. One of these days, he might get sent to Germany or Japan for a considered internship. The director of his department had chosen him for this honorary internship so he would develop his skills further with Western training; he said that when he came back, he'd be a master, training other interns.

Bibi bragged about him and his good fortune every glorious chance she got; while Mother quietly thanked God that He had made such a mistake, giving her a bright boy like that when obviously He meant for him to be born to another mother who lived uptown and had a rich husband.

"Whatever the boy touches, turns into gold," Bibi would say proudly to her daughter. "I'm telling you, dear, God has taken all the talents and given them to this boy." Bibi was right. I was beginning to think that Mohammad possessed some sort of supernatural ability, as if five people lived in him. One day he was a chess champion, another day a frisky ping-pong player, then a competent technician; some days he was a scientist, an inventor, and always a kind brother, a caring son, and a sensitive grandson. Bibi said that he could be anyone he wanted to be and could accomplish anything he decided to do. But now if he continued talking like that, only God knew what would happen to him. *Is he siasi as Ali says he is? He's definitely got secrets.*

Later that night, he gave me a book, *The Little Black Fish*, written by Samad Behrangi, making me promise not to show it to anyone and to read it only when I was alone. "Behrangi was a teacher who dedicated his life to the poor and deprived Kurdish children," he whispered, "teaching them how to read and write. He worked in the villages where the kids never sat on a bench in their lives. Their school is nothing like ours, you know. Kurdistan is very cold and these kids are taught out in the open sitting in the snow. Seeing all that poverty and misery, Samad the Teacher questioned why a country like Iran, with its wealth and natural resources, could not provide the children with decent schooling. He wrote this one book, supposedly for children, but if you think of it, really, it was his message. He simply spoke up and protested the injustice around him. SAVAK, the secret police, killed him and fed his corpse to the sharks in the Aras River. That's what they do in this country when someone has a brave heart and talks and even dares to write about social changes, especially to help the poor. They will *kill* him."

The more Mohammad talked, the more frightened I became. I did not want the sharks to eat my brother's body. I did not want the sharks to eat anybody's body.

# CHAPTER 34

Hossein didn't come home again last night. Mother asked Moham-mad to go and for the love of God look for him. I ran after him. "Wait up! I want to go with you," I yelled.

"That's no place for a girl. Go back home!" he yelled back. When he saw me following him, he slowed down and motioned to me: "Walk faster, then!" he said, sounding annoyed.

Once we passed an empty field, I found myself at the edge of an open ditch. This was where the city dumped garbage and waste. Now, it made sense why Mohammad did not want me to follow him. I saw people in ragged clothes moving in and out of mud huts and shacks made from different-sized tin and cardboard vegetable oil contain-ers—people living in *boxes*. Mohammad shook his head. "And they say there's no poverty in this country!"

Despite the piercing cold, children were running around barefoot and half-naked, their private parts exposed, their bellies sticking out, and their ashen faces smeared with dirt. Not even the gypsy kids looked this bad, not that the gypsies would settle here in such a filthy place. I couldn't believe that such poor people existed in the world, let alone out here twenty blocks or so from my own house. I must've skipped rope a thousand times up to the end of the street; Bibi for-bade me to go past the line where the asphalt ended, and the dirt road began. The taxis and the buses stopped here too. Only trucks and minibuses were available to take people further down to the New Cemetery.

Not too long ago Bibi had taken me to the Old Cemetery where a few of her cousins were buried. Their tombstones were located in front of the two huge white marble lions. Bibi used to make a tray of halva to offer it to passersby on the evening before Fridays in memory of her dead relatives. She'd let me slide down the backs of the enormous lions and Marmar and I would sit on them and pretend to horseback-ride while Marmar's mother sobbed for her dead father, and Bibi drew lines and motifs with a rock-chalk on the gravestones and murmured verses which I did not understand. We stopped going there after the entire graveyard was demolished by huge bulldozers. People were outraged that the souls of their dead were shaken by the monster machines. There was talk that the government was planning some projects. What exactly? No one had the slightest idea. Bibi could no longer go to the cemetery, and she was happy that she did not have any loved ones buried in the brand-new one. We thought there must be some new neighborhood where the Old Cemetery used to be.

"I thought *we* were poor," Mohammad said. "Compared to these people, we're kings. We should be thankful for having such a hard-working mother."

This was the first time I heard Mohammad talking about Mother working. No one in the family talked about anything. No one told us what to say or what not to say; we just didn't talk. Especially my brothers. That boarding school had taught them well. Killed their spirits, Bibi said. Not Mohammad's, though. He always had a curious mind and a head for adventure, always wondering. He said that I was the very "Miss Question Mark." I guess I did ask a lot of questions. "You think we're poor?" I asked.

"We're a working-class family. Of course not as poor as these people or many others in the worst part of the south side of the city."

The south of the city? I have heard it before, from the Ladies who came to our school. Children from the south side, they whispered to each other. "What's that mean? The south?" I asked again.

He told me that cities had good parts and bad parts. In our city the bad part was the south, lower part of the town, where the poor live. The good part is the upper part where the wealthy people live, where the Americans live, where some girls and boys go together to American schools and learn everything in English. Where the Germans and Japanese live. That was called Uptown, north of the city.

He fell quiet. A few moments later he said, "You should've seen the Shah's palace; the Intercontinental Hotel I stayed at while I was in Tehran for the chess championship: the *Kashan* and *Tabriz* rugs, the mirror works and the mosaic arts. All that, it makes you wonder why there should be so much class difference in this world. I wonder if our Shah knows that his people live like this." He looked around angrily.

"But he's a king," I said. "He's supposed to live in a palace. Isn't he?"

"I guess. But his people should live good too. Don't you think? You know our country is one of the richest countries in the whole world. And look how these people live. Like rats. Living under the shadow of God, the King of Kings."

"Ali says it's dangerous to talk about the Shah like that. It's forbidden."

"Well, I wouldn't talk like that if my eyes wouldn't see what they see."

"Bibi likes the Shah. She says he is a much better king than the ones before him."

"That's Bibi. Do you know anyone whom Bibi doesn't like? She likes everybody."

"The British. She doesn't like the English. And the Landlord Feudal. She says they killed her young father when she was still in her mother's womb."

"*Ha!* I forgot. That's right. She does not like the British. And I totally forgot that our grandfather was murdered by a Feudal. He must have been a brave man. I wonder if he's a martyr?"

Days later, when I told Bibi about our wealthy-poor neighborhood, she had a different view of it. She said,"Of course there are the shacks. Wherever rich people are, there are poor people. They come to find jobs. They're forced to live nearby because they can't travel far. They're the beggars, the toilet-cleaners, the pool-cleaners, the washerwomen. To say it in plain language, wealthy and poor end up living maybe not wall to wall, but far and near. And there are some like us, white-faced before God and His people, the ones in the middle. But, alas, before the Almighty, we're all equal, rich or poor.

What really counts are only the good intentions and the good deeds in this world. That's what makes you better than anybody else, not your worldly possessions."

# CHAPTER 35

*Sister* Zahra's voice bursts through the loudspeaker, "Complete *hed-jab*," followed by Torabpoor's scratchy voice, ordering the entire three tiers, including the *normal* prisoners, to gather in the prison yard. The prison yard is finished now; finally, we get to breathe one hour of fresh air in the morning. Even though we are still required to wear our head-coverings at all times, the instant our feet touch the cement, we convert into groups of sun worshipers, darting out, rolling up our sleeves and our pants, exposing our warmth-thirsty skin to a glorious, generous sun. Anxiously, we let our head-coverings slip around our shoulders and comb our fingers through our hair, flattened from being constantly covered. At the beginning, the *Sisters* used to mock our insatiable hunger for the sun rays, calling us a herd of fools, but slowly, they let their guard drop and decided to look the other way. Their sudden carelessness wasn't out of sympathy, but because they, too, feared the rapid spread of skin-fungus disease. It took more than six months before I got to be exposed to the sun once again. Although I am among those fortunate ones immune to the skin-fungus disease, I, too, rush to the prison yard like a crazed person on fire.

Nonetheless, this is not a call for the aeration period. There must be something else.

With the *Sisters'* instruction, inmates from all tiers gather in the prison yard, each tier's prisoners occupying a designated area. The number of emergency-help guards and armed *pasdars* are doubled today, encircling us like a pack of watchful hawks. Torabpoor and a group of armed *pasdars*, as well as a few turbaned and robed Mullahs, enter the yard. One of the bearded men, dressed in a gray out-of-date suit, introduces himself as *Dadsetan* Lajevardi, the Supreme Court Chief justice. Like a good trained dog, Torabpoor opens the way for his master, commanding his subservient herd of repentants, covered toe-to-head in black, to come and sit right above the invisible line he draws on the ground, looking amused and proud. The *normal* prisoners snigger under their ragged, flowery chadors, for they have seen, perhaps for the first time in ages, a turbaned Mullah coming to their Block. Nudging each other, they whisper, "Look, Zari, the Sheikh has come to wed you to Asghar the Bald." They giggle so much that *Sister* Zahra and *Sister* Tahereh escort them to a much farther section of the prison yard and order them to sit quietly under the vigilant eye of a *pasdar* with his Kalashnikov in his hand.

*Dadsetan* praises us for making the wise decision to repent our sins. He marvels at the supreme condition of the prison Block and our cells. "It is apparent to me that you pass your time in an excellent state according to Islamic justice," he says, fingering his prayer beads. He is also pleased about how well we are fed, being given *shish kabob* and gourmet food of all kinds, while the brave soldiers of the land, at this very moment and in such horrifying conditions, are fighting on the front against the ruthless Iraqi enemy. He goes on preaching about how our blind actions and irresponsible thinking, believing hypocrites and infidels, has led us to imprisonment, which fortunately, and thanks to the Islamic Republic's compassion, is the appropriate place for the improvement and cleansing of the soul, mind, and body; so why not take advantage of the situation and respond? And before he bids us farewell, he finishes his sermon, insisting one more time that we ought to pray all day and night, pleading to God, as well as to the people for our forgiveness. Waving his hand a few times, he begins to walk away, encircled by his armed men.

"*Agha*, if I may. Would you care to hear our requests?"

All heads turn in the direction of the voice. It is Banafsheh, one of the most willful non-repentant girls of the second tier. My heart drops. *May God help her and us too!*

"*Agha* is in a hurry," replies Torabpoor without looking at Banafsheh, maintaining his false kindly demeanor.

"Do you see those women?" Banafsheh rises to her feet, ignoring Torabpoor. The girls eye each other and remain silent. Pointing to the group of *normal* prisoners sitting afar, Banafsheh speaks out. "Call us traitors, call us *monafegheen*, hypocrites, infidels, or whatever you may wish to call us, but the fact of the matter is that we are political prisoners, whether you like it or not," she says effortlessly, a hint of vibration in her voice. "We are here not because we committed any crime, but because we believed in an ideology not acceptable to you. They, on the other hand, are ill-fated prostitutes, murderers, criminals. They scuffle day and night, scream and curse all the time. They communicate not in a human tongue but in the most vulgar form of language, cursing to the point that is deafening."

She looks straight at the Chief Justice, and, without losing much time, resumes, "You know better that we are nothing like them. This is an insult to our decent upbringing. Now that you have barred us, why among these people? As political prisoners, we have the right to have a section of our own. You have condemned us to life imprisonment; why, to top it off, must we suffer this kind of cruel punishment?"

*Dadsetan* looks at her from under his thick eyebrows and hastily plays with the prayer beads in his hand. A few more girls from the second tier pitch in. Voices increase. Complaints come from this one and that one. The bearded *Dadsetan* looks agitated, but makes an effort to listen attentively. His men are gesturing for him to walk on. Torabpoor motions for the *Sisters*. Banafsheh was arrested two years ago as an active sympathizer of the Mojahedeen and was sentenced to life imprisonment, but now her case is up for review for the death penalty. She and a few others who live on the second tier are the only ones who protest from their upstairs corridor, calling out to the *Sisters* whenever the *normal* prisoners are like bitches in heat, showering each other with the most offensive curse words ever. She keeps reminding the pack of *Sisters* that it is against human rights' guidelines to keep the political prisoners in such torment. Being in and out of solitary confinement, she's been lashed hundreds and hundreds of strokes, yet she still refuses to repent her anti-government convictions. Now, she stands straight, with all her small, thin body, brave enough to remind this arrogant Chief of Justice of the unjust situation we live in day in and day out.

*Dadsetan* nods his head insistently and says in a polite voice that he will see to it himself to solve the problem. "After all this is an Islamic penitentiary," he says, "and I as its main chief make sure that all the requirements will be met."

Two weeks have passed since the day Banafsheh stood up and spoke on behalf of the entire Block. The *normal* prisoners left this morning, having been granted a ward of their own. Taking their place, the Bahai prisoners were transferred to the third tier, earning officially the label of *soiled untouchables*, separated even from the infidel, non-repentant inmates of the second tier. They spent the entire day sanitizing every centimeter of their new confinement, moving their few belongings to their new cells.

Banafsheh, too, is gone again, this time forever. She was executed last night, among six other young women, *Sister* Zahra confirmed it. No one ever will see her or hear her vibrant voice again. Banafsheh never repented her anti-government activities; she was only twenty-six years old and had been imprisoned both under the Shah's regime and Khomeini's. She is no longer with us, but because of her courage to speak up, we, the repentant, get to do time at last without having to tolerate the constant screaming, the foul language, and the cursing of the criminal inmates. Banafsheh is gone, but I doubt that any one of us in Block 4 will ever forget her, or the day that her brave voice broke the silence in the prison yard.

# CHAPTER 36

The images of those miserable people living in that cold pit did not disappear.

I titled my mandatory weekly essay *Halabiabad*. Before the hour was over, Miss Tabatabaee called my name. "What's this nonsense you're making up?" she berated me; her frown tightened. "There's no such thing as people living in a *pit*. It is not the stone age. And this is a modern country, many thanks to our just Majesty. It might have been like this, well, maybe a hundred years ago. Not today."

"I swear, I saw it with my very own eyes," I blurted. "I don't live too far away from there. And I walk to school . . ."

"Shut your mouth. Or else I have to hand you your school file and have your mother come and take you out of this school. Pupils like you don't deserve to have what our Majesty has done for them. Go thank God that you're a good pupil and the teachers speak well of you. Keep it up that way, and never again write this drivel." Her voice became a bit softer, sort of motherly, like the way Bibi half-scolded me, half advised me when I did something she did not approve of.

"And I promise not to mention a word to Principal Sadati."

"My teacher tore my essay into hundreds of pieces," I told Mohammad. "She said I write nonsense. And there's no such a thing as people living in a pit in Iran."

"How could you be so naïve, writing about such stuff and taking it to school?" he said. "Of course, there's no poverty in Iran. Of course, there's no one living in the villages. Honeyed milk runs in our sink instead of water. These are the kinds of things you should

234

be writing. You'll get the best grades," Mohammad said, mockingly. "Like that essay you wrote on Mother's Day."

*Ah! That essay.* How could I have been such a liar, writing like that. What mother? What love? My mother didn't even know a grain about loving me. All her love went to the neighbors' girls who polished pans and pots and tidied a house like a born-to-be-maid. Getting the best grades at school, all those stars and ribbons I got from my teachers, and even Principal Sadati's Miss Kherad this and Miss Kherad that, none of them, simply, could measure up to making a pot of black tea like the rest of the God-given, gifted daughters that other mothers were fortunate enough to have. Everything I wrote, I meant for Bibi, but there's no such thing as "Grandmother's Day." It was Mother's Day after all. I got lots of praises for a bunch of lies. The whole school clapped for me because I lied.

"What would you wish to be when you grow up?" was the topic of the week's essay. Everyone said what they wanted to be when Miss Tabatabaee asked them. I raised my hand and said that I wanted to be a writer, just like Victor Hugo, even though I didn't know how one became a writer. Miss Tabatabaee, this time, smiled her famous nodding smile. "Miss Kherad, you just keep writing your essays as the book instructs you. Victor Hugo was a genius and on top of it, he was French."

Perplexed again, I went to my very own walking encyclopedia. By then, Mohammad was in tenth grade. At first, he had a good laugh, then he said, French or no French, I could be a writer if I wanted to be. "In order to be a writer you must love books and read tons and tons of them," he said. This was easy, I thought, for both conditions applied to me. I loved books and I couldn't get enough of reading them.

"We have only palaces here," Mohammad said, "We have a Kingdom." He became serious as he saw me looking more confused. "Ah, you, my poor sister. You're so gullible. If anybody tells you that a tribe of monkeys lives on the moon, you'd believe him. The thing is this, there are people and there are governments. Now, the governments don't want people to talk about, you know, *stuff,* because they don't want people to demand changes or reform. The governments are the ones who have the power to do whatever injustice, not the people. Now, in some countries like ours—forget about this rubbish of a glorified country, superior race, splendid history—there's no room for mindful writers. They cannot breathe."

Mohammad's voice turned philosophical again, his head moving in slow motion, adjusting his glasses, nodding, and tapping his chin with his index finger. "Want to know more? To be a true Eve? Then, taste the Fruit of Knowledge. I am giving you a new book, read it, but don't write about it or take it to your teacher. No more *nonsense*, remember? Is that clear? Don't forget, we live under the Shadow of God on Earth. The Walls have Ears and the Ears can Hear."

# CHAPTER 37

In our house, one could always be sure of one thing: never to experience a shortage of Mother's assorted gourmet cuisines, fresh-bought fruits, vegetables, herbs, food, and more food. Whether a person just dropped by to wish a "good day," or if one arrived in the middle of the night, hungry and thirsty for a week of hotel-living, Mother's hot, ready gourmet meals never disappointed anyone, even if she was not home to serve them herself. Regardless of how much food she prepared, one thing she never approved of: squandering them or discarding the leftovers. Nor did she approve of buying any store-bought sweets. Instead, she made her own Jell-O filled with pieces of tangerines, grapes and cherries, made all kinds of jams and marmalades, cherry syrups, and hundreds and hundreds of bottles of sour-grape and lemon juice which she stored in a cool place to be used later throughout the winter. The pans and pots she used glowed so that I could see my reflection in them each time I passed the kitchen shelves. Not a speck of dust was ever to be seen anywhere. When she was not home, everything was prepared and ready to use in her absence; when she was home, she was in constant motion, cooking, organizing, hosing down the entire courtyard, cleaning, or rearranging the furniture in this room and that room.

Borrowing was not in her nature; this unique trait, nevertheless, did not stop the neighbor women from dropping by to borrow an onion here, a spoonful of turmeric or red chilly pepper there, rice or flour, any last-minute forgotten ingredients, and more importantly, money.

To the outside world she was a God-sent neighbor whom even the women from distant alleys fought over to have her cater their special celebrations at wedding ceremonies and *naẓr* of *sofreh*. Within the four walls of our house, well . . . that was another story. When the house was empty of her sons, friends, and neighbors, she'd come out, carrying her concealed basket of anger, frustration, disappointment and weariness that she'd collected to dump on the only flesh-and-blood women in her life: her mother and her daughter.

Now, sitting in front of the pots of sour grapes, Mother squeezed the grapes, salting and crushing them. I watched her as she transferred the crushed grapes from one pot to another. She yelled, "Why on earth are you just watching instead of giving me a helping hand?" Even though Bibi and I had cleaned all the branches and done all the seeding, she still said that we didn't know how to help. I scratched my hands and rubbed more coarse salt on them, but the itching of sour-grape acid would not stop.

It was summer and I knew that this was just the beginning of both her preserves and her complaining. She'd be sour. Right after they were juiced, it would be time for the green limes to be bottled, then for the red tomatoes to be made into paste and sauce for her hearty and flavorful eggplant stews to last us over the winter.

As I walked away, she mumbled, "I'm not the lucky sort blessed with a considerate mother like the rest of the daughters in the world, or with a helpful daughter like the rest of the mothers in the world."

Bibi, who was quiet up to that point, became as sour as the crushing grapes and walked up to the fishpond, leaving the rest of the grapes in the colander untouched. Mother continued crushing the grapes herself, telling Bibi that she was raising me lazy and spoiled instead of teaching me to do the housework. And why on earth did Bibi listen to me reading books when she could be advising me on how to become more useful around the house? "You think you're doing her a favor?" she yelled after Bibi. "Well, the rate she's going, with her head poked into those books, either she's going to land in a crazy-house or end up an old maid. Just wait and see who's going to marry her when she comes of age!"

"Go on and bring me a married one who's a *Shahzadeh*, a princess, and lives like one," Bibi retorted, raising her voice. "I'd like to see the crown of flowers they get to put on their heads that the unmarried ones are going to miss. Destiny is destiny. The rest is a bunch of nonsense." She went back to her room.

I often wondered about Mother's kindness to the world and her rage at me and Bibi. There were times that I doubted if I was my mother's daughter at all. I would ask Bibi if there was something that she had chosen to hide from me. And I often wondered about that day when I first heard Bibi talking in the guest room of Mash Zoleikha. Though I had asked her on numerous occasions, my questions mostly remained unanswered except with Bibi's sighs: "Past is past, dear, you can't undo it." So the past remained a mystery.

It was summer and school was closed. I had just finished the fifth grade and couldn't wait for middle school to start so I'd be out of the house again, six days a week, eight hours of school a day. Completely out of Mother's sight. I would do all the math problems and labor over science and social studies as long as I could avoid her. Feeling the same way, Bibi asked me to accompany her to visit an old friend. Her sight was worsening day by day, but she still refused to wear glasses. "What's the use?" she argued. "It's too late and no piece of glass would cure the cataract."

I decided to go along; I did not want her to fall and get hurt again.

And it was on that day, passing through the narrow, shady, musky *Break-up, Make-up Alley*, that Bibi broke her silence. The air, choked by the high brick walls, was damp and mildewed. The whispers and footsteps of the passersby echoed in the ancient alley. "Your mother used to live a few streets farther down there, in the house of *Sar-e-Do zak*," she pointed to my left. "Your father's fine inheritance," she added, her voice, as always, filled with ridicule when it came to my father, a man I had never gotten to know. I was two years old when he died. I wondered if I could talk then yet, and if he heard my first words.

At the head of the alley, we leaned against the wall to let a line of draft gray donkeys pass by carrying loads of chalk and construction materials. I recalled the first time I walked through those alleys; when I was only a child. I remembered giggling at the name *Break up-Make up Alley*, but Bibi was not in a mood to giggle that day, or to lecture me about the history of this or that place. Later, she explained that the name came from the old days when the alleys were so narrow that the going person had to wait to let the coming person pass. Naturally, out of courtesy, people had to stop and greet the other person with a warm *salam*. Even if they were mad at each other or didn't talk, they had no choice except to face each other, so they made up on the spot and put aside the old animosity. That's why they called it *Break up-Make up Alley*.

It was obvious to me that Bibi did not have much regard for my father or his family. I had sensed her resentment through many of the stories and memories she had told and retold me over the years. Yet it seemed that sometimes she sifted the details.

After visiting her friend, when we stepped out into the busy sunny main street, in the deafening blare of traffic, I stopped at the small ice-cream shop at the end corner and talked Bibi into entering and sitting at a table. I ordered two large portions of carrot-juice-vanilla-ice-cream shake.

"Bibi," I said, searching for the right words, "how did I exactly end up being with you?" I knew she would get really agitated with my questions. I hated doing this to her. But I simply had to know.

"Are you not content that I have raised you, my flower? Have I done bad for you?" she frowned, trying hard not to squint, a habit she had developed recently as she wiped her watery eyes.

"God, no, Bibi," I said. Holding her brown hands in mine, I said, "You mean the world to me. It's just . . . sometimes I wonder why *Momon* gave me up. I know, I know, she had so many kids. And no, I don't want to hear she didn't have money or whatever story you keep telling me. It's just . . . I'm *her* daughter. The only daughter she'll ever have."

"Well. Maybe you're right," Bibi said hesitantly. "You deserve to know, my sweet blossom. After all, you've always been a curious child . . . mature too . . . Even when you were barely three years old, the questions you would ask. Why the color of the sky is not red instead of blue? Remember how you . . ."

"Bibi, you're starting again."

"Why that tone, dear? What, you're becoming your mother now? *Allah-o-akbar*. Well, what can I say? I guess you should know."

I didn't know if it was the smell of hay in those shady alleys that brought her memories back, or if it was the sweet smell of the carrot juice in that cozy café. Or if it was, maybe, that she no longer could bear the everlasting bafflement in my eyes.

"It's not like your mother abandoned you. And besides, I'm no stranger. I'm your grandmother. She . . . your mother . . . well, she didn't have it easy either. She fought. She wanted to have all her children under one roof. But she just couldn't, dear. Years before your *baba* died, on one of those trips to Shiraz, your *Momon* wanted to stay and live here in Shiraz. But your *baba's* relatives wouldn't let her. They, themselves, made Shiraz their vacation spot. At first, they came in the summer to get away from the heat of Abadan. But soon they ended up working in the Shiraz petroleum companies or the oil refinery. The entire clan, one by one, moved to Shiraz, buying houses in the uptown, Ghasr-e-Dasht, Cinema Saadi, all nice places. Well, as they say, when you have money, wherever you go, you won't live bad."

Bibi let out a deep sigh and looked down at her ice cream shake, then at me. "You see, after that clan took my daughter away like that, I sent them letter after letter." Bibi's voice shook. "She was just a little girl. Had seen only nine springs. I begged them to send my girl to me for a few days or I would go to visit her. Mash Namaki, your father's aunt, kept saying, 'It's too soon now. Your daughter is our bride now. Let her get accustomed to our ways, to get more familiar with her husband'. She told me that Golrokh was doing fine. And that everyone was like a servant to her. She said over and over, 'Once the time is right, I'll send for you'.

"Year in and year out, no letter came. No word of invitation. I said to myself, what kind of time is it that's never right? I said I'm no saint. I don't have the patience of the saint Jacob, may I die for all his sufferings. Well, after all, he had more sons than dear Yusef. But I have only this girl. I couldn't bear it any longer, not knowing how she was doing. One day, I took my bundle and got on an *Iran-Payma* bus and headed for the strange city. Traveling in those days was much harder than nowadays, I'll tell you. There, I asked passersby how to get to the address on the back of the envelope in my hand.

"Finally, I was at Agha Bashi's door. I was in a total sweat. My heart beat fast. Well, the neighborhood looked very civilized as they had said, so I calmed down a bit. Back then, they lived in the *Braym* district. The houses were *Farangi*, English style. They all looked the same: same size, same structure, with red rooftops. I rang the doorbell. A young woman, propping up a baby on her hip, opened the door. When the girl returned with the aunt, Mash Namaki said to her, 'Why, what's the matter with you, girl? You don't recognize your own mother?' I froze like a chunk of ice. Mash Namaki said, '*Bah, bah*. Welcome! You brought spring to our house. This is *Golly*, your daughter.' She was a woman of fifteen now, already the mother of a newborn boy, your brother Ali, and I was still expecting to see a little girl. I passed out on the spot. When I came to, they put my grandson in my lap. Imagine! If I hadn't gone over there, no one would've bothered telling me that I was a grandmother now.

"And my daughter acted as if I were a complete stranger. I wanted to hug her, she pulled away. She wouldn't even call me mother or anything. At first, I thought she was shy. Could I blame her? It had been six years since we saw each other last. Her accent was no longer *Shirazi*, but like theirs, *Abadani*, so different in my ears. She acted like them, talked like them and put on airs for me. I hated when they called her Golly. I protested, her name is Golrokh, not Golly. But they said, well, this is a modern city here. It's always good to have short, easy names.

"In the first few days, everything seemed nice and normal. I was welcomed. The house was real nice. Electric fans hung from all the ceilings. It was still winter, but already the fans were running. They had a huge electric ice-chest. The kitchen and the bathroom were indoors. They had *Farangi* toilets, the white ceramic ones you sit on; the kind I can't stand. The good thing was there were no cock-roaches. The houses weren't like ours in Shiraz. The roofs weren't flat, but pointy. I wondered, with this heat, where would they sleep in the summer time? They had two yards, a front yard with sprin-klers and a jasper-green lawn like velvet. I've never seen such a thing in my life before. There were no walls around the front yard, only a one-meter, green-spindle hedge covered the sides of the yard. At the back of the house, there was another yard with a tiny vegetable garden: Very well-kept and full of roses, night jasmine, and mon-key flowers. Lavish, lavish if you ask me. A gardener came once a week. No fruit trees. Poor trees, how could they survive in that heat? There was only a cedar tree shading the backyard, and a tree with the fruit like golden plums that they called three-breast tree. God forbid, who'd ever heard of such a peculiar name, I told your *Momon*. Even their trees' names are not like those in any other place. But, *bah, bah,* what palm trees in those yards and those boulevards, and all over town, along the shoreline! Wherever you looked, there were juicy dates hanging from the branches. If we have great cypress trees here in Shiraz, Abadan is swarming with grand and tall *tall* palm trees. And what a strand! What a fish market! Fish the size of sharks. Mash Namaki would take me every morning to the strand, where fishermen sold live catch in their nets: all kinds of fish, salmon, white, trout, shrimps the size of my fist. And how those Arab women swarmed, pointing and poking at the fish eyes. 'Give me this one, brother! Give me that fat one, brother!' And what seafood dishes my daughter would make, so delicious you wanted to eat your fingers too!

"It didn't take long for me to notice that they treated my girl like a servant, Golly, come here! Golly, do this! Golly, wash the dishes. The Old-Aunt, who was now heavier than a rolling wheel, just sat on that porch with cushions all about her, fanning herself with an Abadani palm fan, smoking a water-pipe, and ordering my child around. When I objected, she raised an eyebrow and said, 'Don't take it so close to heart. She's just doing her wifely duty. It's any good daughter-in-law's job to be agreeable and do the chores for the husband's family. It's both God's and the Prophet Mohammad's command for women to obey'. If you were to ask her which direction Mecca faced, she wouldn't know; but now for me, suddenly the lady was a devoted Muslim. I told her, maybe dear God said to obey your husband, but the size of your family is the size of an Eritrean tribe. There are uncles and aunts and other young and old relatives living in this house. She's taking care of all of them. The aunt just ignored me. And all this time, I thought she was living well. Everyone, my neighbors would say to me, lucky you that your daughter got married into name and money, that she would live like a *Shahzadeh* princess now that her husband is much older than she is. 'You see, I told you, I'd make a lady out of her,' Mash Namaki said, laughing. I was going to say, well, of course you made a servant lady out of my daughter, my bunch of flowers. But, Golrokh bit her lip, signaling for me to be quiet. Poor girl, how she was afraid of them.

"I tried to tell Agha Bashi that I gave my daughter to one husband and not to his entire clan to serve. Bless his soul, he never disrespected me. It was true that he was helpless. Passive and lazy, I'd say. He said, 'Not to worry—life is only two days: the day you're born and the day you die—forget about the rest!' Whatever I said, he just listened, puffed his cigarettes or his opium-pipe when he could. And here I thought my daughter was in good hands. When he saw me surprised by his smoking, he said it's only medicine . . . it's good for the backache . . . good for the toothache, or whatever damage he had. I said to him, the English came, so had their opium. What better souvenir than that in exchange for the oil? But he acted as if I was talking to my shadow. That was him.

"I told myself, you're just a guest in this house, so be quiet. But how could I when I had to see my daughter on her knees. From sunrise to sunset, she was polishing the tiled floors, doing laundry, cooking dinner. As soon as she sat down to hold her baby boy, the aunts scolded her that she was sitting too long and it was their job to play with the baby anyway. Once, I tried to get close to her. I asked her if she was happy there. She looked away and said that was none of my business. I said, I'm your mother for heaven's sake. I'm worried about you. You're just skin and bone, and you have that fat baby to feed. What did these people do to you? She said the house, and whatever Agha Bashi has, is in the aunts' names and that the relatives live nearby in the same *lane*. They're just very close to each other. I couldn't even understand some of her words. *Lane*. She said that's English. What did I know? That's another thing, the black gold was found in this land, so the English came, uninvited. Now my own daughter was talking to me in some imported language. There were turban-headed Indian workers all over town. One of them came to the house one day, doing some sort of work for Uncle Engineer. I opened the door for him and he kept mumbling *'Madame kertahe . . . Madame kertahe.'* His lips were dry and cracked. I said, what is it? Do you want water? Do you want food? Maybe some *pottaato*? What kind of tongue is that? The relatives laughed and mocked my talking.

I said to them, don't tell me what language is. I may be illiterate, but I know the entire *Hafiz Poetry* collection by heart. Half the city is robber Englishman and their horde of servant Indians and the other half is indigent grasshopper-eating Arabs. Speak Farsi, for crying out loud. It took me years to understand their accent and what they said. Couldn't you just speak the human tongue, I wondered. Well, just say *koocheh*, what's *lane* mean? They said the English words potato and tomato instead of the Farsi words. Their streets, no names, only numbers. Lane 1, Lane 2. As if there's a scarcity of good names! All those saints' names. Our good old legends' names. No upper, no lower slopes, no twists or turns, just flat land. Streets came from here. Streets went there. All in horizontal and vertical orders.

"The houses were all alike with roofs colored according to the class and status. Your *Momon* was living in the red-rooftop section; that meant you came from the higher ranks of the oil refinery employees, where the engineers lived. And there were white and blue and yellow roofs in other parts of town, where the aunts wouldn't let us set foot. I think the yellow color was for the simple workers, for the poor. It's like being poor is not bad enough, you have to color your roof, telling the whole world that you're poor. Or look! My rooftop is red, I'm rich. Not only do I own an electric ice-chest, but I live in *Braym, Bovardeh. Cyclane*. The south belongs to the poor. Here in the northern part of the city, we speak differently. We have those foreign words to pronounce.

"Good thing, your mother was in good spirits. Still happy and cheerful," Bibi muttered. "Didn't care to cover herself or anything like that. She wore skirts and short sleeves. At least, that much freedom she had in that house. Sometimes, even, she would hold a round tray like a tambourine and sing and dance with the other women of the family, just like when she was a little girl. And what a baby boy she had, how that family treated him! Like he was a prince. My late husband used to say that the women of my family bear handsome children. We were famous for that. At least God gave us this much luck. Ali was a fat, chubby, white boy with gorgeous, huge agate eyes.

"That day when they put that baby in my arms, I took a pair of gold bracelets off my wrist, and my gold necklace, gave them all to your mother, with two hundred tumans on top of that. She said that this jewelry doesn't look like anything women in this city would wear; they're too old fashioned. Any other girl would've thanked her mother. But she just shrugged and put them on the mantle. The Lady Aunt said, not to worry, she'll wear them later. God knows what the woman did with them. All my hard-earned money from wool spinning all night long. And my daughter had to put me down in front of that woman, black as charcoal.

"Later I found out that she wasn't even allowed to buy herself any clothes, let alone jewelry. Whatever junk the aunts bought her she had to wear. Leaving the house by herself was out of the question, unless one of the relatives went with her. Once she wanted to take me for a walk along the shore. Mash Namaki tossed her a thick black *abaya* to cover herself. I said to the aunt, pardon me, but we're not Arabs. That's not our traditional attire, covering ourselves with a black *abaya*. If you want, put a light colored scarf over her head. Mash Namaki turned sour and said, 'This is what a Muslim woman should wear, especially in that part of town you're heading to,' I said, I'm a Muslim and respect God's words. The holy Koran doesn't say to cover yourself with a black abaya. It says cover, now be it with a potato sack or a piece of silk, whatever. She's a young woman, not a black crow, I told her. I just couldn't stand watching all those bad things. I had to leave after a few weeks."

Bibi looked at me and patted my head gently. She hesitated, but it seemed as if she was rolling under an avalanche of sorrows and regrets, tumbling downhill, expanding, growing, too late to stop. She breathed hard and continued, unfolding . . .

"Year after year, word came that she had another baby, boy after boy. Everyone kept saying how good for Golrokh, such a fertile woman to bear that many boys. She was like a commodity for her husband, especially in that family with all those barren women. Some of them were way past their marriage age, thirty-something; some old maids still waiting for someone to ask for their hands in marriage. Even if someone showed up, they'd shrug: this one is bald, that one is old, the other one is not educated enough or doesn't have a respectable job. Well, poor things, they weren't all that pretty, bookish though, and very well positioned, teachers, nurses or doctors. Some of them even worked in that oil refinery, shoulder to shoulder with men. They did all kinds of office work, I was told. What else do you expect when their fathers were engineers and had money and connections all over town?

"They sent their girls to good schools. In those years, when women stopped going to school as soon as they finished sixth grade, these girls went all the way up to the university. Not like my poor daughter who never got the chance for any schooling, ending up being their servant. Only I knew how they treated her. She was not even in control of her own children. The Grand Uncle Engineer was already claiming Ali as his adopted son. The man was married for a long time to the Grand Aunt, but the woman could not bear any children. It was such a dilemma for awhile in that house. Finally, the Grand Aunt divorced herself and let her own niece be married to her husband, so the Grand Uncle Engineer could have children of his own. With all her ignorance, at least Golrokh had that much sense not to give up that child. And the rest you know, dear. Your poor brothers didn't exactly live in paradise either.

"I remember the first time I returned from Abadan," Bibi continued, "I was barely back to my life in Shiraz when a letter came that Agha Bashi's newborn boy kisses his Bibi's hand from the distance. So I had to pack up my bundle and head back to Abadan. The more babies she had, the longer my trips lasted. After she had four boys, I told her, *babam*, you've got enough children. You're still young and strong. You'll suffer when you're old. Don't be so harsh on your body. Enough is enough. You brought Agha Bashi and his relatives plenty of boys to be proud of for at least seven generations to come. Know your worth. You're not made out of steel. It's just a body, not a hatching factory." She laughed. "Agha Bashi said the more, the merrier. Children are God's blessing. I said to him, you're not the one who's giving birth. You just have to stick your head under the covers, and you think that the rest takes care of itself.

"When your sixth brother, Hossein, was born, I just stayed in Abadan. I thought what's the point of going back home to Shiraz when three months later she's pregnant again. I might as well camp out in Agha Bashi's backyard, waiting for another baby.

"So it happened again. This time, unlike before, she was sick all the time. She had constant nausea, slept most of the day. She was cranky and for the first time she craved weird food to eat. She crunched so much dry rice you wouldn't believe. The weather was awful too, hotter and more humid than usual. She vomited and could hardly eat. The smell of frying fish that she cherished so much drove her crazy; she couldn't even cook for that army of a family.

"I always wondered how she survived all those pregnancies? She was thin as the water-pipe stick. Never gained a kilo on that skeleton body of hers, just a big belly. On the other hand, her boys were fat, five kilos and more. Big boys. Handsome too, just like my own dead boy. With skin as white as milk and golden hair and colored eyes. The aunts wouldn't let the boys leave the house by themselves or play in the front yard without any supervision. They were afraid someone might kidnap them. The neighbors called them *golden boys* because most Abadanis are bronze-skinned. They like to say it's because of the sun and the heat. But, if you ask me that's what you get when you couple with Arabs, you know. Sometimes, when the aunts were in a good mood, they'd say, 'We knew what kind of breed to choose for Agha Bashi's children.' Well, the boys really took after your mother and grandfather, my own husband. Coming from them that was, well, a lot. They're so snobbish, they tell their own buttocks, don't walk with us, you stink.

"I guess, God was with her, with that small body of hers. She had no problem giving birth to those big boys. I'm glad she didn't take after me. I had an awful pregnancy, with these big breasts and fat body. She was nothing like me, she had four of them without even having the midwife around. She did housework until the last minute before she went into labor. I remember, she would simply say, she had backache, as if it was a slight chill or a headache, and right there in the yard or wherever, in one of those rooms, she would squat down with her water bag broken, like a mother cat. Not even half an hour of labor. Her babies would plop down like ripe peaches. May I die for her strengths. With all her bad, God bless her. She would get up the next day and do the chores around the house as if she didn't just give birth. Her sisters-in-law had these commotions and threw such a big fit as if they were giving birth to the very Prince Valiahd. The bad thing was she didn't have much milk.

"Before you knew it, another few months, she'd be pregnant with another baby. And to top it off, during all that times, they moved from this area to the next area, from Braym to Bovardeh, to Bahmanshir, and finally to Cyclane. Since the houses belonged to the oil company, the employees would live there for only a few years, and they had to move again to a new house in a new vicinity. Don't ask me why, I never understood the English anyway. And they call *us* nomads.

"The house in Cyclane was smaller, but the backyard was very charming with a nice garden, full of palm trees. I couldn't leave your mother alone now that she was in such a miserable condition. She was moody and felt tired all the time. I told her, 'Your nature and temper have changed, this one is a girl.' I just knew it. All the signs predicted a girl. And what do you know, it was this beautiful spring afternoon; she went into labor. Right there in the garden. We were planting lilacs and marvel flowers and your *Momon* was trimming the white roses, sweet briars, and wallflowers. Poor thing, what an awful labor she had. She was in so much pain, she bit my hands and squeezed them so hard in her fist that I thought I was going to lose my fingers over Agha Bashi's newborn. She screamed and yelled so that even the next seven neighbors could hear her. 'Get it out of me . . . get it out of me . . . this is the last time I'm going to have a baby . . . that's it . . . I'm done with babies.'

"When you were born, the midwife gave you to your mother, 'You have to give me an endowment. This one is a girl,' the woman said. I cried with joy, thank you God, at last, we've got a girl in this house. But the moment your *Momon* saw you, well what can I say, she sulked. The aunts said, *Voy, voy*, why is this one so dark? Why is she so tiny, like a kitten? Look at those eyes, like two black buttons. I said to them, Ah hush! Don't you dare talk like that. Be thankful! This is a gift from heaven. I told Golrokh, *babam*, you're just used to all those white boys. Not all five fingers are the same length. So she doesn't have colored eyes, what's wrong with that?

"I guess she was afraid that you would look like the rest of the Agha Bashi family's women, dark-skinned and not pretty. I took you from her arms. Now, I have held so many babies in my arms, but I never felt the way I felt when I held you to my chest. You squeezed my index finger so firm, it just touched my heart. I raised my head to the sky and said, dear God, you never gave me good luck in this life, and you didn't give any to my daughter. Let's make it up to this girl for all the suffering we went through; give her a white forehead and good fortune.

"The aunts all wanted to give you a name, someone's dead mother or sister or some old grandma's name. Agha Bashi was as happy as if you were his first child. He held you in his arms and named you after his dead mother, Narges. But since you were born right there in the garden by the white rose bushes, I named you just that, the White Rose.

"Next year, she got pregnant again with her seventh and last boy, Amir. Poor thing, he was only six months old when your *baba* died right there on his prayer rug. My daughter had barely turned thirty when she became a widow.

"After your Baba passed away, your mother put both her feet in one shoe and insisted on leaving, now that her husband was dead. But the aunts told her if she wanted to leave, she had to leave without her children, with only the clothes on her body. She protested, said she wouldn't leave without her children. She fought for the house and whatever belonged to your *baba*. The aunts told her that Agha Bashi didn't own anything to pass on to her or to her children. 'He was poor when you married him, and he was poor when he died. And according to law, the children belong to the father's family after his death. So, we have their custody. Now there's no money, so why don't you go and live with your mother. You're still young, you'll marry again and have more babies,' they told her. That's why she had to move into the house of Sar-e-Dozak, whatever estate left from your father, and, of course, she had to share it with Mash Namaki and the leftover clan. She stayed there in that shabby house, putting up with all that ill-fortune, hoping one day she'd leave when her kids were at the legal age."

Bibi paused again, this time she looked around the café. There were only a few people sitting at the far corner tables. A little girl with black curly hair pulled at the hem of her mother's skirt, pointing to the ice cream cones lined on the counter.

"Whom can you tell tales of misfortune like this?" Bibi murmured, rubbing her chubby chin with her fingers. "It's like sprinkling salt on my old wounds, *babam*. You and your curiosity. Well. . . ."

I wished I could stop wondering about all this. The last thing I wanted was to hurt Bibi by calling up unpleasant memories. But, once and for all, I yearned to know, and Bibi was my only channel to the past. She looked at the little girl for a long moment and when she noticed that I was waiting for her impatiently, she lowered her voice and went on.

"Well. What can I say? They were trying to send her out of the house where she'd worked hard for over twenty years of marriage, as if she was a slave and now *wooshhhh*, free to go. The soil of her dead husband's grave was not dry yet when the aunts wanted her to marry this Kuwaiti Arab man. They said she'd be better off without the kids. 'After all, who wants to marry a widow with so many children?' The Kuwaiti man, God forbid, had a nose the size of a potato. His stomach walked one meter ahead of his body." At this point Bibi stretched her arms to the sides as far as she could, performing an effortless pantomime. With her big chest and belly sticking out, she swayed her body right and left, making sure that she drew an accurate picture of that bulky Kuwaiti man. "The man came to my house, bringing his *sogoly*, his first wife, to choose his fourth lawful wife, asking your *Momon*'s hand in marriage. I said to my daughter, 'Maybe once I was a fool and you were a child and didn't know what marriage was, but now I'm wise and you're a grown-up woman. You don't have to listen to Agha Bashi's relations anymore. You're free. Think of yourself.' But was she listening? All those years, whatever they said, she said yes, Khanoom, you're right, Khanoom. I . . . I was an old village woman, that's how she thought of me. So, I didn't deserve her respect. I said, I'd burn the back of my hand not to ever mingle with your affairs. You do whatever you want to do. If it is your wish to let them make you small, it's up to you."

Any other time, I would've been thrilled with Bibi's animated recounting. Not today. She stared out the window and wiped her eyes with a tissue. When she saw me looking so serious, waiting for her to go on, she waved her hands in the air, sighing.

"It was the snowy year. There was one meter of snow on the ground for many weeks. Imagine white snow here in Shiraz. Well, one day, your *Momon* came with you sick in her arms. She said that the aunts had sent the younger boys to a boarding school and wanted to put you up for adoption. I was furious with them all, squandering whatever the man had left behind and doing such a heartless thing to those delicate children. I couldn't bear the thought of it, let alone to witness giving you up. You grew up so attached to me from day one. I cut your umbilical cord myself. When you were a baby, I held you in my arms until you fell asleep. I said to her, they would do such a thing over my dead body. I promised to keep you under my wings until she got her life back in order. I said whatever I eat, this child will eat too, one extra mouth to feed won't kill me. So help me God."

Bibi held my frozen face in both her hands, brushing away the strands of hair from my cheeks and pushing them behind my ear. Even though she was aware that I no longer approved of her affectionate gestures in public, yet she knew that it was only her kind caress that could hold back my tears in that cozy café.

"You see, my bunch of flowers. Your *Momon* didn't have much choice. You have to understand."

# CHAPTER 38

"Have you had any visitors on Monday?" Torabpoor asks, the usual wryness absent from his voice.

"Yes," I say, "my mother came to visit."

"And the Monday before?" he asks again.

"Yes," I answer, perplexed. Why is he questioning me when he surely knows my mother hardly ever fails to come visit? With the exception of the two weeks she fell terribly ill, she has been my faithful visitor during this past eight months of my imprisonment. Hasn't he witnessed her enough standing in the notorious visit lines in front of the prison yard in pouring rain or scorching heat? The *Sisters*, who know exactly which family members are visiting, report every detail to him. Not to mention the invisible male and female guards who overhear our conversations; they even drop a word of warning here and there once they feel the conversation sounds dubious. Have I said anything suspicious according to them, I wonder? I should never come back and stand in this begging line. "Can I see Mohammad, just a few minutes, that's all I'm asking," I repeat the same damn sentence even though each time I swore that this would be the last time I uttered it. This time he looks right at me. Our eyes meet for a good long moment. His eyes tell something that his lips refuse to utter. "Perhaps next time," his mouth finally shoves the words out. The girls in line shake their heads slightly as I pass by them. How bizarre. Something strange drifts in their eyes. One even reaches out and touches my shoulder gently.

At the threshold of my cell, the girls turn quiet as I approach. Why the sudden quiet? Lately, my cellmates seem to have an eye on

253

me, somehow more attentive; they talk to me in a softer tone than to each other. How strange, the girls from the second tier walk close to the bars and peer down from upstairs whenever they notice me pacing in the corridor. The other day, one of them even formed words without making a sound, asking if I was all right. I nodded quickly, wondering why she wanted to know that. I had received my verdict and that may have surprised everyone, but why should it, really, and why now? Just because I turned myself in and the *Sepah* promised my mother I would return home the same afternoon, that did not stop the *Hakim* judge from issuing me a two-year sentence. Did it?

"She hasn't been exactly as cooperative as she was expected to be," Mother was told when she confronted Torabpoor, asking why and on what charges I had to be sentenced. "You should have advised your daughter not to worsen her situation by misbehaving," Torabpoor scolded my mother at the end, taking the upper hand. So I guess I misbehaved, whatever that means. And I had to be punished. All in all, I know that when I notice concern in their eyes, it's really my brother's verdict the girls are thinking of. If they ask me if I'm all right, it is really Mohammad's situation they are wondering about.

It has been a few weeks since the horrible news, execution of several of the *oldies*, Mahnaz's husband included. Just like a hawk, the *Sisters* watched Mahnaz the day her family informed her, pacing back and forth in front of her cell as she prayed on her prayer rug solemnly and recited verse after verse of the Koran. The girls stayed away from Mahnaz's cell that day; we knew that no one was allowed to get near her or express any word of sympathy or condolence. We knew that we were being watched by the *Sisters* more now than ever. No one heard Mahnaz crying, but we all knew she was in a veil of tears. I knew she was shattered inside. I was shattered myself. Mohammad was among the twelve oldies and his verdict, too, was surely a death penalty. On that Monday, right after the news of the oldies' executions, my mother came to visit along with three of my brothers, all dressed in black, their eyes hollow and pink, their faces sullen. "Why are you wearing black?" I barely dared to ask. "It's Moharram, dear," Mother answered. "It's the mourning month. One ought to mourn." My brothers hardly ever wore black in the mourning months. The whole world is turning upside down, I thought. Nowadays, everyone always mourns, everyday is Ashura, and everyone wears black as if it is the only acceptable color.

Yet I wasn't convinced. During the following two visits I kept asking my mother if she had visited with Mohammad, if he was all right, and she kept giving me the answer I wanted to hear, "Yes, dear. Your brother is all right." Although I sensed a bitter tinge in her voice, I was afraid to push it. What if Mohammad was executed too? I did not want to know. I still wanted to believe that my brother lived another day and another and another until there was a miracle. Until somehow, one day, something extraordinary would happen and everyone would be free. All of us, once and for all.

Now, among my strangely solemn cellmates, I wonder about Torabpoor and the unusual flicker in his eyes. My entire body begins to shake. My stomach churns. Could it be true? Is Mohammad gone? No. Torabpoor is much too malicious not to make this public. He would have thrown it in my face when I begged him once again for a visit. Then again, could it be that he's having his little joke and savoring it secretly? He wants me to go and beg him even though he knows that Mohammad is gone. "Gone"—I hate this word. You mean dead. This word should be wiped out from every dictionary in every language. Execution too, and hanging, and murder, and solitary confinement and torture; I detest all these words, alarming words wrapped in fear and dread. Why am I feeling what I'm feeling? I feel like I'm going to vomit. Why are all eyes on me at all times? Mrs. Hashimi cried the other day when I stopped to say a hasty *salam*.

All day I gaze in a kind of stupor; I see things in a blur and hear peculiar voices.

I have nightmares as soon as my eyelids close. In my dreams I see Mohammad running and I run after him but I can never reach him.

I brood over the questions and the foreboding in my breast and wonder whether or not on my next visit I should ask my mother to tell me the truth.

"*Momon*, why didn't you tell me?"

"What, dear. What didn't I tell you?"

"Mohammad. About Mohammad." My mouth feels dry and my voice is barely audible. I gather all my courage. "I already know,

*Momon*. That day when you were wearing black. And Rahim and Ebrahim. I knew it then." I didn't know, nor do I want to know now. I hesitate. Why am I saying this? Mohammad is fine. I turned myself in; the Revolutionary Court will definitely take this fact into consideration. I hear my mother's cry. "I wanted to protect you, dear. I knew you'd find out sooner or later. I just didn't want you to hear it from me."

"So, it's true," I say in a whisper. "Mohammad too? Without saying goodbye?"

"Ah, my God! You didn't know." My mother gasps, covering her mouth with her hand.

The receiver slips from my grip. I lean my head against the wall of the cubicle. My mother's voice seems far away, pleading with me not to cry, that the *Sisters* are watching. There are no words, just a lump in my throat. My knees are too frail to hold my body weight. I need to use the bathroom. My stomach churns. My head spins. Sister Zahra is behind me. "Compose yourself!" she orders in a very low voice. Without looking at my mother, I walk away from the cubicle, hold on to the wall and keep walking. Everything is blurred—everything. Jumbled blur of people. The walls draw closer toward me.

How did I drag myself through the long hallway to the cell block? Sister Tehereh jolts me. A line of black shrouded girls pass me . Who are they mourning for? Women in black, the color of mourning. "I need to use the bathroom," I mutter. "Compose yourself," Sister Tahereh reminds me in the same ttone Sister Zahra did. "Stand up straight," she says. I should scream. I should cry. But there is only a hard lump in my throat. No. I shouldn't cry. I wouldn't give Torabpoor the satisfaction. That bastard, he knew all along, and yet let me go and beg him for a visit with someone who was already dead. Dead. My brother is dead. Gone forever. Executed. How do they make these kind of decisions? Who gives them the power to take a human life, just like that? Even a sacrificial lamb entails more ceremony than this. It requires permission. I have seen butchers slitting a lamb's head on the Day of Sacrifice, even beheading chickens. They always kiss the head of the animal, whisper words of permission and gratitude for offering their flesh to humankind, for contributing to the continuing circle of life. What kind of permission was there, what ritual, what rationale, when they killed my brother?

I go directly to the bathroom, rinse my face under the cool running water, then drag myself toward my cell. The cement floor beneath my feet has turned into a thick molten tar, clinging to my steps. I should pray or pretend to pray. But I do neither. What's there to pray about? To whom? God of justice? Where is He now? How can He bear all this horror done in His name and remain silent? I would not pray, not to Him or to any gods. I sit in a corner and stare at the empty wall. Motionless. My cellmates say nothing. What's there to say? They know it, knew it all along and perhaps wondered when it would be my turn to find out. Who was going to tell me first, my mother or Torabpoor? What would I do with this lump in my throat, the thumping in my chest? I want to sleep. A deep sleep; maybe I will see Mohammad in my dream, free at last.

*Boom ... boom ... boom ... bam ... bam ... bam. The tabla players play rhythmically. Someone is crying on the second tier. Mrs. Hashimi calls out her children's names, Sohrab, Parvin. Bahram. Babam, babam, babam, where's Bibi's voice coming from? Is she calling me or Mohammad when she says babam? There's Mohammad! Why is he on a white horse? Where is he heading to? Mohammad, Mohammad, where did you find this horse? The gypsies sing and dance, jumping over a huge bonfire. Why are these fields so barren? The grass so brown. Why is it so hot here? What happened to the running brooks? I'm thirsty. The animals are thirsty. Someone ought to water them. Is that Bibi dancing? What a beautiful white scarf she's wearing. Women in black dance and sing, Killili ... killlilli ... killilli ... they run after Mohammad. What a beautiful smile he has. Roaya is running too; why isn't she hiding in Bibi's room? Her mother is chasing her with a water pipe stick in her hand. She's tearing off her top, cupping her breasts and screaming. Mother calls out to Bibi, 'A mother should have dignity,' she yells, 'these kids deserve to have things just like the rest of the kids with fathers. And look at my Mohammad, everyone! Look how my son's riding that white horse.' Mother. Mother. Wait up. I can't run as fast. Why is Mother crying? And look at her large droplets of tears. Who's she calling after, justice, justice, justice ...*

"It's all right. She's just running a bit of a fever. That's all. Just a nightmare. It'll pass soon." I hear my cellmate's voice. It must be Parvin's. She's talking to someone. *Sister* Tahereh is standing in the threshold, looking inside our cell. I feel thirsty. My entire body is drenched in sweat. My face twitches. My mouth has the taste of rusting iron.

"If this cell is too hot for you, you are much more than welcome to invite yourself to the second tier," *Sister* Tahereh tells me. "The air feels much cooler up there, don't you think?"

It's not a question. It's a warning. I must have been whimpering in my sleep again and she must have heard me before my cellmates could have awakened me. The last thing I want is to jeopardize their situation. I remind myself of *Sisters'* orders: Compose yourself!

I am grateful it is daytime. I wish the days would stretch with no nights to follow. When the nightmares attack.

I hear my name called over the loudspeaker.

Torabpoor motions for me to step forward. It is not the five-minutes-begging day and there's no line behind the curtain.

"I see you have cut your visit short with your mother," he says under his breath, leafing through some papers on the desk in front of him.

*They* have already informed him of my "misbehaving."

"I know about Mohammad," I tell him without looking at him. "I no longer need a visit with my brother." I turn on my heels toward the curtain.

"If I were you, I would be extra cautious with my behavior," he warns. "You should think of your wretched mother; the woman came to visit you that day, right after she buried her son. The things you and your kind do to your mothers."

Why is he doing this? Should I break in front of him? Should I tear this lump out of my throat and scream out loud? Why don't tears come? You bastard. How dare you tell me that I ought to think of my mother. For months he warned me to consider my brother's circumstances, now, he warns me that I have to think of my mother. And I wonder if he and the others and those stone-hearted Mullahs in the Central Revolutionary Court have ever given a grain of thought to why a mother should have to bury her innocent 24-year old son. No mother deserves this, no mother. I hear these words only in my head; if only I could speak them.

I walk back to the corridor.

If only I could scream.

If only I could scream.

# CHAPTER 39

It is almost the end of winter. Finally, I have seen the entire four seasons of prison; though in the cell block, this bottomless lopsided abyss, really, there are only two seasons: the season of fear and the season of waiting. Indefinite, colorless season of waiting where branches of phobia, blankness, restlessness, and hopelessness grow savagely in each and every direction. There are only two temperatures: either too cold, or too hot. Not mild, not comfortable, never just right. It is winter and the cement floors, the cement walls, the cement corridor, every bit of the cell block, this oval foul mouth, breathes out cold. The fear is cold too. The chill in my bones is no longer an alien, external foe, it is part of me. We have become well acquainted, the chill and me. The heat and fever too. Chill and Fever always come looking for us, lurking from this cell to the next, drifting from this body to the other, reminding us of their caustic presence, sometimes even claiming the entire tier, the entire block, depending on their mood.

Soon it will be spring. The beautiful spring of Shiraz, this ancient city of poetry and wine, gardens and nightingales. The city of Sa'di, the great poet, thinker, and philosopher who traveled the world only to come back to his birthplace so that he would be buried in its fragrant soil; the city of perfect climate he called it, where no other city in the world was like it. And the city of Hafiz the Poet, the pride of Shiraz, the poet of Bibi's heart. How I wished I could recite his poems now. How I used to recite them at school, and to Bibi. I wonder if someone will ever recite these great poems to her. I wonder if anyone will ever recite them in this city of mourning, in this country of mourning.

The New Year is around the corner. I wonder if my mother has already begun the spring cleaning as she always used to do around this time. It is *Esfand*, the last month of winter. And I wonder how she will celebrate this New Year, still mourning for her son and worrying about her daughter in prison. How do the mothers of Iran celebrate this year, I wonder. History has never been this cruel to the mothers of Iran. In every street, in every alley, there must be one house in which a mother mourns her child's death, either killed in this unjust and bottomless war with Iraq, or executed or disappeared. I wonder what kind of poems Sa'di and Hafiz would write if they lived in this mourning era. What would they say about their beloved city, their homeland, their people drowned in this sea of wretchedness? Would they still drink the crimson wine from the hands of the intoxicated Shirazi goddesses, reciting verses of love and emancipation in the company of nightingales singing in the jasmine and orange blossoms filling the gardens of their Shiraz?

"Are you daydreaming again?" Afsaneh nudges me, smiling.

"What else is there to do except daydreaming and perhaps," I reach for the ruby-colored frame of her unusually large glasses, "taking these ugly things off your eyes. Why do you have to display your eyes like that," I sneer, "as if they're not slanted enough already?"

Afsaneh laughs, her lighthearted laugh. I love her laughter. I envy it.

"You wish to have my eyes, almond shapes and . . ."

"Ha, ha, and crooked." I titter. She does have large brown almond-shaped eyes, but constantly wearing glasses has given them a squinty look. "You know, the first thing you should do," I roll to my side, cupping my head in my left arm, "is to buy brand-new chic frames as soon as you get released. Or else you will scare away all your suitors now that your chicken-hearted fiancé has gone bye-bye."

"First, let's see if I get freed," Afsaneh puts her glasses back on, still smiling, "then if that happens, I'll come and knock on your door, giving you the honor of choosing a pair of gorgeous glasses for me that you like; what do you think of that?"

"You got yourself a deal, dear cellmate. But as for me, I still have another year to go," I say. "That is, if Freedom ever will show her face to me."

"I'm like you. My verdict is also two years, in case you've forgotten. But you know, it's the New Year. Didn't you hear what *Sister* Zahra was saying the other day? They're already talking about
amnesty. Maybe you and I will be included, too. We have light sentences. I'm really hopeful."

"One could only wish. I don't know, Afsaneh. I wish I could share
your optimism, but I'm rather doubtful." I think of Mohammad and I
think of the day I turned myself in and I think of all the promises that
*Sepah* gave my mother that day. I don't tell Afsaneh any of these, and
I hope she is right, but I have my reasons to be skeptical.

Afsaneh's predictions came true.

In observance of the New Year, there is an amnesty indeed, which
does not include any of the inmates from the second tier nor the deso-
late Bahai inmates of the third tier. Some of the girls' sentences are
lowered, for instance, from life in prison to fifteen years, or from
fifteen to ten years. Most of us who are included in the amnesty have
already been given short-term sentences, under three years to begin
with. One of the girls has only three days of her sentence left when
Torabpoor announces the names through the loudspeaker.

"You really didn't deserve this," Torabpoor says as he approaches
me standing in line. "I just had mercy on your mother," he says
coldly. "But we will still have an eye on you, just to make sure you
don't stray from the right path."

Afsaneh, too, is granted freedom.

The news of our freedom is bittersweet. We don't know whether
to celebrate, congratulate one another before the eyes of those
rejected yet still hopeful for their release, or pretend it's not really
a big deal. We do the latter. We tell the other girls that soon they
too will be released, perhaps in the next amnesty. Soon, very soon.
There are not that many girls who are given amnesty and truly they
all deserve to be freed, Mahnaz included, whose son is growing up
without a father, who was executed, and his mother, who is still in
prison. As for me, I am happy and I am distressed. I am happy that
my mother will no longer have to endure exhausting waiting lines
in the prison yard, humiliated and mortified by the prison guards,
only to see her daughter behind the glass barrier. I am happy that at

last I can see my grandmother, I can sit next to her and listen to her warm voice. I am happy because I can see the sky once again, the moon, the streets, our house, the trees, and that I can breathe the fresh air again and hear the sound of fruit vendors coming to our alley. But I am sorrowful because I know I will be entering a world in which my brother is buried, a house in which Mohammad will never again set foot. I wonder how my life will be after prison. What would my imprisoned Iran have to offer me? I think of Torabpoor and his words, and I wonder what kind of liberty I am being granted in the world of watchful eyes? Would I, really—or in fact any of us—ever be truly free?

Those of us granted freedom are ordered to line up at the gate. We say our hasty farewells to our cellmates, we embrace each other, holding back our tears, whispering again words of courage and hope.

I find a plastic bag from under the cot and cram in it all my belongings: a few pieces of clothing, a couple of overwashed, faded hand towels, my white prayer chador, my Koran, and a pair of bread dough prison-made prayer beads. I adjust my black chador meticulously over my head, making sure that all my hair is covered, and set out for the line. I look back at the long corridor stretching behind me and wonder how many times I have paced it. I glance at the second tier and the cellmates standing behind the bars; I know well that my memory will forever trace their hands clenched around these bars, their hollow yet hopeful eyes, their sealed lips, their thin bodies, I will remember them all and I know well that they deserve freedom as much as I, perhaps even more. My eyes search for the Bahai inmates on the third tier. Not even one of these wretched women is included in this bogus amnesty. I see a few of them pacing slowly in the narrow corridor before their cells, and suddenly now, I detest this amnesty. I imagine that the women of all the tiers are hurrying downstairs, that no one is packing up anything, leaving everything behind, that everyone is laughing and singing pre-revolutionary emancipation songs, knowing that their families are waiting outside in the prison yard, celebrating a new revolution, exchanging sweets with each other and saying that the Mullahs have fled the country just as the Shah did, and that the entire nation is free, free of war, oppression, misery, and mourning. Free at last. No more prisons, no more executions. Only liberty, justice and equality for all.

In separate Range Rover patrols, and blindfolded, we are transferred to the Sepah Detention Center.

In a small, almost bare room, a male voice orders me to remove my blindfold. He points to a metal folding chair across from his desk. On the facing wall, there hangs a picture of Khomeini, his piercing, punishing eyes look down on me. A bearded, serious-looking young man gazes at the papers in front of him and, without looking up, announces that I am free. He tells me that I should pray for Imam Khomeini and his forgiving, pure heart for granting freedom to me, a hypocrite. He says that from this moment on I should serve the country and the nation by doing good deeds—whatever that means—to cleanse myself from the past sins I have committed blindly. He mentions many other things I should be thankful for, but my mind has already left this place. I listen to the sparrows chirping in the branches outside the window. I wish the man would shut up and let me listen to sounds that I have not heard for over three hundred sixty five days. He tells me my rights: I am forbidden to contact any of the freed prisoners, any former activists, any political parties and anti-government organizations, even though he assures me repeatedly that the brave *Sepah Pasdaran* had exploited the entire enemy, broken down all the organizations; I am forbidden to leave the city without court permission and I have to report to the *Sepah* once a month and whenever I am called upon to follow up with the authorities' orders; and most of all, I am forbidden to visit my brother's grave; and I am forbidden to discuss anything contradictory about my imprisonment and the prisoners I have come to know. He informs me that I am free on bail guaranteed by my mother's house as collateral.

When all is said and done, and I am blindfolded again, a *Sister* leads me back to the front entry cubicle where she removes my blindfold, hands me my plastic bag of belongings and sends me out the door to my collateralized freedom.

My mother walks up to me. We hug each other for a long moment, trying our hardest to hold back our tears. Behind her stands my brother Rahim, the engine of his taxi still running. He, too, hugs me without uttering a word. His honey brown eyes are filled with tears.

In quiet, he drives us home. I look out the window and breathe the freshly rain-kissed air. The day is not too bright, not too threatening; the streets are washed from the rain of the night before and not yet too crowded with the ordinary midday traffic. People seem to go about their business as usual. It's been almost two years since I have last seen the streets and the outside world. There are tiny waxy green leaves on the trees along the boulevards; a boomerang of birds fly overhead in a gray-blue sky. Perhaps tomorrow there will be a much bluer sky. A spring blue. A new day. A new season. A new beginning, perhaps.

# CHAPTER 40

I enter our courtyard, it smells like winter, the gardens stripped of any flowers or blooms, the tree branches bare, trimmed down savagely, no birds' nests, no fruits, no blossoms. No one is home to greet me. Not even Bibi. Rahim, too, leaves the house to continue with his shift. As I enter the parlor, I am faced with Mohammad's framed picture—a black ribbon crossed diagonally—placed on top of the television set. Mother goes to the kitchen to prepare lunch, and I am thankful for that. I walk up to my brother's picture, the last picture he ever posed for nearly four years ago in a photographer's studio. There are many things I want to say to him, but the words do not come. There are many tears I want to shed, but the tears do not come. My memory returns to the day I first saw Mohammad, the day I woke up on that cold winter morning and there he was sleeping ever so peacefully in Bibi's bed, his bandaged foot falling out of the covers. And now I cannot help remembering what Bibi used to say, "This boy will surely be somebody some day!" I caress Mohammad's picture and stare into his green eyes. *Where were you running to, all these years, brother? So this is it? Have you foreseen our destiny to end up like this, dear Mohammad?* There is a lump in my throat. I had lost my father many, many years ago, before I could have any memory of him, before I was old enough to understand what his loss would mean, or to feel the pain; but oddly now, I feel that I have suddenly become an orphan. Abandoned. I feel utterly numb and I do not even know how to grieve this sort of loss. They have taken my brother. I am brimming with rage.

266

"*Momon*, why didn't you bring Bibi ?"

My mother, expecting this question, says that she wanted to make sure that I was home. "You never can trust what they tell you," she says, referring to the *Sepah*. "I already asked Rahim to go get her. He'll bring her over soon."

None of my brothers are home and the house feels ghastly quiet. With the exception of the persimmon and the lemon trees, I know Mother has managed again to keep the trees and the arbors bare of any fresh green branches. "I guess you cut down the trees too far this time," I say to Mother as she strains the bubbly cooking rice into a colander. "It's almost spring, but the gardens look completely empty. The trees should have blossoms by now."

"I just didn't feel like sweeping the leaves day in and day out," she says, oiling the bottom of the pot and emptying the strained rice from the colander. "They'll grow back soon," she adds without looking up.

"Do you need any help?"

"Not much to do," Mother replies. "Why don't you go rest a bit."

"Rest?" I shake my head. "What do you think I've been doing all along? I wish I could run or do some jump-rope somewhere. I need to move my body. Look at my legs. All swollen and puffy."

"The water in the shower is boiling. I turned the heater on this morning. Why don't you go take a nice, long shower?"

"Good idea, *Momon*. I need a hot shower more than anything. There was never hot water in Adel . . ." I stop short.

My mother pauses and looks directly at me. "I know, dear. Try not to think of that damn place anymore. May it be abolished some day soon. Go take a shower and let me know if you want me to come scrub your back."

Rahim finally comes home, holding Bibi's hand. If my mother has aged ten years, Bibi has gone virtually blind. She has sight only in her left eye and not too much vision at that. I almost shriek the moment I see her, flabbergasted. She holds me in her arms as if I am a four-year-old and kisses all me all over my still moist hair and face, thanking God constantly and crying bitterly. My mother, too, begins to cry; quickly she goes back to the kitchen and busies herself so that I won't see her crying. "She's losing her sight," I whisper to Rahim.

He nods. "Can you see me, Bibi?" My lips quiver.

"Ha, my father, my brother, ha my bunch of flowers. May my eyes be bright at the sight of yours. Let me smell you, *babam*. Let Bibi kiss your face. You're free at last. Praise be to Allah."

I am glad that I took a shower before Bibi came so now she can smell my freshly shampooed hair and soaped skin rather than the damp smell of prison. She touches my hair and when she notices its length, wonders why I had to cut it so short. I give her the same explanation my mother gave me with about the trees. "It was hard to manage, Bibi," I say. "It'll grow back soon."

I hear my mother chuckle.

One by one, my brothers come home; they hug me, but none of them asks me how I felt during my imprisonment and what my days were like behind the walls. I know their wounds are still open and their pain still fresh, but most of all I know they are not good at asking questions and very good at avoiding touchy subjects. There are many things I know I have to repress now that Mohammad is gone, and now in the presence of my other brothers, I begin to grasp the many things I will have to do without: the lengthy conversations with Mohammad on politics, at times fervent, at times hasty and nervous; our talks about religion, history, poetry, the forbidden books we read, or just everyday things. Most of all, I know I will miss our laughter together, which now seems so many years ago. I know that I will yearn to replace what I shared with Mohammad with any of my living brothers, but I know also that that would be only wishful thinking. We had a small world of our own, Mohammad and I, where the other family members did not fit in or perhaps we did not fit in their world. And I can not help wondering, more than ever now, if Mohammad ever belonged to our family, so different he was from the rest of my brothers. He was caring, studious, and most of all articulate. Perhaps, all along he had belonged to a different place, a much happier place, perhaps, where he could simply be himself. I know my brothers mourn him now, but it hurts to think that Mohammad will soon be forgotten. Soon they will go on with their ordinary lives, unmindful of the outside world, get married, father children who would never know that once their brave uncle fought for democracy and lost his life for this country. Something horrible, a cruel injustice was done to him and to my family.

# CHAPTER 41

I walk along the green pathways of the cemetery, from where the patches of a cloudy sky are visible through the sycamore and willow trees. I watch row after row of marble tombstones with framed pictures of young soldiers who died with the promise of an eternal life in heaven. Groups of black-dressed mourners splash water on their faces from the glorious fountain in the middle of the square. The crimson water cascades out of an immense tulip figure in memory of the red blood of the young who lost lives in the war with Iraq. They are *shahid*, the martyred, the honored.

The air is cool, filled with the verses of the Koran coming from the loudspeakers over the blooming plaza. A mild wind blows the green-white-red national flag. I walk the entire length to the end of the cemetery, where a line of tall green cypress trees end and the dirt road begins. No taxis or buses pass this point; an abandoned field lies on the horizon.

As I near this deserted place with no trees or green shrubs, my knees weaken. I look carefully for the signs my brothers have left here to find Mohammad. I know I am endangering my life. Only the mothers are allowed in this part of the field on Fridays. My mother holds my passport and the plane tickets to Istanbul. She begged me not to go to the graveyard, but I cannot leave this land without saying my final goodbye to my brother.

I kneel at his grave, a nameless, fractured, rectangular cement slab surrounded by brown weeds, among hundreds and hundreds of other nameless scattered graves. I pour rosewater over his grave and cover the surface with pink and white rose petals and orange blossoms I have picked from what was once my grandmother's garden. I try to say a prayer, but my heart is no longer a place for worship. I do not plead for justice. I leave the praying to my grandmother and the cursing to my mother. I choose to cry bitterly out loud. I know it is forbidden to cry on the grave of one who has been hanged and buried quickly in the middle of the night, but this is my brother and I want to mourn. This is my brother who gave me Tolstoy, Dostoyevsky, Ahmad Mahmood, Daneshvar, Dr. Shariati. . . .

My eyes wander the hushed field. Above my head, the sky turns from a misty gray to a gloomy dark ashen. I hear only the sound of my sobbing. I do not hide my tears and let the drops of rain wash my face, for I do not know if I will ever be able to feel the rain of my country's sky again. I finger the moist soil around my brother's grave. This is the soil he lost his life for, yet he is not called *shahid*. I wonder where my final resting place will be and it hurts my soul to think that it might not be in this land, the land of my childhood.

I have only to close my eyes to hear Mohammad's voice in the eerie execution yard. *Down with fanatism. Freedom for Iran.* His face materializes through the dense clouds, the familiar smile in his green eyes.

As I rise to my feet, I gaze one last time at Mohammad's grave and the entire graveyard. I am surrounded with images and whispers, and voices forcefully silenced.

*May your soul rest in peace, my beloved brother. You will always be alive in my heart.*

# CHAPTER 42

Standing in the center of the international terminal of Mehrabad Airport, I try to read the black departure screen over a human wall to see if my flight is delayed, a typical occurrence these days. Flight 367, Tehran-Istanbul flashes on the screen, ON TIME. Still three hours to final boarding.

My eyes scan the crowded airport. Men walk in their black mourning shirts, a distressed expression on their bearded faces. Women linger in their black chadors, or their adopted knee-length, loose, dark manto. Their heads are covered with the tight long navy blue maghnaeh, the government mandated head-covering. Some even wear black gloves. Men and women speak without looking at each other, yet another new sign of modesty and virtue. Wherever I look, people push in the zigzag lines, at the departure gates, at the ticket counters, in the cafes, everywhere. They embrace and greet each other with excitement. Some laughter is heard here and there. But mostly, they are crying. The recycled air is heavy with nervousness, anxiety, and anticipation.

In the snack-bar line, waiting to buy a bottle of Schweps, I watch the transformed surroundings. Victory, proclaims the headline of the Keyhan newspaper: "The resistant holy army has defeated yet another nest of the anti-revolutionary enemies on the western border of Kurdistan."

The walls are covered with life-size pictures of the Ayatollahs, along with religious slogans and phrases written in a mixture of Arabic and Farsi. The language is being infused with Arabic words and phrases, replacing English ones. A country with its stolen revolution, with signs of Westernization evaporating day by day.

I walk to the small corner tea house across the hall, where my mother sits at a brown table, sipping tea from a slim crystal cup. I place a bottle of Schweps in front of her; she slides it toward me, saying it tastes like dry hay. She still refuses to drink or eat anything canned, bottled, or without gourmet packaging. I wish I could buy her some fresh lemonade, but I can't find it anywhere. The prices are going through the roof, she says. She had to pay twenty tumans for that cup of tea. The same cup would have cost only two tumans a year ago. Inflation, I tell her. Currency devaluation, scarcity, and all that economic stuff I had learned in high school.

She catches me glancing at a young man leaning against the wall. "He's going on the same flight," she says. "I overheard him talking to his family. He's quite handsome. Isn't he?"

He is, I think to myself. A tall, slender, twentyish young man with sharp features and a self-consciously stylish hairdo.

"Maybe you'll get lucky and he'll sit next to you, keep you company," she says. Disappointed with my lack of enthusiasm, she leans back in the red chair and murmurs, "Your hands and feet are made of wood. I'd be surprised if you ever managed to find yourself a husband."

My mother can make you cry and laugh at the same time. Her sense of humor unfolds even in the most awkward situations. This is how she maintains her calm. Her face is fatigued with the lack of sleep from the night before. Whenever I turned over in the twin bed next to hers, her eyes were fixed on the ceiling or wet with silent tears. The dark circles around her eyes appear deeper than usual.

She still has difficulty covering all her hair. A gray strand strays from her black headscarf. She's been prematurely gray ever since I can remember, and she refuses to color. She blames it on my grandmother's genes. It troubles her that I had begun to turn gray as a teenager. "Nothing good came from Bibi," she says. She mumbles something to herself I cannot understand. I listen closely. "We inherited her gray hair, but not other traits. Couldn't she pass to us her big bosom trait, for instance?"

She suggests that once I settle in Germany, I should go to a doctor and have them ballooned up. I tell her I'll worry about it once I'm over there. Right now, I'm happy just to be alive. She leans toward me and whispers, "Don't get married too soon!" A hostile smile appears on

her face. She tilts her head back and faces the crowd. "Who's going
to marry you anyway? You're like a dog, you bite. Maybe a bald fat
man will marry you."

I am surprisingly calm, and ignoring her comments, I just listen
and smile. If Bibi were here, she would have snapped at her. But I
have grown to understand that this is how my mother communicates
with me. We're not like other mothers and daughters. We have never
been and we're never going to be. I struggled with this for many
years, until the reality hit me like a brick. We're more like two nagging sisters who fight and bicker all the time. I searched for her love
in my grandmother's embrace. She says I got all the love from her
mother, all the love she deserved to have. At times, I felt sorry for her
and for myself. At this moment, however, I crave her love.

I am as quiet as she is talkative. I know she is agitated. My grandmother and my mother both become wordy and repetitive when trying to hide their nervousness, a trait I do not share. She says I should
never marry someone fat and bald. She won't approve of it.

"And don't forget! Tall. He has to be tall," she says. "You tell them
my *Momon* likes them tall and handsome. No children! Remember
that! What's the point? They leave you. Or you lose them to drugs
or to the hangman's rope. Do you hear me?" she says in her adopted
Shirazi accent. It's Ali she's thinking of; he's become a drug addict.

I am still quiet. I watch her from the corner of my eye.

"Well, maybe a little girl. You don't want to disrupt the family's
female lineage."

I am the fifth generation as the only girl in the family, from my
great-great-grandmother to me. "If you hadn't been born after six
boys," she says, "our female generation would have ended with me."
As if trying to make sure that I hear her, she waves her hand in front
of my eyes like opening a Japanese fan. "Hey. Am I talking to your
shadow on the wall?"

"I heard you, *Momon*. No boys are allowed in my house. Satisfied?"

"Men should wish to have you by their sides," she says a few
moments later. "They should be honored to have you as a wife."

I shake my head and stare into her eyes. "Make up your mind,
*Momon*! Which is which?"

That's when she breaks into tears. She can no longer hold them back. Through her sobs, she says, "If I left Bibi, I came back to her. At least Bibi has me, now that she is old. But you are leaving me and your poor Bibi who raised you, thinking you would be the cane for her elderly hand. God knows, she'd go blind crying over you."

I would prefer she would keep tormenting me with her ludicrous comments rather than say that. It tears my heart to imagine not being able to see my grandmother, to sit next to her on the front porch of her house and listen to her warm, inviting voice. This is the mother I have come to know from the fruit-lady I resented in my grand-mother's garden. Has she watched me grow up as I watched her change from that elegant fruit-lady to this scarf-headed woman who sits across from me, trying to hold back her tears? Her presence was only a shadow on my childhood. She missed watching me grow to a young lady behind the bars of Adelabad Prison and the glass barriers in the visitation corridors. Now, she will miss seeing me become the woman she might have remembered as her young self. This is the mother I did not choose, but at this moment, I understood the meaning of the proverb heaven is under the mothers' feet.

I fight the image of that mean fruit-lady, my grandmother's daughter, pinching my thighs, leaving purple bruises I tried to hide from Bibi in the shower. I remember, instead, the woman who kissed the stranger's hand for giving me shelter when I lived underground. Why should bitter memories matter now? I wish I could bow to her. I wish I could hold her hands and kiss them the way I kissed my grandmother's, the way Mohammad kissed them in that last visit he had with her. But perhaps I am too young and vain or too conceited to do so.

I want to remind her once again to take care of my half-blind grandmother, yet I change my mind. She knows I belong to her mother. But at this moment, I want to be my mother's daughter. I want to feel her presence close by my side, as if she and I were alone in this crowded place. I want to hear her warm southern enunciation with traces of Abadani accent still in her voice.

"I am the one who carried you in my womb for nine months," she reminds me for the hundredth time. "What a pregnancy, all that kicking and jumping you did as if my belly were a soccer field. You were impatient from day one, wanting to come out as if the whole world was awaiting your arrival. I gave birth to seven sons without a bit of pain. Five minutes of labor," she holds up five fingers. "But you had to announce that you were a girl by making me ill for the entire nine months. And if it wasn't for the home childbirth, I would have thought someone had exchanged my baby for a tiny gray kitten with eyes as black as two round buttons."

I remind myself what Bibi always says, that I should not pay attention to my mother's sarcasm because she was used to bearing fat light-skinned boys with golden hair and hazel eyes.

As if reading my mind, my mother reassures me. "You know perfectly well that I would never forsake her. She may be your grandmother, but she is my mother."

All these years, I felt I was like the icing of a twin-cookie, connecting my mother and my grandmother. I cannot help thinking of the women of my family. My grandmother is right. We're all rebels. A bunch of gypsies. Nomads. We take off in our youth; our roots seek another land. My mother was married off to my father in a faraway Peninsula in the Persian Gulf. My grandmother left her village when she was barely seventeen. And I—I'm not marrying or just leaving my Shiraz, the city I never thought I would have to leave. I am leaving my country. Bibi would say, wherever you go the color of the sky is the same, "Don't alter your ground my *babam*, change your destiny!" Why did all this have to happen to us?

My mother reminds me not to call her on Fridays. I nod my head. I know she'll be at the cemetery with the rest of the mothers, sharing their buried children's memories. I want to say that I will call her on Wednesdays, but I remember that was Mohammad's visit day. She had waited for those fifteen-minute visits for almost three years. At one point, she had to commute across town between Adelabad Prison and Sepah Detention, to see four of her children behind the glass barriers. That is, if we were not lashed and could walk that day. The rest of the weekdays, she had to endure the never-ending human lines at the Revolutionary Court in order to find out our verdict or to plead for a visit, especially with Mohammad.

"I'll call you on Mondays," I say before remembering that it was my own visit day. I want to change it, but she says, "Mondays are

good. At least I don't have to travel across half the city to see you
from a glass cubicle." Her wet eyes gaze at an unknown distance.
"The bad thing is," she cries, "I won't be able to see your face. Only
to hear your voice from another continent."

"I'm no educated person. You're the bookish one here," she says.
"In all those books you've read, was there any resurrection day? Any
justice?"

I do not know what to believe any more. I have been exposed to
many versions of Islam: the Islam of the Ayatollahs who in the name
of God and his Prophet kill and execute youths for their beliefs; who
use innocent village teenagers as human mines to feed their war with
the promise of heaven; the Islam of the ghetto, the aimless flagella-
tion and self-torturing devotion on the day of Ashura; the symbolic
and state-enforced Islam of the Shah in the dominating Muslim Arab
region; and the Islam of my brother Mohammad and his beloved Dr
Shariati, this modern version of freedom, equality, brotherhood, and
classless society. Above all, I have witnessed the Islam of my grandmother, with her endless affectionate stories from the Koran that I
fell asleep with and grew up on. The compassionate Islam of Bibi,
this illiterate woman who, on the wings of imagination, took me to
the land of Ebrahim, to the house of Zoleikha the Beautiful and Josef
the Moon-Face. Who taught me the meaning of love, respect, emancipation and benevolence.

Even if I were to have read all the books in the universe, I still
wouldn't have the answer to my mother's question. My faith has been
shattered over these years of turbulence and loss. And this is all I
have to leave with now, this shattered faith and this broken heart.
They say the heart will mend. And maybe, someday, I will have my
faith again.

So, I tell her, "I hope there's going to be a resurrection day and
that justice will be served."

I hold her hands in mine and try to comfort her and myself by
feeling the heat of our hands. She is silent. Slowly, I kneel in front
of her, cross my arms over her lap and look into her face. With her
rapid weight loss over the past few years, her body seems to have
shrunk each day. I study the deep lines around her mouth and on
her forehead, the two vertical lines between her arched eyebrows.

"*Momon*—I want you to promise me you'll take care of yourself. You know, I will feel it when you cry."

She fumbles with the white Kleenex in her hands. "The days are more tolerable," she says. "It's the nights that are too long and never end."

I know my mother will wake in the middle of the night thinking about Mohammad. About the last visit she had with him, when she said her final goodbye, knowing that her son would be walking to the execution yard as soon as the visit was over. In that same hour.

I want to cry for my mother. How did she get home that night in the dark, carrying Mohammad's few clothes and last belongings neatly packed in his green backpack? My heart aches.

She hardly talks about that night. Sometimes, she grieves and says that he was relieved at last. How many more days could he have tolerated to live in that two-by-three-meter solitary cell without seeing a ray of sunshine? How many more midnights did he have to bear waking up, to be interrogated with closed eyes, or lashed on his back and feet? I gather, if it weren't for all these recollections, my mother could never have endured getting up another day.

She strokes my head and says that Mrs. Bahrami, the new neighbor, told her once, "In Germany people buy fruit by the piece. Unlike here where there are so many kinds of fruit coming to the house." She promises that as soon as I get situated in Berlin, she will send me all kinds of dry fruit and vegetables.

I listen to her warm voice, capturing this last image. She is the one who brought me fruit when I was a little girl. She is the one who brought fruit when I lived underground. She carried her fruit basket in the cold of winter and the heat of summer to Adelabad Prison; and at this last moment as I'm leaving this land, she is still worried that I will have enough fruit to eat.

I glance at the big, round clock over Gate 15. It is almost time. I have given my passport to the airline authorities the day before. No *pasdar* or any frontier guards have disturbed us yet. We've been told that the system is not computerized nationally, at least not completely. My heart pounds in my chest. Humming sounds drum in my head. My palms won't stop sweating. My mouth is dry. My knees tremble under my thick black pants. I try not to go to the lady's room too often, for I do not want to worry my mother by revealing my anxiety. Holding the side of her body with her hands, she straightens her back every now and then. I know she is suffering from a backache. I can feel her pain in my own back.

When my flight is finally called, my mother rises to her feet, uncertain whether to hug me. I look into her brown, glistening eyes, the eyes I saw first in the deer's face in the picture hanging in my grandmother's prayer room. I do not wait. I draw her to my chest as if she were my daughter. I hold her in my arms for a long moment and smell the familiar soap scent rising from beneath her black mantaue. I kiss her forehead and her cheeks, hot and wet with the smell of salt. I try to hold back my tears, but I fail. This is no longer the fruit-lady I am saying goodbye to. She is my shahid brother's mother. My Mother. "Stay in the background, in case I get arrested," I try to convince her so she'll be safe. I let all the passengers get on board and make sure my mother knows her gate number. Her flight back home, from Tehran to Shiraz, leaves in less than an hour. She says she will wait. She wants to watch my plane take off from the waiting area's windows, still annoyed that I am not flying on Lufthansa instead of Iran Air. "What would happen if one of those ungodly torturers sees you and reports you?" I assure her that this way is less suspicious. Besides, I'd like to fly on our domestic airlines.

I embrace her one last time. She bursts into tears again. My mother's cry is the most painful cry I have ever heard. She says in a muffled voice, "My children are disappearing one by one before my eyes. What have I done to deserve such cruel punishment?" She raises her head as if calling out to the saints.

I can no longer stand her tears. The pain in my chest grows stronger. She pleads again that I call her as soon as I get to Istanbul.

"I will, *Momon*," I comfort her.

As I walk toward the boarding area, I am aware that these may be my final footsteps on Iranian ground. I feel my mother's heartbeat in my chest. I know her eyes are fixed on the stewardess's hands. The uniformed woman extends her arm to me with my passport and my boarding card. "Welcome aboard Iran Air!" she says, with a faint smile.

I turn and look to see my mother through the blur of tears.

"May God's hand be with you wherever you go, my daughter!"
I hear my grandmother's prayers in her voice.

# GLOSSARY

*Abadani*: referred to people from the city of Abadan in the southern part of Iran

*Abaya*: (Arabic), head-covering worn by local Arab women

*Adjan*: (French), policeman

*Afarin*: bravo; awesome

*Alhamd-o-lellah*: (Arabic), praised be to Lord

*Allah*: (Arabic), God

*Allah-o-Akbar*: (Arabic), "God is the greatest," often recited in prayers

*Alvat*: bunch of hooligans

*Areh*: (colloquial), yes

*Arrack*: hard liquor similar to Vodka

*Ashura*: 10th day of Muharram in the Islamic Calendar which also marks the day of mourning for the martyrdom of third Shiite Imam, Hossein, grandson of Prophet Mohammad at the Battle of Karbala in today's Iraq

*Askari grapes*: very sweet, yellow grapes

*Baba*: dad; father

*Babam*: my child; my baby

*Bah-bah*: expression of awe; literally means wow!

*Baha i*: the Baha i Faith is a religion founded by Bahaullah in nine-teenth-century Iran

*Barakat*: abundance and blessing

*Barbari bread*: a type of Persian flatbread

*Basij*: a paramilitary force founded by order of Khomeini in November 1979; there is a local Basij organization in just about every city in Iran

*Besmellah*: in the name of God

*Brothers, sisters*: referred to the male and female prison guards

*Buffet*: china cabinet

*Chador*: (Farsi), a traditional, long, black piece of fabric, which covers from head to toe, and is often associated with Islamic women's head covering in the Middle East; also referred to as hijab

*Crepe-de-chine*: (French), a kind of slippery and fine fabric

*Deh*: village

*Esfand*: the 12th month of Iranian calendar, also the last month of winter

*Eyes*: penitents who report to the prison guard; the informers

*Fada i*: the Marxist political party of Iran

*Faludeh*: a local ice desert similar to ice cream

*Farangi*: a term referred to the European

*Ghaz and pashmak*: local sweets, specially made in Isfahan

*Giveh*: woven shoes worn commonly by villagers

*Grading system* in Iran is from 1 through 20 years as the best number, equal to an A in the U.S.

*Ha*: (colloquial), yes

*Hajji Agha*: respectful title given to a person who has performed Hajj pilgrimage, also a cleric

*Hakem-e Shar*: the religious judge

*Halal*: lawful, also kosher

*Halva*: a distinct sweet made out of flour, sugar, and oil

*Haram*: (Arabic), forbidden; unlawful according to religion of Islam

*Hezbollah*: literally party of God is the first paramilitary organization founded in the aftermath of 1979 Iranian Revolution

*Hijab*: Islamic head coverings

*Houries*: (Arabic), angels of Paradise

*Iftar*: (Arabic), referred to the evening meal for breaking the daily fast during the Islamic month of Ramadan

*Imam*: religious leader; a title given to Ayatollah Khomeini

*Jihad*: (Arabic) Islamic term; a religion duty of Muslims

*Jinn and Dives*: legendary and invisible beings, who constitute a world almost parallel to the human; The Jinns are believed to be created out of smokeless flame, while man and angels are from clay and light.

*Kafer*: believers in religions other than Islam; nonbelievers

*Khan*: a title for a ruler or the head of the tribe

*Khanum*: Mrs., Miss, Lady

*Khourgeen*: saddlebacks

*Kleem*: hand woven tribal rugs

*Kowli*: local gypsies

*Kuchulu*: little one

*Kuh-e Nur*: (literally, Mountain of Light), the most celebrated diamond in the world

*Kulucheh*: sweets; cookie

*Laleh abassi*: miniature summer flowers

*Lamb, lamb cloud*: dense, white clouds; cumulus clouds

*Lavashak*: dried fruit

*Mafatih al-Jinan*: (Arabic, Keys to Heavens) by Shaikh Abbass Qumi is a compilation of selected chapters (surahs) from the Koran

Majlis: parliament

Mantaue: (French), a knee length overcoat used by women in public as Islamic clothing

Mashk: goatskin or leather container

Mashti: also mash, (colloquial), Mashhadi, a respectful as well as a religious title earned when one has visited the Shrine of the Eight Shiite Imam, Reza, in the holy city of Mashhad

*Mehr*: the seventh month (also the first month of fall) of Iranian calendar

*Merci*: (French), thank you

*Meter*: metric system of measuring length

*Mini-joop*: (French), mini skirt

*Mobarak*: congratulations

*Mohandas*: engineer

*Mohr*: prayer stone

*Mojahedin*: the political party of Mojahedeen-e Khalgh-e Iran

*Momon*: mom; mama

*Monafeghin*: literally means "hypocrites," a slandering label given to the Mojahedin Party by the Islamic Republic

*Moshgel-gosha*: literally, the resolver of difficulties; also various mixed-nuts and raisin which one gives to people in order for their vows or urgent wish to be fulfilled by God

*Muezzin*: (Arabic), a person who recites the prayer calls at mosques

*Naa*: no

*Nahj al-Balagha*: a collection of 241 sermons, 79 letters, and 489 utterances by the fourth Caliph and the first Shi a Imam, Ali, also the cousin and the son-in-law of the Islamic Prophet Moham-mad

*Na-mahram*: men not related to a woman such as father, son, hus-band, brother, uncle and grandfather

*Namaz*: reciting the five-times daily prayers (Islam)

*Nastaran*: sweet briars, white rose

*Nazr*: an urgent wish

*Pari*: fairy

*Pasdar*: the Islamic Republic guards

*Podegon*: (French), military base

*Qashqa'i*: a sect of Nomad tribes living around the city of Shiraz in the southern part of Iran

*Rahbar*: leader; here referred to Ayatollah Khomeini

*Ramadan*: the Islamic, fasting month of Ramadan

*Rozeh sermon*: the reciting of the Koran and prayers and the narration of stories of battle of Karbala, usually held in mosques for men and in houses for women

*Saghez*: a hard chewing gum collected from the sap of mountain trees

*Sahari*: the meal eaten before dawn during the Islamic month of Ramadan

*Salam*: greeting, hello

*Salavat*: (Arabic), saying to wish peace upon Prophet Mohammad and his entire progeny

*Sangak bread*: a kind of bread baked in the wall oven of hot pebbles

*SAVAK*: (National Intelligence and Security Organization), the most dreadful institution and secret police of the Shah's regime, for its association with the foreign CIA intelligence organization, and its torture of regime opponents

*Shahid*: (Arabic), martyr in the way of God

*Shater Khan*: Mr. Baker

*Sepah Detention Center*: the temporary detention center where they keep new prisoners before being sent to Adelabad prison or for those kept in solitary confinements

*Shah*: King, here refers to the last King of Pahlavi Dynasty, Mohammad Reza Shah

*Shahbanu*: The Queen

*Shahi*: the smallest unit of the old Iranian currency

*Shahrivar*: the sixth month (also the last month of summer) of Iranian calendar

*Shemr*: the murderer of Imam Hossein, the third Shiite Imam and grandson of Prophet Mohammad

*Shiraz*: the cultural capital city of ancient Persia, famous for its beautiful gardens and poetry, located in the southern part of Iran

*Siasi*: literally means political, yet often used by the government as a derogatory remark, labeling dissidents

*Sigheh*: temporary marriage

*Sofreh*: a piece of clean cloth spread on the floor on which food is served

*Sogoli*: the first wife

*Sormeh*: distinctive eyeliner made from natural carbon and coal

*Sweets eaten usually in Ramadan*: zulbia, bamieh, halva, baghlava, tarhalva

*Taaorof*: an offer made out of courtesy and etiquette

*Taxi-bar*: pick-up truck

*Tekyeh*: temporary stands during the Islamic months of Moharram to commemorate the third Shiite Imam, Hossein's martyrdom

*Toman*: Iranian currency; Rial: the smallest unit of Iranian currency (one toman=10 rials)

*Ulama*: (Arabic), the clerics

*Waay*: wow!

*Well of Zamzam*: a famous spring in Mecca visited by Hajj pilgrims to honor the memory of Ibrahim's wife, Hagar, and his small son, Ismail